And Then God Said...
Then *I* Said...
Then He Said...

Volume One

ISBN 1-4392-4632-7

A special acknowledgement for a special person

We wish to thank Ann Ulrich Miller for the job she has done with all the technical aspects of taking this book from its CD manuscript form and formatting it into the book layout for the printer. Ann also took the background that we had Created and transformed that into the cover. It is a great deal of work, and we do not know anyone who could have done a more professional job. Ann is also a novelist and editor. She is the creator and publisher of her long-running metaphysical print magazine, *The Star Beacon*. The Web site is www.earthstarpublications.com.

And Then God Said...
Then *I* Said...
Then He Said...

Volume One

This book contains information God transmitted to Celestial (Celest) Blue Star of the Pleiades, David of Arcturus and Suzanne (Suzy) Ward, a dedicated "Way Shower." There are also special messages from Blue Star, Matthew, Hatonn, Melena, Tomás, Serapis Bey, Horiss, Commander Theda, Mother Mary, and one other very special unexpected Voice who has asked to be heard.

CONTENTS

Foreword

Introduction

Foreword

Celest — In every lifetime experienced here on the Earth Star planet, each person who enters here does so with the innate ability to know "right" from "wrong." Each "knows" to act in accordance with Universal Laws which were Created by the God of this universe, as well as by Other Highly Evolved Beings. Throughout the history of this planet certain "teachings" are sent to all of humanity for the pure purpose of maintaining Spiritual stability within the hearts and minds of each individual.

Spirituality does not "know" if an individual is black or white, yellow or brown. Spirituality is the nucleus of All That Will Ever Be. This dynamic force is an exquisite extension of all the Higher Forms of Creation; of love *without condition*. The God of this universe, in His wondrous compassion for all other aspects of HimSelf, gifts each person with "awakening moments." These are the life changing, life defining, episodes that prompt each Soul to use their "free expression" (free will), to release all conditionings that have been imposed upon them from the time of their emergence here as infants.

A part of these awakening moments is the timely release of God's Truths, which are intended to re-inform each person of the true existence of *HimSelf* in all His myriad forms; thereby negating the bastardization of His Truth. Dis-information has reigned here for as long as humanity has been. Although there is never a day gone by when the true realities cannot be found, it is when humanity as a whole is on the verge of great transformation that the most important of all His Words are once again heard. This is in part for the purpose of not merely enlightening the populace, but also to render staunch support for all those who have endured so much in their quest to "be a difference," oftentimes at great personal cost.

Of all the reasons that are relevant to the evolution of the human race, the greatest reason of all is to ensure that humanity can and will ascend and be "in awareness" once again in *conscious* fashion, that each person is "God in physicality." We are now in the mid-time of the "balancing of the scales." This is the time period for the greatest ascension of the Light of All Lights on this planet, and the final severance from the dark. Those beings who are part of the "un-illuminated forces" and the people, who for whatever reason have chosen to refute the truth, are determining their own destinies. Although this madness has occurred before many, many times here, this time all truths of the Universe are melding to form into one concentric configuration. As a result, especially over the last two hundred years, many "Speakers" have either chosen to be the recipients of His Words, or were "elected" to do so.

Speaking for myself, I do not have any "remembrance" of "volunteering" for God's Book; I did not know this was part of my mission. On the afternoon of August 10, 2006, I went upstairs to take a nap, or so I thought. I was preparing to lie down and did not even have time to close my eyes when suddenly, *poof*... God appeared. He simply told me, telepathically of course, that He wanted me to write His book. I "intelligently" thought "what book?" God did not give me a moment to ask any questions. He simply showed me through "imagery" the title of the book and the cover that was to be Created. He was quite firm about the title being written exactly as He had stated. Well, after He "left," I went downstairs to speak with David about this. I wanted to ask him if he would like to participate in the book. Of course I did ask and receive permission from God first. Come to think of it, I never did ask God, "Why me? Why now? What happened to my planned nap anyway?"

David — In short there was to be no compromising on the works He wished for us to transcribe for Him. We did learn from Him that it had been decided long ago that we were to be His messengers, His voice that is to be heard once again. For far too long the Children of the lesser gods have stated that their words are His Words. We are living in a timeline to correct all misinformation and lies delivered through corruption and deceitful enterprises that are in opposition of His Truths. As time progressed and He slowly started sending us His "topics of discussion" in the form of chapter titles, we had a "quantum thought." We thought it would be a good thing to ask Suzy Ward if she wanted to be part of the book too. We asked God and He said, "Ask her and see if she can make the time." So we did. Suzy is not only a good friend of ours on a personal level; she, too, is in contact with many other "off world beings." Of course it took her approximately 15 seconds to "jump on board." As you will see when reading the book, many other "off world family" members, of all of ours, excitedly asked to participate in this work.

There comes a time in everyone's life when the search for the ultimate truth, meanings and purpose to their existence becomes paramount in their minds. "Now" is that moment. In my own earlier years I could not bring myself to follow any religious practices, there was a gnawing at me each time I tried. I know now that I had already researched those for validity in previous lifetimes, guess you could say, *"been there, done that, don't need to go down that road again."* I must tell you of the High sensation one receives when re-connecting with the Almighty, there is a peace and calmness to be felt that equals the calmness and serenity of being in a mother's womb. These words you shall read in this book are God's words, His messages to all of us because of His eternal love for all His Children. I, for one, shall lend Him my ear.

It took me many years to comprehend that I was, we are, all of us, "The Ones" we have been waiting for. God's patience with my questions, His calmness, His delightful humor, His unexpected bursts of laughter while working within the confines of my self-imagined, self-imposed, once limited understanding, gave me a much more enhanced outlook on life. His guidance, His friendship, His trust, His love, needs to be shared by all. I say "He," for the ease of communicating His words; He Himself does not limit Himself to one energy pattern or modality. He is androgynous as are all of us, and as such you may call Him by whatever name you see fit. I understand that the possibility exists that there will be resistance to the acceptance of this God-umentary. I can only speak for myself and say, *"yes, these are His Words, not ours"*; I know this, because I was there.

Suzy — I feel it's a joy and a privilege to receive contributions for this collection of invaluable messages. And it's good that I do because God says this is a *responsibility* I chose, just as I did with the Matthew Books, which He told me are HIS books and so is this one.

Since I don't remember signing up for any of this, I think of my participation as a natural extension of my passion for peace, truth, fairness, and spiritual wisdom to prevail in our world. Messages like these that you are about to read let the light in our souls spark our consciousness to remember that we are eternal gods and goddesses, all of us. We have unlimited potential to help restore Earth to her Eden self and know (once again!) that we are members of God's universal family.

My 35 years immersed in Christian dogma are showing when I say "He" meaning God, who is neither only "he" nor "she," but androgynous, the perfect balance of energies. What we call the Supreme Being in our universe isn't important. But knowing that each of us is an inseparable part of that being and so are all the other souls in our universe IS important. Explaining this and more is the purpose of this book.

The words of God have not been altered by us in any way.

Introduction

God (*received by Suzy*) — The parts of this book ascribed to me are my words and mine alone, *my* messages that I gave to these dear souls to pass on to you. I do so wish that all of you knew that talking with me — and I mean *two-way* conversation — is as natural as breathing, but in this moment most of you, my beloved children, aren't remembering that. In time you will, and what a great day that will be!

Oh yes, I'm only too familiar with this widespread falsehood: "Talking to God is good, but if someone talks back, that's Satan." Does that even make sense? Your mind may believe what you've been told *ad nausea* — God is invisible, silent and all-powerful, and from some distant nebulous place runs your life and everything else in the world — but — your heart, the "seat of your soul" — knows the Truth. As you read, let this Truth ring loud and clear!

****

God (*received by Celest*) — Celest and I had discussed the all too likely probability that many people would consider the words in this book to be "delusionary" or just as bad, that My Book is a "feel good book." Neither is true! I have My reasons for insisting that this book be written in **"My Own Words." YOU** are the reason. Each of you. I am here to prepare you for the times ahead as well as for the times present.

I can do no less for you Children whom I love so dearly. So I request that you read My Book with an open mind and an open heart. That is all I ask of you. Now, sit back, relax and "strap on your seatbelt," I have awaited this timeline for a very, very long time.

****

God (*received by David*) — The times you have all awaited are staring you smack dab in the face. You, My brave Children, have fought off the continuous onslaught of those whose intent was to use and abuse you. You have done so for many, many lifetimes. And yet, you came back to this planet time after time to make a difference and be of service in the world that you called **"home."** I know this has not been an easy row to hoe but the fruits of your labors will soon be realized. There is evidence of this appearing everywhere you look. I ask you to follow your hearts, for they will never lead you astray. Stay out of logic, which will only confuse the issues at hand. I promised you a long time ago that I would always be with you in your times of need. *Promises made, promises kept.* I also promised you that My presence would be felt by all as well as known by all. These good-hearted scribes worked very diligently to record the words that I have shared with each of them. I give My loving thanks to them for writing My words, as well as all of you for reading My words. Peruse these pages at your leisure and when questions enter your minds, quiet your thoughts and listen, for I will answer those questions of yours. I Am the God of this universe and My love for each of you is unconditional as should be yours as well.

****

Chapter 1

Oh yes, it IS all about Me! (*and* You)

God (*received by Suzy*) — My dear children, this is God here. A lot of you have been wondering where I am when so many bad things are happening to good people, and others are blaming me for all of it. I am here to tell you that I'm right where I've been since Day One of this universe — everywhere! — and that it is YOU collectively who are responsible for what happens for good or for ill in your life and your world.

Now then, there are the soul contracts that each of you makes each time you go back to a spirit life and see the big picture of how you've lived in all of your lifetimes. All of those lives on Earth and in the world you call heaven — please call it by its right name, Nirvana — and other places in my universe that you don't remember. Each time before you take on another body, you choose what you need to finish up uncompleted business, so you can move upwards in spirituality and intelligence. All well and good — clearly, evolving is in your best interests, and so it's your contract goal every time.

The thing is, you have free will to do whatever you want to, and if you decide not to stick with your pre-birth choices, that's fine. But when that lifetime ends and once again you're living in Nirvana, once again looking at the big picture, and you see that you still haven't done what you had expected to, you choose it all over again. Occasionally you pat yourself on the back, in a manner of speaking, and move your next physical experiencing up a notch or two. All of this is for balance, you see, and balance is what makes the world go round.

Well, you've been making your world go round and round and round a lot longer than I thought you would. Now, I did put Earth in her place in the Milky Way and set her orbit in motion, taking care so that she doesn't bump into any other big celestial body, but I'm not the one who set her in third density mode where darkness lurks at every corner. Earth's residents did that over the millennia of treating each other and the animals and Earth's body in ungodly ways. That's how those souls before you chose to behave, and some still are, but I assure you, I'm not the one who decided that was the way things would go.

Long before I came into being, Creator gave every soul in the cosmos the privilege of freely expressing whatever the soul wished, and all of us "supreme beings" who reign over the universes are bound to honor Creator's law. This means that regardless of what any of my children in this universe do, I have to sit back and let it happen.

You still think I am in charge, because if not me, then *who?* If so, it must be because you don't understand who YOU are. I'll tell you. Each of you is a part of me — we're inseparable and have been from the Beginning. You are not a physical being who simply happens to have a soul — you are an ETERNAL SOUL having just one more physical lifetime, and it's not my job to tell you how to run it. If your birthright to make your own decisions suddenly went pooooof, and I started mapping out every one of your lives, I believe I would hear howls of protest.

Ah, it is lovely to see you thinking: So, *if everyone in the cosmos has free will, then God does too, so why doesn't he/she change the bad things that people do?* Indeed I do have the same right as you to express myself, but NEVER may I use it to deny YOUR choices to interact on whatever level you choose, and once you've set in motion the energy streamers from your motives and actions, I can't interfere with those either.

I must tell you that I would be much happier if all of you chose to let your obvious differences enrich your lives, not divide you into "enemy camps." I would love to have my various cultures, races, genders, ages, philosophies and life forms that you collectively are living together harmoniously and cooperatively. And I'll admit that in a way, that is self-serving. I know your every thought, I feel your every feeling. Can you imagine the state of mind and emotions that puts me in? It would be tough enough to deal with only Earth — and she's not just the sum of her humans; she's all of her animals and plants, her seas and soil, her skies and what's beneath her surface — it's her entirety of polluted and desecrated planetary body and sorrowing soul that I feel. I won't even mention the rest of your solar system, let alone your galaxy and all the millions of others — just try to imagine the turmoil and agony I feel from only my parts that Earth herself and all of her many billions of life forms constitute. No, of course you can't do that, and I wouldn't wish it upon you!

You're wrong if you think I love my "good folks" one iota more than those you may consider "bad 'uns." That would be like your loving the cells in your liver more than the cells in your fingertip — each of the countless cells in your body is essential and you don't consciously favor some over others, do you? I don't either. Some of your cells may act up on occasion and are a real pain. Sometimes my children are like that, too. But all of your cells and all of my children are individual, yet in-tandem functioning parts of the Whole, and neither you nor I can separate our parts, now can we?

Furthermore — and this is important! — you are there to help each other achieve the balance that all of you are striving for. The very soul you think is despicable may have volunteered for that role to provide many others the experiencing they chose. You don't know who's who, so you'd better see the god/goddess in every person. You want to see the Whole God of Earth? See yourself and all others in every giraffe and jaguar, oak and redwood, stream and ocean, ant and pebble, and respect all as the parts of me that are there for your joy and learning.

It is **my** joy to see how quickly you are learning! For far too many generations my messengers and their messages were ignored or distorted, and Earth grew tired of it. She decided to go back to the vibrations of her body's origin, and in her travels, she's absorbing more and more light. Many of you are feeling your own light expanding as your hearts grow more loving and your visions set on higher horizons. And glory be to you — you're being responsible for your own trip ticket at the same time you're helping pay for your **planet's!**

Still, most of the light paving the way for Earth and her companion travelers is coming from other star nation families. You see, in honoring Earth's free will, I can authorize my children in higher civilizations to help her get where she wants to go and her you go along with her. I'll be glad when you know how much help they are giving you and your world, and the day is nearing when you will. Some call it the Golden Age, and that's a nice name for it — you'll understand then the Sun of God and the Sons and Daughters of God that you all are.

My love embraces you and is within you — feel it, LIVE it! LOVE is the key to everything glorious in OUR universe!

This is an overview; I'll let others give the details. **Questions or comments, anyone?**

Celest — All right, God, one of the greatest hurdles we encounter here is teaching people that challenges are not the horrid issues they think they are. Too many people feel if they are "enlightened" people, they should not have to deal with the same issues that "ordinary people" deal with; what do you have to say about this?

God — Yes, I agree with you, the greatest challenges for each individual Soul to adjust to, and to adapt to, are the hurdles that each Soul Creates not only for themselves, but which invariably impact upon others. If each person saw themselves as a tree, some would see saplings, others would see sturdy oaks, others would see junipers and so forth. An entire forest would be perceived as covering this world, this Earth Star planet in **Nirvana-ly** majesty. Each Soul in human guise then would <u>know</u> without any need to be reminded by MySelf, or any others of the Divine Forces, that each tree, to a certain degree, is dependent upon all the others for growth, for strength, for the harvesting of the beauty that is the stimulus of the tree. Each would further <u>know</u> that *"one tree alone does not a forest make!"*

Yet in reality, the first tree must be here and in "awareness" of who and what it is before other trees can then take root and become the staunch symbols, the sentinels, the eyes and ears of MySelf and the Creation. So if you think of the "Adam and Eve" archetype, think of two trees instead, it would be more truthful anyway. Each tree would be here with a specific mission, each to be fruitful, each to multiply. Each would also give My birds and other life forms ample protection and food and shelter. Many of My Earth Children have wondered about how it happens to be that trees bend with the wind rather than "go against the flow." I take credit for that one! Surely you can know that if I was able to Create the tree for a multitude of purposes, then I would teach the tree to bend rather than break.

So we have a "tree," the tree as the image for collective unconsciousness, so to speak. Each Soul as an individual person now grows slowly just as the tree does, while its roots continue to spread out and downwards, ever seeking more nourishing ground from which to enrich itself. Billions of Aspects of MySelf in different insect forms are attracted to the tree, some seek nourishment from the tree itself while conversely others give nourishment to the tree. Each *in this sense* are dependent for a while upon one another to enhance the life force of each iota of themselves/MySelf. Just as "like attracts like," so does one organism attract another organism that constitutes **the entirety of the whole.** Now, still using the tree as a *prima facie* example of an individual Soul walking the human walk in physicality, the persona of any individual is the direct reflection of the state of their Soul.

No, "small tree" does not mean "small Soul," I thought I better head that one off at the pass! "Persona" then means to ME, that regardless of what color you have chosen to be, regardless of your financial state or your sexual preferences, or anything else of minuscule nature that is part of the Earth Star Walk, it is your own Soul Self, your own Soul Voice that you will exemplify throughout the ages. You each began as a seedling, then slowly progressed to sapling stage and so forth. There are many different Soul levels, Soul stages. Each was designed to allow you the greater freedom to be who and what you truly are.

Which means you are Me and I AM you; yet I know this and most of you do not. You are each your own "tree," you selected the type prior to your first incarnation, yet should you be a "birch tree," now you can choose to be a "ponderosa pine" at another time. This is part of your own "free expression" (free will). If you make those changes of species, it will not affect you as Soul, in most cases it will provide an enhancement. Obviously, if you choose to be a sickly seedling or an ill sapling of any of the species, that would not be an auspicious sign for your present/future reincarnation. There are exceptions of course. Those Souls whose Contracts call for them to choose the experience of genetic illnesses or becoming sickly as a result of noxious substances that have been infecting My Planet have personal reasons for those experiences. Those reasons are **very** personal and private and shall remain that way.

There are those who for as long as *they have been* have chosen to keep one tree as their own, foregoing the "choosing" to be anything else. **You, Celest,** for example, have always been a "Christmas Tree," statuesque, healthy and fully decked out in lights and glittering ornaments. Each individual Soul has the right to not only be whatever they have chosen to be, but to **do it right!** It is only when an individual has lost sight of not only their Soul objectives and Soul ideals that turmoil of the most anguishing kind afflicts that individual. Do I feel it? Well, of course I do! Just not the same way that you do. As I stated earlier, I feel, sense, see, all that each of you do. BUT I must remain passionately detached from the dramas.

You would too if you were in My shoes...well, you are in My shoes... yet it is the walking in human form that can cause the individuals to temporarily "forget" their purpose. They then "forget" about the real Me, which is the REAL *you too,* and lower themselves into a long period, a lifetime for some, of disorganized chaos. Being an "enlightened" individual does not mean there is nothing more to learn! It **really** means there is a tremendous responsibility for continuing to move ever forward at whatever pace you are best suited to. It means... YOU are now an example. It means YOU must now live up to what you are! Let's go back to the trees again; if we see the trees now as a spreading healthy force, then we can see a segment of collective consciousness as a massive independent WAVE of healthy Souls aligned once again with the others they had chosen to be here with for their own evolution. Not merely as the progressive movement of Soul Clusters, but the magnificence of the single FORCE of a Soul that cannot be defeated. I must tell you, you make Me look good!

Celest — All right, God, here is a question that so many people are puzzled by, "Soul Contracts," why are they important and are we ever permitted to read them?"

God — Well, Celest, the relativity of the importance of Soul Contracts is indeed paramount to each individual Soul. These Contracts were devised for the purpose of not merely providing guidelines for Souls to pay attention to, BUT they are a necessity for the Souls to journey forward on the most progressive paths that ultimately lead to the returning to Source. In this sense the "return to Source" is relative to the timelines each Soul experiences as Soul moves forward and not merely is pureness in thought, deed and action, but "ascends" ever further into Myself and all of the Divine Forces. This means as this occurs, each Soul releases any/all final dross which may have impacted on Soul and is finally attuned to the Highest of all Vibrations; the totality of Oneness with MySelf. You see, it is all about states of perfection and levels of integration. The Contracts are given to each Soul EVERYWHERE to "sign," so to speak, each Contract may vary *in action but the purpose of the "destination" of a Soul is clearly understood.* Those who are still "baby" Souls as well as those who are yet... a tad immature... have contracts that are slightly different in nature. Each Contract is geared to each <u>individual</u> being, as well they should be.

It would not be fair to expect one who is on a different level of learning/experience to immediately "elevate" their levels, expectations and/or abilities just because an "Old Soul" is able to accomplish those things. Contracts are a way for Soul to have received a "teaching" and a gestation record defining what Soul can do, and what Soul is advised not to do. Contracts are specifically geared to each Soul, I REPEAT this statement! There is not, nor ever was any "clause" containing any form of retribution to any Soul for whatever he or she may involve themselves in that is contrary to their Contracts.

If a Soul cannot soar freely and learn from all that Soul experiences, then there **cannot** be any **Evolution of a Soul.** However, each Soul does have the free expression to retain the memories of all that was experienced in any given life experience. These memories are housed within the matrix of each Soul and brought back into activated form when Soul has returned "home" during the in-between lifetimes. It is then that Soul can and does examine the previous experiences and compare them with the memories of previous lives. It is also then that Soul CAN review his/her own Contract. Let me be clear about this, this does not mean that Souls can erase what is part of their Contacts; they cannot invalidate the Contract in any way, shape or form. Do not presuppose that Souls would want to do this; I am merely making a statement defining what cannot take place. You see, these are such important periods for each Soul, these periods require adaptability to CHANGE and the innate desire to first understand what, where and how, they may have made errors of judgment in any given life experience, then to augment those previous times by implementing new thought forms to replace the old.

I cannot "make them" do this, I am God, I am not permitted to do that. I cannot interfere with their free expressions when they are home, any more than I can when they are Earthbound. The game of "trivial pursuit" as played out by the dark energies on Earth, who have been determined to keep humanity spellbound with lies, dictated that some gloom and doom **Judgment Day** awaits people when they pass over from physical life. To that I reply,"AARRG!" Although **your father, Blue Star the Pleiadian,** has been known to use that word on occasion, I feel it is the appropriate response to that falsehood. When the physical life here on Earth has reached its conclusion, each Soul "reappraises" ItSelf, each Soul uses all of Its sentience to determine what **changes** It can/should make, predicated upon the Soul's own unique desire to correct ITSELF!

Never underestimate the Soul you are and, remember, you are only the outer persona of Who you really are. You are Soul in physicality; as such it is expected that you shall make errors of judgment. Speaking of which, I really wish you would all learn not to be so hard on yourselves when you stumble on the Earthbound path. After all, it is only a matter of non-time before you pick your-selves up and start anew. I do believe part of the misconceptions you have about "Contracts" is that unwittingly you tie the term into some manmade conception; one that is a bitter pill to swallow. So stop doing that and think of your own Soul Contacts as "a teaspoon of sugar to help the learning go down."

Celest — One last issue, God, people need to understand that none of us want anyone to become obsessive about their Contracts; also people should understand that each Contract is "privileged information," for God's Eyes only.

God — Celest, I know that has been bothering you. I agree with you, I say a resounding **Yes**, people need to be aware of the existence of Contracts. **But** We do not want them to become infatuated with the subject. All of what you have said is true about the Contract issue! Although We will all be speaking about the Contracts throughout the book, under no circumstances do We want any of My Children to dwell overmuch on this subject. By the end of this book all will know as much as they need to **at this time**. No one needs to know more than this about their Contracts while they are in physical form **unless** the individual Soul decides it is necessary for the person to know more. As Soul evolves, while an individual is walking in human form, Soul will permit certain information to be received by that individual as Soul deems necessary. Also, I caution all people not to seek psychics, mediums, etc., and ask them to reveal information about another individual's Contract. There are penalties that can be imposed for trying to find out about matters that are Sacred to another being. No one on Earth should attempt to violate another person's Soul by asking for information which is not their right to know. Have I been clear enough about this, Celest?

Celest — Yes, God, you have. I thank you for speaking about this now before anyone attempts to do something that is against "God Principles." OK, I feel better now.

God — Good, when you feel better, I feel better too.

David — I have heard from many people, and I also share this thought at times, who wish to read the fine print of their contracts. I also hear so often from you and others that *"you are on a need to know basis and right now, you do not need to know, when you do, we will tell you."* Any comments on this?

God — Throughout your many lifetimes, David, I have at times shared that thought with you. I thought what a novel idea it would be to let a Soul read the fine print and allow them to straighten up and walk forward, instead of consistently swerving sideways. But alas, that is not to be and for good reason too. If I were to make an exception for one person, can you begin to *imagine* the aftermath of events that would occur because one did not wish to follow his/her own chosen path? Ah ha, so the twinkling of remembrance is still there and you do see that the cause and effect of any action is or could be an equal and opposite reaction leading to unknown arenas of disorganized chaos. My dearest ones, as much as I would love to honor your requests, the fine print that exists within each individual's contract is there for specific purposes. It is not to be tampered with by either MySelf or any of My other Children. That is why I **gifted** you with your many intuitive gifts; those that are there for you to see by looking beyond yourself and your physical vehicle and peering into the vast realms of possibility. Every personage, whoever you are at this time, who is there now on My planet, has this ability. Do you understand? OK, let me see if I can clarify this a tad bit more. Let's see, how shall I delicately put this? NO, you may not see the fine print on your Soul Contracts.

When you as Soul leave the planet, you will have more than ample time to peruse your own Contracts, as well as examine the cause and effect of all those who interacted with you in that lifetime. You will see that what one did, or did not do, ultimately affected the outcome of another. The easy part is planning your individual life experiences for the growth opportunities that each lifetime possesses. The hard part for many of you is actually playing out your designated roles. It is not always easy, for if it was, what lessons would you have learned? Each must challenge themselves in order to gain the wisdom needed to evolve into a finer aspect of

Self. At this time you may choose to interact with those who were not true to their Soul's nudging, and it may be that you may feel that they cheated you out of your true calling. Now if this were true, which of course it isn't, would there have been any reason why there would have been any provisions for such an instance to be added to all the active participants' roles? Every "t" was crossed, every "i" was dotted, checked and rechecked by all consenting participants well before the timeline for your arrival on Earth.

The status of any good Soul Contract will have provisions and loopholes to allow you to move into another different arena from the one you may have originally chosen. Yet each has its own rewards. Perhaps by looking at the brighter side of things and acknowledging that you may have just moved forward up the ladder of life another rung, realizing you did not even consciously know that you did this, is a good thing. To me it would make sense to take advantage of every opportunity that presents itself, whether it be a window of opportunity or a doorway that opened. Your presence there at that time made it possible for you to experience that "once in a lifetime gift" that was handed to you on a silver platter.

Let me make one thing perfectly clear, there are no coincidences in life. Each and every one of you will be at a predestined place at a predestined time if that is what you had written in your Soul Contracts. Each and every opportunity realized or unrealized has been accounted for. Have you ever heard the expression, *"This is a movie?"* Well, there you go, and now you are here to play out your chosen roles to the best or worst of your abilities. As I said before, I feel everything you do, can you imagine this? I did not think so. Yet when all is said and done, is it not you and I and the rest of My Children who benefit from each other's triumphs and tribulations?

For now put your mind at ease, whatever you wished you had done and failed to do, whatever grievous thing you may think you have done in your life, can be rectified and opportunities will arise to correct all perceived wrongs. Please remember, all wrongs are not by accident either, someone has to play the bad guy in order for you to be the hero or heroine, whichever the case may be. Let me ask you a question and please take your time in thinking about the answer.

Would you really like to have lived a life with no mistakes and every-thing went according to plan? If so, tell Me, dear Children, what would you have learned? In order to be a great warrior, you must first have lost at least one battle, how else would you know what defeat is? Would you be satisfied later on, knowing that you had cheated yourself and did not even know it? I did not think so.

The human mind has a tendency to be far too harsh on itself, the games that it plays are but a moot point here. What each must realize is that it was *each of you* who trained your intellects to respond the way they do, it was not I. When all life was first conceived, the *"communication"* was always to be with Soul Voice. The intellect was designed as a failsafe mechanism, not as the con-trolling entity it has evolved into. I *MySelf* am the soft subtle voice in your heads reassuring you, encouraging you to do what is best for you. I hear all your prayers, I even answer all of them. Sadly I must admit that **you**, My Children, simply do not hear Me anymore. Yet times are a-changing and what was once old will be new again. What was once thought "lost" will make its presence known. What will be, will be, and neither you nor I can change that and who would want to? If all were known, what fun would life be?

Many of My Children have expressed themselves well through their individual gifts of "insight." These gifts are known by you as "Clairaudience, Clairsentience, and Clairvoyance." This is not a special gift set aside only for them, yet they have earned it through their many lifetimes. However, not even my Celestial daughter, who sees so very clearly, knows everything. You could ask her what she would say if asked, "Would she want to know everything before it happened?" Her answer would be, "Of course not, what fun would that be?" You see, she knows as well as do Suzy and you, David, that you would not at any time, for any reason, wish to miss out in all the fun. And that, My Dear Children, is what life is all about. It is about growth experiences, momentous moments, and inspira-tional breathtaking moments in time, that for most would be shared only with themselves, to treasure for all of eternity.

Well, David, as to the second part of your question, when I feel "you have a need to know," then and only then shall I answer you.

You see, My Children, it was I who said I would never leave you,

you would never be **alone**. I did not, however, say that I would not leave you to your own devices. I did tell you I would be there for each and every one of you while you walked upon My Beloved Terra. You see, the Earth and the human being was a great experiment of momentous proportions. As such it was agreed that all who were brave enough and willing enough to go on this journey would never be "left alone." What was never My intention was that so many of you would become ensnared in the dualities of existing in human guise. It was also never My intention that so many of you, in fact all of you at one time or another, and some for many, many lifetimes, would decide to ignore Me and quit listening to *My Song*.

Now the very young Children and those who are young at heart never did. In all their innocence they knew instinctively that it was I who was conversing with them. This, too, changed as their parents and guardians started impressing upon them their own ideals, ideas and preconceived notions of how things were. Again we go back to the **CON**-ditioning which those of the dark intent cast upon the innocents with their webs of lies in order to control and enslave them. It was at this point that even the young Children lost their connectedness with All That Is. Now this was not My Intention. My promise to you was to always be available to counsel whoever was in need. It is not I who went off and left you, it was you who stopped heeding *My Song*. Now that you are leaving the drafty confines of the third-dimension behind, once again you shall embrace your universal families along with MySelf and start remembering that *"We are All One."*

David — God, perhaps people will start *living their lives* instead of regretting things they had done in the past and wondering **how** they should have lived them. Thank you, that was most en-light-ening. Do you have anything to say about those who are curious about their previous incarnations?

God — David, please pass this on to all those who are obsessing with the past. The past is gone; it is over and **please** start living here and now in the present. There are reasons for knowing the past lifetimes you have endured or enjoyed. However, from My point of observation, I see that some of you are so busy trying to figure out the past, to see how it may relate to your present lifetimes, you forget to live for today. The present is what is occurring all around you. It is this which requires the entirety of your focus in order for you to keep your wits about you in the days ahead. These will be challenging times even for the most stout of heart/mind and Spirit. The past has already occurred; the lessons that you are faced with today are the ones that will offset the unfinished lessons from the past. You, yourself, set up these events and I would encourage you to keep that foremost in your minds. That should do it, David.

David — Thank you. I think that should settle that question, at least for the moment.

Suzy — Hi, God. Can you please give a concrete example of what we do that's not in our best interests because it's not in our soul contracts?

God — Very good idea, Suzy, and I have an excellent example on the tip of my tongue — pettiness. It's that clutter-clatter of attitudes, interests and activity that keep you preoccupied with trivialities that aren't worth even one bean in the hill, yet have the power to prevent reasoned, sensible thoughts, evaluations and actions.

All of you need to think about how you spend your time. How much do you devote to light-filled thoughts, conversations and actions — BEing the light you really are? How much do you spend in silence and solitude so peacefulness can ease away the pressures of daily tasks? How much goes to playing with your families and animals, smiling and laughing, listening to melodious music or reading something that expands your mind, or connecting with the beauty of Nature? How often do you see and feel thankful for the blessings in your life or go within your deeper self and listen to the song of your soul?

"I'm too busy!" won't cut it, my dear children. What I just mentioned is restorative, rejuvenating, energizing and essential for balance in your days and within you. When you oust pettiness in its

many forms, there IS time for uplifting experiences.

Because I am you/you are me, I know what your petty stuff is. I'm suggesting that you sort through that vast heap of mindless TV programs and gossip sessions, inane chattering and pointless spats, worries about "what if" and rumors of dire possibilities, jealousies and nit-picking, nagging and griping, and letting mere curiosity rather than core interests occupy your thoughts. Consider if giving those your time and energy is as important as LIGHTening your mind, body and soul.

Like I was saying, most of you have been on the merry-go-round in lower vibrations over and over, and some of you MANY times over and over. NO, I'm NOT faulting you for this, and it's NOT because you've been "bad!" It's because you got stuck in the mind control that the darkness levied through its religions and their various dogmas. That orientation led you to accepting the words of other "authority figures" without questioning, like those who send many of my children off to wars to kill others of my children. You are born with an amazing capacity to think and reason, but the collective influence of "authorities" dulled your use of it and, without resistance, you bought into the rhetoric and followed the instructions.

The thing is, your soul DOES resist. At that level you know that being a "sheep" isn't what you signed up for, and this soul-to-consciousness conflict becomes problematic. Part of you wants to rebel, the other part squelches it — after all, you're only following what the assortment of authorities tells you. So you live with conscious, or maybe subliminal, anger and resentment instead of feeling the light of self-awareness and self-worth, and your escape into pettiness naturally follows.

So my suggestion that you compare the benefits of escaping vs. light-filled pastimes and outlook is not criticism, my dear ones, it is wise and loving motherly/fatherly advice. Like I've said, there still is time, but not much, to realize your soul power and USE it. LOVE-LIGHT is the way to get off that bumpy merry-go-round ride, and it automatically will come when you exchange pettiness for knowing and LIVING the value of BEing your SOULSELF. The choice is yours and whatever that is, I honor it in infinite eternal love. There, how was that, Suzy?

Suzy — I don't have any questions about what you said, just how you said it. You sound different when you talk to me than when you talk to Celest and David — it seems that you always speak more "plainly" to me than to them. Why?

God — Suzy, dear little soul, I simply talk to you the way you think and speak and to them the way they do. You don't get that, do you, because you're remembering what Matthew told you, that telepathic communication is an energy transfer of the source's thoughts into your mind. And he's right, of course, about himself and all the others who talk with you. But you and I are One and the Same, so naturally we both use your expressions, your kind of thinking and style of speaking, your frames of reference. Let me make a simple comparison here. Say you're a scoop of chocolate ice cream, others are cherry or vanilla or caramel, some are orange, lime or lemon sherbet, and still others are a strawberry sundae or a banana split. I just follow suit whatever flavor the scoop or serving is.

Suzy — Well, your sense of humor gets to all of us anyway! Thank you. That's it for now!

Celest — Well, God, referencing back to your previous statement; I have been called many names, not all of them pleasant but "ice cream" is a new one on me. Hmm... I will have to think on that for a while. Don't bother to reply, God, just think "sweet thoughts."

Chapter 2

What is it about *change* you don't understand?

God *(received by Suzy)* — Good morning, dear little Suzy, and yes, that is my choice for this chapter's title — it's my *intention* to rattle some cages.

However paradoxical it may seem, the only constant anywhere is *change*. Your world is teeming with greater changes than ever before, and I assure you, you wouldn't want it any other way! Many who sensed a need to make changes are doing so confidently, but for some of you, moving out of the familiar space seems scary. *"Whatever will happen if I change my job or location or even my mate? Oh NO, not my* beliefs *too?!"* You'll get on with what you chose to experience, that's what will happen. Is that so bad, that you'll get yourself out of a rut and get on with Life's Adventure that you signed up for?

Of course not everyone needs to change jobs or mates or relocate, but many DO need to change beliefs, and here are the first two if you believe that (1) Your individuality means you're separated from everyone else, and (2) I am the cosmic superpower that makes everything happen. You're definitely a unique individual, but also you're an inseparable part of me and all others *everywhere*, and it's ALL of us in this universe who make things happen.

Hmmmmm. So you're a bigger deal than you thought and maybe I'm not such a big deal after all. Not exactly, my dear ones. WE ARE, together, ONE amazing powerhouse with infinite and eternal potential — so yes, you better believe I AM powerful! And it's not because I control you — I *don't*. It's because you and all other life in this universe are my BEing in all your experiencing forms — *collectively WE ARE this universe!*

I have more to say about beliefs, but let's talk about why I don't control you, which is much like your idea that I let bad things

happen to good people, so I'm going to expound on that "fre
business I talked about in Chapter 1. This is how it goes: Cr
ruler of the cosmos — that's all the universes — gave you free wi
express whatever you want to and gave us universe rulers a law we
have to obey: *Stay out of your soul parts' choices!* Eons later Creator
made the one exception to that law: *"No nuclear wars anywhere,"* so
now we rulers have the authority to stop all efforts to do that.

Otherwise, it's like I said, your choices all the way, and
actually, that's an excellent basis for your multiple lifetimes
around our universe. If you stray from the path you chose in your
soul contracts —those pacts you make before you are born so you
can grow beyond that stage of evolution — I can't mess with that. I
do have a hand in it, though. Creator thoughtfully put a loophole in
that free will law that lets me put conscience as an ingredient of
your souls, and that's what can keep you on your straightaway
path, *if you want it to.* Like everything else, it's your choice to pay
attention to it or ignore it. Conscience should come with a warning:
Ignore me and I'll become extinct. Well, just as you don't come with
copies of your soul contracts, you don't come with a warrantee on
your conscience either. You have instinct, intuition, inspiration and
a sense of honor, too — those are other ingredients I put in souls
that also help you know what's right and what's wrong for you.

But — sometimes "but" is necessary, and this is a big one —
what you may think is right may be wrong and *vice versa.* You don't
consciously know what's in your contract, and you sure don't know
what's in anyone else's. Your contract is your part of the pre-birth
agreement made by the souls who want to be in on the "give-and-
take" lifetime of shared experiences. The agreements provide
growth opportunities for every soul, so you can see that they're all-
around win-win situations.

So think about this: You (or they) *chose* to be on one end or the
other of "bad" things and you (or they) did it for one of two reasons,
both of which provide experiencing that balances other lifetimes,
and balance is essential for soul growth. One, you (or they) needed
to feel what it's like to endure hardships and others volunteered to
provide the circumstances that let you (or them) do that. Or: *"Been
there, done that"* and this time around you (or they) are the

volunteer(s). You can call this karma if you like — just don't interpret this opportunity to achieve balance as a reward or a punishment for yourself or anyone else.

Something else you need to know about those agreements is that *unconditional love* is the basis on which *ALL* the souls fill their various roles. Out of love, some agree to be the "heavies" for those who choose the "rough way to go" — I explained the reason for this see-saw experiencing. The thing is, you've been stuck for only I know how long on this bumpy see-saw of third density, where deceit, tyranny, violence and corruption are part and parcel of everyday life. You're sick and tired of it, so this time around you chose — again! — to get out of it, and believe me, you wouldn't want me sticking my finger in and doing anything that might keep you *in* it! You have no idea of the domino effect if I meddled in just a few lives, no matter how good my intention! I'm not allowed to do that anyway.

Now, some of my children aren't on Earth to wind up their karma — or if you prefer, call this universal law Divine Grace — they're there to HELP all the rest of you do it. And you'd better be grateful that they are willing to temporarily leave their families and homelands in higher planes to help you fulfill your pre-birth choice to deal with third density and be done with it.

Since doing that may require you to make some changes, maybe you'll welcome more suggestions for going about that. Foremost is: DON'T GO INTO FEAR! If you think you have any enemies, you'd better know that fear's by far the worst. From my point of view, it's your ONLY one, and I strongly suggest you give my opinion of this careful thought. My messengers have told you time and time again that fear isn't only the fuel that keeps the dark ones alive and kicking, it's also their favorite tool because fear's energy forms a barrier between the soul and the consciousness that light can't penetrate. They have said as well that you need light to physically survive in the vibrations where Earth is heading — reason enough to stay out of fear, and you don't need me to expound on that.

But you've also been told what results from fretting about "what if this or that happens," yet whenever you hear something *"scary,"* far too many of you leap back into fear, so I am going remind you why you shouldn't. Energy is neutral — you could even say "mindless," because it can't distinguish between what you want and what you don't. Energy streamers simply pick up attachments, those countless thought forms from every soul in our universe since Day One, and they're all swirling around in the universal pot. The energy in your worries shoots out to that pot, finds the most similar forms, boomerangs back to you and lays at your feet the circumstances that best match those in your head. *Voila!* You have just "bought" yourself something to really fret about. And when a bunch of you focus on the same thing, the result is exponentially more effective, whether it's what you want or the furthest thing from it.

There's something else about fear — it rears its ugly head in a number of ways. Actually, everything you may think of as "negative" has fear at its root: tyranny, war, greed, deceit, prejudice, corruption, violence, jealousy, vengeance, guilt, anger, despair, hopelessness — the whole spectrum of attitudes and actions that make life in third density formidable for those on the receiving end. OK, there are those soul contracts, but you don't get any extra "brownie points" for *repeatedly* experiencing what you chose!

Another thing is, "Judge not..." — some things in the Bible are right. You do know that I don't ever judge you, don't you? "Judgment day" — I don't care much for that term — is when you review your past lifetime in the context of ALL your lifetimes, see where you need to improve things, and based on that you choose what to put in your soul contract for the next time around. Anyway, not judging is a key to helping self and each other evolve and so is gratitude. Feeling thankful for the help is as important as not judging the helpers. That doesn't ever mean approving of greed or viciousness or violence — you certainly don't have to do that! Gratitude is acknowledging and appreciating that some of you agreed to play the "heavies" because others need that to wrap up their last remnants of third density. It would be good, too, if you also feel thankful that you wanted *and were selected* to participate in this magnificent time of Earth's entry into the Golden Age.

"Golden" because only light will prevail on Earth, and how she will rejoice! She is a beloved part of me just as you are yourself, and price she paid to give her humankind many, many, MANY chances to get it right and "see the light" — it nearly cost her planetary life. I'll tell you more about that, but the point here is, she's giving all of you this one last chance to wake up and wise up. Part of that is, you have to stop confusing religion with spirituality, and that brings us back to beliefs.

I'm not saying that all of you are clinging to beliefs that are based on false teachings, but if you believe that your religion is better than all the others, listen up. My messengers whom you attach to the various religions didn't set those up. In a nutshell, the very concept of religion came from the thoughts of dark ones off-planet, and today's religious teachings are based on what a few of my self-serving parts on the planet said a long time ago: *If you don't obey God* — or some other name they gave me — *you're doomed*, and they said that was "My Word." Those few folks wanted to control everyone else, so they wrote the rules of "obedience" that spell "doom" to falterers. And I have to tell you, Christianity is THE major digresser from the truth that my messenger came to give. Yes, the one you call Jesus, and oh my! how they changed his life from the factual to the fictional — it's hard to know where to begin to set the story straight.

The FACT is that Jesus was never put on a cross, so there was no crucifixion or resurrection. That rather blows the whole foundation of Christian dogma, doesn't it? For how, then, could it be that "he gave his life to save sinners"? Sinners means the whole lot of you, according to those who came up with the idea that everyone is "born into sin." Oh dear me! The *only* "sin," if you will, is interfering with the growth of a soul, your own or anyone else's, and the result is DEvolution with as many more chances as needed NOT to do that.

Then there's Mary Magdalene — how wretchedly the Bible portrays her! She was Jesus' wife and ultimate soulmate, and after the Sanhedrin flogged her husband and warned him to get out of their territory — they didn't want to make him a martyr as that would give impetus to his teachings — they went to the East, where Jesus had spent the "lost" years learning from the masters how to perform "miracles" and where he knew his family was safe. He and Mary had a large happy family there, and years later they all traveled to the West and settled in what now is France. Eventually Jesus returned to the East and along the way continued teaching My REAL Word — the Bible includes some of that, but everything in the early records that didn't support the self-serving ones' cause got left out — and he lived to a ripe old age. Although in their later years he and his adored Mary were apart in body, they were so highly attuned spiritually that they were together then, as now and evermore, in spirit and celestial visitations.

Later leaders of the Roman Catholic faith made up absurdities like "the only son of God," "virgin birth" and "immaculate conception" and made layers of saints. They did that to put *still more* distance between "my ONLY son" and all my other children — and ME, who is ALL of you! — as well as making themselves the gate-keepers to heaven. Or hell. Actually, neither exists as portrayed, but that's another story.

Those leaders were greedy, too. In the centuries during and after Jesus' life, the same few people ran church and state, and along with unfair taxation of their poor countrymen, the church of Rome came up with a two-edged sword to cement their control: *You can atone for your sins* — they made those up too — *if you confess and pay money, and a portion of everything you have must be given as well.* That spread to other churches and you know it as tithing. Something else that church did now and again was demand of their priests sexual abstinence, as if denying that strong nature in humankind made them more "saintly," and you know what that led to. Then there were all those wars and inquisitions and brutal killings in my name!

Later movers and shakers of the Roman Catholic religion decreed that birth control is a sin and, more recently, so is abortion. With the wanton killings they've caused or sanctioned throughout the ages, it's hardly sanctity of life that interests them. No, it's to keep the population growing that financially supports them and bows to their authority. From Day One of the papacy, the appointed one and his close circle have lived in opulence that has been paid for by the masses they brainwashed into believing that the church's rules came from ME.

If it sounds like I'm picking on that religion, it's because its

31

headquarters, the Vatican, has been the biggest hotbed of darkness from its beginning. No other religion has it all right or all wrong either — strands of truth are in the "holy books," but the Bible is by far the most seriously distorted to keep unquestioning followers mesmerized. And while the original basis of individuals' faith may have been pure long ago, fanatical elements have defiled that purity to the extent that some of you think they represent the religion itself.

Realizing that EVERY soul is a precious and EQUAL part of me and I love each and every one unconditionally, let's look at the collective soul-selves "religiously." Fundamentalist Protestants say that unless you accept Jesus as your "lord and savior," you'll burn in hell for eternity — I notice that they tend to leave me out of it. Some congregations have split over accepting or scorning my beloved children who are homosexual by *birth* choice, and they choose it for good reason: It's an advanced stage of balanced masculine and feminine energies, and all my children experience those lifetimes as they progress toward androgyny. Islam is seen as rewarding its followers for "killing the infidels," and my women children are deemed inferior to my men children. Zionism, a political militant movement, hides behind the skirts of Judaism and cries "anti-Semitism"; and the pacifist Far Eastern religions, which have adhered most closely to my messengers' teachings, are deemed by the others as out of touch with reality. As if those painful departures from SPIRITUALITY aren't enough, this whole situation has become so befouled that even Satanism with its diabolical tortures and human sacrifice is an established religion.

It's been like the plaintiff wail of a broken record but with far harsher, far sadder effects as generation after generation, my Earth soul-selves have been mind-controlled by religious "authorities." Once the people were stuck in those clutches, governments and all other institutions that impact life on Earth easily became authority figures too. Lifetime after lifetime after lifetime you heeded their words and failed to hear mine.

How did that whole sad state of affairs come about? It was the work of the off-planet dark force that is without conscience, without light except the spark of viability. That force "captured" my weak-willed children of Earth who got caught up in the lure of power and money and, performing as the force's puppets, they kept all the rest of my children in the bondage of fear, poverty and ignorance. The souls' need for *balanced* experiencing kept it going until now — that ages-old merry-go-round is stopping. There's more to say about that, but I want to give you a good example of ignorance.

"All life began in the sea and apes are humans' ancestors." OH?! I'm not saying that primitive sea life and apes and their relatives aren't parts of me, but can't you see how DEMEANING the very idea is that *that* is how I started you, my HUMAN souls?! You credit me —well, some of you do — with making you "in my own image," and I assure you, my drawing board didn't start with you as amoebas, some of which I "inspired" to move to dry land and grow into apes, and then I picked which ones of those I wanted to become humans. Your ancestors are such highly spiritual and intelligent beings that you can't even imagine it! Yes, your "theory of evolution" was in there somewhere, but not as you understand it. Nothing's "black or white," the way you think.

Now about the price Earth paid for enduring the darkness throughout the millennia of the insidious workings of religions and other sources of near equal dark persuasion. She kept giving her own light to sustain the lives of her humankind as they slaughtered each other and destroyed and polluted her Nature until all the bloodshed and devastation nearly claimed her own body, your planet home. Her soul which stayed in its high plane of origin, as her body spiraled downward into low third density, was in deep sorrow and despair. Her planetary self survived because she cried out for help and my children in civilizations far advanced from you spiritually, intellectually and technologically — yes, some are your ancestors! — rushed to infuse Earth's body with their light so it could survive. She wanted to give you this one last chance to open your minds, "light up" your consciousness and shake free from the shackles of that dark force.

And this brings us to *why* that LONG merry-go-round ride that you're sick and tired of is stopping. So is my beloved Earth fed up with it! She's on the fast track out of third density where, until recently, the darkness has been quite successful, but its time is up

— ...e dark force "has left the building," so to say. Only the lingering effects of its influence on its Earth puppets remain and those are fading fast. The truths "coming to light" are exposing once-hidden agenda, and by the impartial law of physics regarding form and frequencies, the puppet's refusal to accept the light will cause their demise along Earth's ascension path. Your dear planet is home-ward bound to her soul's blissful plane, and all who go with her will live in harmonious cooperation with your benevolent "space" family. The trip ticket is free, but with strings: You need to know and live the TRUTH of who *WE* ARE. This isn't complex — it's as simple as paying attention to what your soul is telling you! "Going within" automatically connects you *consciously* with soul-self — that's you and me — and all the rest follows naturally.

I never take sides — how could I when I'm ALL of you! — but I do have my druthers, and I'd love to have all my children choose to live together peacefully. So I hope you will believe what I've said and act on it, but I can't make you — it's always been your choice to believe what you want, do what you want. All I can do is add my voice to the messengers who have told you the very same things through their Earth receivers. What will happen if you don't believe us? What will happen to the souls who will never know about our messages? They will go to a placement attuned to the energy they put forth in deeds and motives throughout the lifetime.

Some will journey with Earth because they are living in "godly" ways simply by heeding their souls' messages. They live from their hearts, where unconditional love, kindness, honor, truth, compassion and desire to help others lie.

Some will go through it again — the tyranny, violence, corruption, lies, the hold of religions — and they'll come in with the brain power to question and reason, yet another chance to break free of dark control. But not on Earth. There are other third density places in our universe where rampant disrespect for life will go on until all my soul parts know the truth of their god- and goddess-selves.

And some will DEvolve and start over from scratch. They're the ones who persist in choosing darkness over LOVE, the same Creator Source energy as light. Constantly light will be beamed to those souls, who will start with only basic instinct, and when they accept the light, they'll recall a smidgeon of intelligence. As they accept more light, they will remember a modicum of reasoning ability, and so on and so on. This isn't punishment, it's a chance for those parts of me to start over without even a hint of darkness.

It's quite a lot to think about, isn't it? There is time, my beloveds, but frankly, not much, to decide what you want. Whatever that is, I will honor it, and if it's help, ask and it shall be given!

David — *God*, I know this is a lot of information for many people to swallow, is there any reason for them to seek confirmation on your words of this day? Many will find reason to disagree due to their previously held belief systems and will stop reading at some given point, what would you say to them?

God — David, you know as well as I do from all the emails, personal contacts. etc., you have made with others that not everyone is going to be willing to adjust their entire life's belief structure in one swift movement. There are many who will need reassurance from others that what their "gut" feeling is telling them is true. I encourage all of you to follow your instincts, always use discernment in all that you read, watch or listen to. What is "true" will resonate from deep within the bowels of your being, this is Soul Voice along with My own encouragements that are leading you on the course *you* have selected. The advice I most heartedly give at this time would be the same as I would give to any of My Children, no matter what their location or evolutionary status. If it resonates and feels like the truth, then most likely it is. If you feel resistance of momentous proportions, then perhaps it is either not true or you simply are not ready for these revelations at this time. Either way the choice is as it always has been, yours to make.

I am not a scolding, overprotective parent, although like most, I do wish only the best for all of you. Nor do I have a desire to impose upon your thoughts and ideas that would go against everything that you believe in. Unfortunately, far too many of My children do not believe in themselves, much less anything else, they are simply skating through life with no purpose, nor direction to be

.. How would you suppose I reach out to them, I too must abide by the *Laws of Non-Interference*? You see, it is a quagmire of untold proportions. If I were to make it mandatory for all to believe in Me and to do as I say, would I be any better than the self-serving parts of Myself that for eons have controlled, enslaved you and kept you in ignorance of who and what in totality you are? Each part of Me comprises the whole, and as such each part of Me expresses themselves to the infinite degree in the realities that present themselves every moment as possibilities. I would love for all of you to be able to join My beloved Gaia into the Golden Age, yet I know that this is not possible at this present time period, for there are far too many disbelievers in Me.

Which brings us to "agnostics." Oh boy, the direction some Children take. If they do not believe in Me, how can they possibly fathom the very concept of their own God-liness? I have not washed My hands of them, nor will I throw them out with the bathwater. Gauging how the amount of the controlling religious hyperbole has been force fed into all of you for so long, who can blame them? How can one believe in something that they do not wish to know exists? If one does not believe in a God or Creator, if one does not believe they hold the **key** to their own immortality, if one does not wish to fathom any connectedness with each other, how can they possibly join the journey so many are now participating in?

It is really quite simple, be kind, be helpful, "be yourself," be your GodSelf without even knowing it. Some of the best teachers don't have one iota of a clue that they are, they just "are," there are no pretenses to be found. I would also tell them to Love with all their heart, trust and believe in yourself and that will radiate outward to all receptive others, allowing them the courage to believe that they too can make a difference, no matter if they lack complete comprehension of the whole picture or not. Their Spirituality lies within them, surrounding them, awaiting the right moment to make its presence known. They do not require a plaque or a master's degree in theology, or a list of credentials to show that they are doing My work, much less do they need to know that they are. Just because they do not believe in Me does not make them bad people, quite the contrary, actually. They are expressing their free will choices, just as are all of you in your search for the meaning and purpose to your existence, your be-ing.

I send delighted blessings to all who have the courage and curiosity to pick up this manuscript and venture into an area that may be unknown territory to them at this time. Also to those who have the desire to start remembering that which they had long forgotten. There are many who will understand and resonate with all that I have said these many days. I also understand that a great many will come across a phrase, or My choice of words, that does not appeal to them. I also understand that opposition, as a result of long-standing beliefs being *challenged,* will always be the forerunner to any great undertaking or massive **change**. Which brings us back to why change is so important. If you thoroughly understood the previous chapter, then that should not be a question in your minds.

"Resistance is futile" is not one of my favorite Earthly expressions. I believe that belongs to the Borg species from that well known sci-fi series, *Star Trek.* Much to My dismay, however, many people will feel resistance to change and that is their right, yet "resistance" will be futile in the end as those who do not wish to accept the overwhelming influx of Light will be fating themselves to repeating lessons that could have easily been avoided. Eventually all will move into the Light of Awareness and will come to recognize their true God/Goddess selves. The world you are now currently residing on has great desire and compassion to be of assistance to all who have the intent and desire to be able to find completion from their karmic pasts. However, please remember that there is good karma and there is the not-so-good karma; both work hand in hand. There has never been a time in Earth's history where it has been possible to complete all this in one lifetime. This is another fine example of My *Divine Grace.* In your current times of "now," you have the means at your disposal to take quantum leaps in your own evolutionary station. You all knew this coming in to this dimension. Evolutionary progression was promised to you as a "possibility" or "probability," when you all agreed to participate in the Greatest Show on Earth, just as you all willingly volunteered to help rid My beloved Gaia of all vestiges of the darkness that held control of Her physical body. There were timelines set up in advance for all of you to awaken, yet the masses who are still among the **walking asleep** still roam the wastelands of Spirit-less deserts.

That brings us to those that are love-less. These ones have not yet come to understand that to love without limits, nor without conditions imposed, without judgment, is the greatest gift they can bestow upon *themselves*. In order to truly love another, one must first love themselves in the same capacity, unconditionally. They must first be their own "best friend," so sorry, I guess that means you are going to have to start liking yourselves as well. If you look into a mirror and do not like what you see, then perhaps it is time for you to initiate the changes necessary to correct that oversight which was of your own doing. Love can be likened to an infectious disease. It can cause great distress and discomfort to be loved by another without you first knowing that love which comes only from within. Love knows no bounds, it is limitless in its capacity to lift the very essence of a person's Soul into the ethers of Creation. It is not bound by any dimensional limitations, nor jurisdictions. It is timeless, yet it withstands the **tests of time** in of itself.

I gifted to all of you the ability "to do," "to be," to accomplish anything, to Create something, anything from nothingness. I gave you the ability to expand upon yourselves to the Infinite degree omni-directionally, all aspects of your Soul's desire to express itself and enhance all facets of itself at the same time. You have the ability to manifest the realities necessary for you to feel at peace with yourselves, to overcome yourselves, to challenge yourselves and to Love yourselves. You have an unlimited capacity to love, to appreciate, to wonder, to explore alternative options that will lead to a higher understanding and increased Soul growth, and yet at the same time, to be of assistance to another aspect of the Universal One. Yet most people do not use this gift.

When Earth rises to Her rightful place in the higher frequencies, all who are with Her will once again be able to Create through thought everything that they need or desire, to make their lives more purposeful and fulfilling. There will be no more need for monetary compensation, for all will work for the Greater Good. All will work in complete harmony with nature. There will be no more dis-eases to cause you distress. Your retirement homes, your sanitariums, your dependence on governmental assistance for your well being, will become a thing of the past. In that frequency when a Soul reaches that particular stage when they have gone as far as they can go, or care to go, in any given lifetime of experiencing, they will simply allow their physical body to die so that they can journey into another higher realm of understanding and Spiritual clarity.

There is much to look forward to, yet you still hold on to your material possessions with the utmost care. You fear the unknown, yet you embrace petty desires. For most, holding on to the past with such a stranglehold on their memories means that you/they forget to live here and now in the present. You cherish the memories of your lost, departed or fallen ones by mourning and building shrines to them, instead of simply honoring yourself and them by saying, "thank you for be-ing," thus allowing all concerned the freedom to move on. You worship, you idolize those who are in "tune" with the **physical** world, not realizing that it is but a masterful illusion. Illusions are holographic, they can cause the truth to become disrupted or distorted at any time. They cause you pain and angst for you do not know how to see through them.

You want what you already have, yet you still know it not. I cannot give you what you already have, what I can do is to help you realize that you are already there. What you do with it now is completely up to you.

David — Well, God, this should give those that require "food for thought" something to chew upon.

God — How right you are. That is the Soul purpose of this entire manuscript.

Celest — God, I think you just answered David's question pretty completely. Can you think of something to tell the teachers, whether they are on an evolved level of "knowing" or not, that could help them during their natural periods of frustration when dealing with people who try to challenge the teachers' beliefs? I tell other teachers to not try to prove something intangible for it cannot be proven in the old third-dimensional way.

God — Celest, I heard your thought forming while I was answering your David — well, your and MY David. Yes, I know of which you speak of course. I have borne witness to the onslaught of challenging questions that seem to follow My teachers when attempting to speak of My Truths. The ones of My Children, who are still stuck in mindless theology and bastardized truths, are always the Children who taunt the true Wisdom Speakers. I do not endorse this, of course, but it is the way it is. I do not watch the teachers' Spirituality waning, I do not see any loss of faith, BUT I do see their intense frustration and sometimes justified anger when they listen to the provocative taunts being hurled at them. No, it is not right, and yes, it will continue for a while longer yet. I like the way you phrased it, though, "do not try to prove something intangible for it cannot be proven in the old third-dimensional way."

I address All My teachers now: You must remain firm in your beliefs, to do otherwise will but cause you to become one of the mindless masses intent on promulgating mis-information that will be deleterious to all My Children. Even when you feel you are not making a difference, remember you are still planting a seed. In time, mayhap it will require many upcoming lifetimes for these other Children to evolve, but with each level of evolvement achieved, even if it is an unconscious action, the seeds you have planted now and in the past are/will germinate. And in closing out Celest's question, remember, during those times of strife, call upon your Guides and off-world families for encouragement and support. Send "the call" and "listen for the answers."

Celest — Thank you, God, I felt that You having said this rather than any of the three of us would be received better by the readers.

God — Don't underestimate yourself, Celest, you have been telling people this for a long time.

Celest — Touché, God!

Chapter 3

Communication with God

In accordance with God's instructions as to what is to be in this, HIS book, a chapter given by Hatonn for the fourth Matthew Book, Voices of the Universe, *is to be included along with this preface from Hatonn. Hatonn "wears many hats," and during this time of Earth's ascension process, he is especially active in his roles as commander of an intergalactic fleet and master of communication in the universe. In another chapter of* Voices *he answered my question about what he was doing with those two major responsibilities:*

Hatonn — "Communication is the more challenging by far because of all the wrong ideas folks have about telepathic communication, the DISinformation coming through, and that mountain of layers I was talking about [*NOTE: This is in reference to his message in the book chapter below his preface*]. The commander function is easy by comparison! We're all in a holding pattern, performing our various technologies that are helping your planet recover from the eons of neglect and abuse and ignorance."

"As far as settling in and identifying ourselves as your 'space brothers' — including those of us who are living right there with you — your world is not ready for this at this exact moment. You're uncovering the darkness with each breath, and when all the uncovering is done that could pose a life threat to us 'aliens' showing up in our crafts, then the landings will come. The same goes for those 'aliens' who are walking your streets to properly introduce themselves. We *all* are eager for that day!"

Hatonn — Hello, dear Suzy! Hatonn here to emphasize the importance of ones giving attention NOW to my longer message that will follow.

The times they are a-changin' fast, and you'd better start ramping up your awareness that you are part of God and there's

NEVER a need for any intermediary between you. Why *would* there be when you and God are *ONE*! Oh yes, indeed you are an independent, inviolate being, but you're also an inseparable part of the eternal All That Is. Of course that idea is as taboo as what many of you have been taught: *By all means, pray to God, but if you hear anything back, that's Satan talking.* Now really, isn't that just plain unreasonable?

Linear time, which is what you live by but won't be much longer, is moving into the timelessness of the universe — the continuum — where everything is NOW. So, in *your* sense of time, there's not much of it left for discovering that you are an inseparable part of the Oneness and telepathic communication is your birthright. What if you don't discover this, what happens then? No punishment, simply you'll get another chance to do it in another 3D world. But look around you — do you want another lifetime in a world like yours is right now, or do you want to go along with Earth into the pure love and harmony of her journey's destination?

I think the big snag for you ones who can't wrap your minds around being part of God and entitled to enjoy conversing with Him is believing that you have to study your way out of the layers that religions devised between you and your Maker. Instead of checking within to see if it really is OK to believe you are God and therefore certainly qualified to chat with Him/You, you keep attending classes or reading books about it. Just DO it! NOW!

Go within and ask, then listen — it can be words right off the bat or start out as intuition, either way it's AHA! — and you won't need to look further to understand "Who am I?" "Why am I here?" Nevertheless, I'll tell you. All the answers to everything you want to know and all the power to manifest whatever you imagine is Who you are and helping Earth move out of that 3D morass is Why you're there.

Suzy, that's it. Thank you for receiving my message — you know how urgent it is that people wake up to the truth. Now please copy what I gave you some time back for another book, that chapter that God wants in this one, too.

Suzy — *You're welcome, Hatonn, and yes, I do know. Here's that chapter:*

Communication with God

May 13, 2003

Suzy — Good morning, Hatonn. I could hardly believe it last night when you said you want to give me a message "for the new book." Didn't you know that I just finished one?

Hatonn — Suzy, dear child and friend, yes, of course I know. And you know I'm in charge of communication between there and everywhere else, so you know how important this subject is to me. It's been talked about in the other books but not with the point I wish to make now.

Those whose minds are ahead of their hearts in this matter are unwittingly lagging. The folks who think they have to study this or that to work themselves through their perceived layers of separation from God are just *making* a separation between themselves and God! That is their chosen pathway, so I have no quarrel with it, but it is so *unnecessary*! Especially now, with everything speeding up, they need to know that their spiritual connection with God isn't achieved through mental exercises or incantations or invoking the help of ascended masters — it simply IS! Every soul is a part of God, every one **IS** connected with Him! How could it be otherwise when it's the physics of the universe at work here?

This, now, is my presentation, Suzy.

This is Hatonn speaking to you. As master of communication between Earth and the rest of the universe, I am telling you the simplicity of the answer to your soul-searching: You are a part of God and your connection with Him is your birthright. **God IS. You ARE. You and God are ONE**. How much more simple can it be? Your soul knows this, and you need only to align your conscious self with your soul, your godself.

You may search through books to learn how to make the communication connection, but those are merely others' ideas of how to reach a stage of spiritual awareness, and that is not

43

_cessary. It is as simple as ASKING! Say, for instance, *"God, I am you, you are me, so please let me hear you."* Or say nothing, just feel it in your heart — God hears that just as clearly. Allow your mind to be still and listen to your soul giving you God's message.

As for searching for God's "will" in your life, as so many of you do, you could say that since you are God in fullness and He is you as a part of Himself, yes, He has a pathway for you. But your own soul as the God part you are *chose* the pathway it needs for growth, and the purpose of your life is to consciously discover that pathway. Conscience is your guide, and so is your intuition. But those can become hidden in the labyrinthine pathway of esoteric studies, lessons, seminars, books — all designed to heighten your awareness of *yet another obstruction* between you and God.

I am not saying for a moment that your studies and sessions are a waste! But how accurately are they assisting you in the direct course to being the god and goddesses you already ARE? You are yearning to feel something that isn't in books or graphs or seminars. It is the private pathway to your godself you need, not the mysterious mountains and valleys to travel for years and years. Nevertheless, if you have spent years in this journey, start connecting directly with God without further delay!

Think of this: A child comes into an Earth lifetime with knowledge of that direct God connection, that absolute intuitive knowing, that total sensing of inseparability. The child hasn't studied, hasn't spent hours in seminars or been treated to sessions of calling upon help from the ascended masters. The child simply IS the godself! Only by orientation away from that does the passing of your time bring about the separation. Then you search for your connection through those various forms of "how to" reach what *always* has been yours, *always* has been **YOU!**

Suzy, my friend and mutual servant, as we do indeed serve each other, thank you for heeding my call to come to the computer. I'm a soul of few words usually, as you well know, and I have extended myself on this occasion. Sometimes it's necessary to put a hammer to a head to get the attention, so I have done that with this message.

Suzy — Thank you for your message, Hatonn. May I ask you some questions?

Hatonn — Of course you may ask your questions, but please relocate our further discussion to a different chapter. [*NOTE: As a reminder, this part of Hatonn's message is a chapter from* Voices of the Universe, *the fourth Matthew Book, that God wants included here; the chapter to which Hatonn refers is in that book.*] The essential need for people to recognize their constant, direct communication link with God is best left alone as the first message in the book.

Celest and David — Hatonn, we — as always — treasure, honor and respect your many contributions to the human race as well as to all of Creation. We know your obligations are very demanding and because of this we will withhold our questions for a future time. We do however wish to thank you for sharing your words of wisdom with those who shall benefit from the truth you have shared with us. In time, they may also teach others. As you know, truth needs no validation; it shall and will stand on its own.

Hatonn — I, just as all my brethren everywhere, have had our "ear" to the wind following the progress of this which is "God's Book." Its receptivity is paramount for each of your entries into the upper realms. I might suggest you pay attention now to "life episodes" as you never have before, as this current chapter of your *present* life unfolds.

Commander Theda *(received by Celest)* — Theda is a Commander of the Arcturian and Pleiadian Peace Keepers Forces, chief Officer of the Interplanetary Diversionary Project, expert on holographic projectile infusions and former explorer of ancient worlds. We (Celest and David) physically made "first contact" with Theda early in 2004. Her communiqués were not unexpected. She is a unique individual who had been hovering overhead, awaiting a specific linear timeline before connecting with us, as she herself stated, "again." We have spent the time since then retaining our connection with Theda and listening to her sage advice. Theda generously consented to allowing us to interview her.

To date, Theda now can speak when necessary in 134 languages. Many languages are Earth Star "lingo." She was issued her own ship 614 years ago, in her time-measurements. She was given her own fleet 126 years ago. Without further ado, here is Theda, to share her perspectives on:

"God and I"

Theda — We are well aware of the human propensity for questioning the reason for their existences as well as their wondering if there is in fact a force outside of themselves that has in any manner contributed to their Creation. Our Earth Star cousins are not so much naïve as they are ignorant of the reality of the Prime Creator and the reality of God. On our home planets, we are from the very moment of conception consciously aware of the Divine Force. Those of us who inhabit worlds that use the conception process for propagation are fortunate to carry those vivid memories with total recall as we enter the world as babes and later enter the adult world.

Those Star Keepers, whose home planets are those where propagation is achieved through other means, still have the same total recall as do we. When my cousin Celestial asked me to explain to you my personal relationship with God, I had to stop and ponder the situation. It is difficult at best to explain something that is so natural, so normal. How do you explain inhaling and exhaling? Do you count your breaths to ensure that you are breathing enough? Do you have a regimen to follow that maintains the steady breathing process even while you sleep? Of course not.

I have however reached far back into my memory-banks and viewed the images there that depicted the Divine Gestalt from the first moment of my first breath. The first awareness of myself was the incredible White Light similar to a gigantic starburst or super-nova, which was in front of my closed eyes. The warmth that emanated from this glorious illumination was felt by me throughout every fiber of my body. I was aware of a certain cadence of tonal effects

46

that permeated this light. The depth of peace surrounded me, yet I was shown images of a life yet to be for me. Of course when The Divine Force "speaks," it is a mind-thought link; here on your planet it is called "telepathy." I was told that when I emerged into the world I would be known as "the gifted one."

Many of us have different specialties, unique abilities that we must hone well in order to be of service to others. My attributes are so varied, so "ancient," that it was decided that the use of that phrase would further my self-determination, my motivation to be all that I could be for the good of all. We learn at home, <u>to live up to our names, never down to them</u>. The Divine Force is present at the emergence of each new life form. This happens on the Earth Star planet as well, it is just that the babe cannot maintain conscious recall because of the conditioning that occurs here. I entered into the world encased in love and in light. Yet on some instinctual, survival level, I was aware that the peace that our race of Star Keepers had struggled for centuries to possess, and then maintain, was a peace that we, as the new generations, would have to protect. We would be called upon to fight when necessary and die if needed.

Throughout all of my growing-up years, I have called upon the GodHead when I have sought answers to situations that did not make any logical sense to me. More often than not, He would already be speaking to me about events to transpire before I had the opportunity to ask. When our human cousins turn to their best friend for assistance or advice, **we turn to God.** We do not throw ourselves down on our knees and pray to Him, nor do we subject our bodies to torturous yoga positions to "meditate" and seek answers. You see, we <u>KNO</u>W that God and The Creator are very much in existence and that their love and guidance envelops us at all times. How can we doubt what we already know? We cannot. It is not necessary for Him to perform "miracles" to convince us of an established fact. We need no proof. We KNOW.

I shall make an attempt to explain to you something that really should not need to be explained. However, I am taking into consideration the human primitive mind-thought. The Divine Force of the Creator, The Creation and God exist as separate entities, yet they are as One. Every mote of dust carries the imprint of the Creator, of the Creation and of God. Using our science of schematic geometry, this Force forms a Sacred Pyramid. This pyramid is an *entity* which supersedes all other life forms with the notable exception of The Creation. The Creation is a process of manifesting that which God chooses. The triangle is non-tangible, yet They can be seen, felt and tangible when He/They choose to be. The triangle is androgynous; the triangle is everywhere at once. So, the triangle is in all universes, raising vibrations and altering frequencies, promoting the life force of all incoming life and defeating the dark legions through us, through knowledge and through love.

God is the totality of wisdom and honor. God is the all-seeing compilation of the Sacred alignment of the Creative Forces. God exists through us and for us; we exist for God. We are God as well, as are you. If you wonder how we "see" God, maybe you should reconsider how YOU see Him. We see His Brilliance everywhere we go; He lives within our community-type family lifestyles; He speaks when spoken to and speaks when we need Him to. At times we clearly hear Him speaking in the wind; His "voice" is a harmonic melody that immediately invokes images and grand prisms of color. His is a language of Infinity. His touch is a gentle but comforting one that causes an acceleration of the electromagnetic currents that function within our bodies. Your jaundiced and deliberately misled belief systems promulgate His "judgment day." This is a deliberate and malicious lie! You may believe that truth is relative to the believer; I do not. What is true is that there are infinite realities that exist within realities.

However, what you see is not always what you get. The existence of "free expression" on this planet you are temporarily visiting allows you to experience the reality you create for yourself. It is part of your remedial training, your remedial education... until you get it right. Since you refuse to see God here, there is but one option left. It will not be until you leave this unhallowed place to return to Nirvana, some for but a short stay, that you will see that beyond this place down here, beyond the space time continuum, there is but one reality. The BIG one. That will be a real ball buster experience for many of you. There you shall <u>see</u> God. You will also see yourself.

Celest and David — Thank you, Theda. As you always do, you have hit the head of the proverbial nail once again. We believe one of your most admirable qualities is that you never mince words; you speak your truths as well as live them as all should and most will, in the days ahead.

Theda — Once we three were re-united, the combined light force of all of us together brings to Earth a melodious tone that echoes, reverberates and complements that which is God. Can each of you imagine for just one moment if all life there on Earth was to unite in harmony, the chorus that would envelop and permeate the universe? Just a thought. Till next time, when we speak again, until then I shall of course continue to *live up* to my name, I Am Theda. I am a thought away and for those who are able to see clearly, I am in the skies overhead, watching and waiting.

Blue Star the Pleiadian — (*received by Celest*) Blue Star the Pleiadian is a member of the Pleiadian Guardians; he is a teacher and warrior. He commands a star ship called the "Sedora." Blue Star is a part of the Galactic Federation and works with the walk-ins on the Earth Star planet as well as with all those other of his brethren engaged in humanitarian efforts. He is as old as the Creator but not as old as the Creation. His original ancestors were the Lyrians, many of them later founded Lemuria and Atlantis. That was after The Great War. When peace reigned once again on his home, the Pleiades, The Divine Force issued a prime directive to him. He was asked to organize a parley, to format a program that would assist the Earth Star planet humans in finally attaining peace and freedom from the Illuminati. Although God and The Creator cautioned him that this would be a formidable task, he was well aware that the success of this Spirit endeavor would be well worth the journey into madness. Now here is Blue Star to share with all of us his intuitive knowledge of who,

"God Is"

Now, I have observed over my long, long lifetime that far too many humans concern themselves with the affairs of the intelligentsia rather than the affairs of the GodHead. I have seen more schemes hatched since 1866 for the dual purpose of controlling other humans and obliterating those who do follow the path of Spirit, than any previous times in this planet's rather dark history. Commander Theda and I have discussed many times that the possibility exists that humans in general require severe "wake-up" calls before they abolish their own slavery and advocate true freedom not only for themselves, but for all others of the human race. We are also in agreement that only when you people are pushed to the limits of emotional and mental distress do you "suddenly" <u>find</u> God. This fact is self-evident in your aberrant behavior and attitudes towards your own races, your cultures, and your philosophies. Why does it always seem to require a calamity to take place before your wondrous hindsight of helping others occurs? Why is it that each race here must not only see themselves as better than other races here, but feel threatened by those who are different?

Now, it does not require anyone of genius mentality to see that the duality that exists here is in great part attributed to your religious and Spiritual beliefs and disbeliefs. The Illuminati know more of God and the Creator than do you. The Illuminati know more of the Creation than do you. Of course in their case it was a point of "knowing the enemy." As God has pointed out on more than one occasion, our Earth Star cousins are not consciously aware that *the enemy lies **within***. You yourselves are your own worst enemies. This is sad. The allies of your enemy-selves are: ignorance, disbelief, prejudice, vanity, narrow-mindedness, jealousy, hate, greed, drugs, alcohol, spitefulness and the adamant refusal to acknowledge a God of love and justice, of the sentience that prevails within the true God Force.

So it is that in general humans would rather fear God, would rather imagine that the God Force is wrathful, vengeful and callous. In a bizarre twist of a reality shift, humans fear what they do not understand, yet what they do not understand they disallow as part of their personal realities. As this occurs the temptation is planted deviously in your minds by the Illuminati and their legion, the dark horde, to halt any belief you may still have about the goodness of God and the very existence of this Being. It is then like the contagion that it is, that disbelief fosters anger and hatred towards your very selves and others. Those among you ones who see themselves as pious will pray for redemption from a God they fear; others will pray for peace yet do nothing to cause it to happen. This is a contradiction in terms, so to speak. If you ones do not want to be afraid, then why are you so fear-filled about taking a **stand** and **standing** in truth? Not the lying rhetoric fed to you by the current dictator of America and those others like him in other countries, but standing back and looking at life in general and saying "NO, this is not OK!"

You see, you do not confuse shall we say, President Bush, with God...and a good thing too! So how can you confuse yourself by equating God and fear? When your life is running smoothly, you thank God. When your life is filled with pitfalls, you plead for a God that you do not really believe in to help you. When your life is filled with strife, war and death, you blame God. Make up your minds already. NO, this is not OK! The GodForce is not now nor has He ever been responsible for the deadly foibles and the deadly games you participate in here on this planet. He is not a "governing body," He is Everything that is real and nothing that is static. The Creator granted permission for you ones to be permitted to indulge yourselves in all manner of creativity. The Serene Awareness of the Creator and the Creation foresaw that with this enormous gift to you ones was a tremendous responsibility you each have.

You were granted *freedom*, yet you knew it not. You were granted protection, yet you sensed it not. You were granted the ability to manifest and materialize all that you required here, yet you used it not. It is why linear time was Created for you ones; to function as a "governor" to assist in keeping you from speeding totally out of control. To a great degree this has succeeded, much to the chagrin of the Illuminati. And they were doing so well with you up until that "time." A commonality that exists amongst each of your races is the insatiable need to be the best of the best. This is highly illogical. Who among you has stopped, looked and listened to find out who or WHAT feeds that need? Who is it that keeps the holocaust alive and well in your memories? Who is promoting war and who is countering with peace?

Tell me, oh illustrious Earth cousins, does a god of death and destruction work for peace and harmony for all life forms? Does a god of dominance send his warriors and teachers here to walk among you, promoting the Spiritual aspect of life? Does a GOD OF LIFE SUGGEST THAT YOU MURDER YOUR OWN PEOPLE? Like it or not, you are ALL RELATED. Deal with it. Subterfuge, hypocrisy, the illicit use of power, these are the tools of the children of a lesser god. Again and again, throughout the centuries I have impressed this upon you ones. Again and again, a few, a very few, have listened and responded. You ones in general stubbornly refuse to heed all our warnings of the true overlords that fight us as they seek the total control of this planet. We fight for your freedom-to-*be*. You have become so involved in your everyday life situations that you are now blind; as such the dark overlords are steadfastly battering at you by hurling religions and biblical propaganda into the morass of your confusion.

They have sought your Achilles heel and they have found it. The same Divine Force that birthed your presence is not about to allow you ones to cease as a life species. We were granted our rights of intervention in order to preserve the planet and you, yourselves. The same Divine Force that so many of you decry is permitting you largesse of movement in your individual quest for immortality. Whether you find it or not is really up to you. For many among you ones, it is a moot point. I have had many, many conversations with the Divine Force. Not at any time did I, or have I, felt anything but the deepest love and warmth that only the Infinite Divine can offer. Yes, indeed I do understand the precarious lifestyles so many of you live. Please to remember that is your own Creation. In essence, God is All That Is and All That Ever Will be. Believe me or not, I don't care.

Salude... Blue Star the Pleiadian

Celest — Thank you, Father, for words of wisdom.

Chapter 4

Awareness

Celest — God, we know that it was You, not any of us, who chose the chapter titles, why is it that your selection of "Awareness" is so important to this book?

God — "Awareness" is a term that can be taken in many ways. I KNOW that it is important because of all that I have always seen on the Earth; all those billions of peoples who have not been "in awareness" for many a year, some not for many a lifetime. It is when the curtain of your "remembrances" falls when you reincarnate here, that reality takes a back seat to "illusions and deceptions." Many of My Children feel they are aware of all that is truly occurring, yet in fact they are not. They may know some truth from deception, but the heavy burdens they each carry while walking this walk, causes them to at times... too many times for some... accept that which is false, or worse, replace truth with the illusions of reality. This is obviously not a good thing.

It is important that all of My Children come to terms with truth, that they come to terms with themselves and have confrontations with the "devil," if necessary. There are different levels of "KNOWINGNESS," which is "Awareness" in a different guise. When you KNOW something, it means that "you are sure on a conscious level" about a person, place or thing that has some connection with you in everyday practical life. Unfortunately, too many people take it for granted that what they think they KNOW, and what they really KNOW, are the same. In fact quite often, they are two separate entities. It is like My sky, there is "day" and there is "night," one is different from the other in APPEARANCE, yet they are each an aspect of the ONE sky. It does not mean, *"day will become night and night would become day,"* it is the reality of two aspects of one entity sharing themselves as one unit.

Many people KNOW that the conditions of their lives are, to say the least, in disarray, they then begin to contribute the mess of their lives to all different people, places and things which they THINK have somehow contributed to the situations. Some people will actually have the...strength...to acknowledge that in actual fact, only they themselves allowed such and such to happen. Had they been **AWARE** that none of those distasteful or tawdry events could have occurred unless that individual PERMITTED them to take place, then OBVIOUSLY any sane person would have kept it from happening in the first place. I have just given you a very practical example of any everyday situation; I did so because it is My hope that in this manner you will be able to follow the rest of what I have to say.

What occurs on the conscious levels of KNOWING can be easily filtered through the *"intellect bugaboo."* Don't get me wrong, I love the intellect, after all I did Create it, you know. BUT it was not My Intent for the intellect to control the AWARENESS which you each bear as an aspect of your Soul Self. The AWARENESS of all that you each are, all that you each have ever been and the POTENTIAL of all that you still MAY ascend to, lies quietly in the Super Conscious realm of yourself. The Super Conscious can and does transmit the AWARENESS into and through your subconscious. However, the subconscious can filter through to you only as much as your CONSCIOUS MIND can accept at any given moment.

This is one of the primary reasons that the dark energies have had so much success here on this planet. The "mind" is a gigantic computer, in a sense; it had followed the dictates of the impulses of "reasoning and logic," for the most part, so of course those dark ones did all they could to control *"your computer."* "AWARENESS" has nothing to do with the computer; AWARENESS is a subtle realization of reality, the "real stuff," not the manmade variety. AWARENESS is a by-product of Soul KNOWLEDGE; the AWARENESS FACTOR cannot take its place of pre-eminence within the mind, heart and Soul of any of My Children until there is a blending together of "mind and matter."

You see, many are born into AWARENESS here, but lose or temporarily forget about that intangibly tangible aspect of their

54

Soul until or unless something jars them terribly awake from the sometimes self-induced stupor. As long as the conscious mind controls the thought forms, actions and deeds of each person, or groups of like-minded individuals, AWARENESS must await the needed catalyst before walking forth inside of you in its great majestic form. Are you getting My Picture yet? If you place this situation under your nonphysical eyes and scrutinize the conditioning that had taken place which subjugated you to the lower realms of KNOWING, then you shall better understand why AWARENESS is the key to your own immortality and why the dark so fears this Aspect of Soul.

Many of you KNOW that you are not "separate" from your AWARENESS, you KNOW that the AWARENESS is an integral part of who and what you are. It is a "part," not "APART" from you. It is when that KNOWING reaches the conscious mind that the Super Conscious, the subconscious and the conscious mind can interrelate and quietly integrate the SOUL memory you have been permitted to bear with you. These are the memories that are dependent in great measure upon your individual abilities to ALLOW information to pass through the channels of your mind and thusly into your hearts; since this all actually originates as Soul MOVEMENTS, it will not pass back to Soul again, rather Soul will radiate more as Soul reaches upwards to bring you onto yet another plateau of BE-ING.

So AWARENESS must not only be thoroughly understood by you, it must be respected, cherished and honored. You each have a responsibility here and that is to willingly bring AWARENESS into conscious manifestation. It is no longer enough to say, "I am aware of all that is going on here," NOW you must really KNOW what you are saying. The time for "lip service," is over. The bridge that once existed between Nirvana and Earth is becoming a moot point. You no longer have *old-fashioned linear time* to fall back on; to once again assist you in "COMPLACENCY." Whew!! Boy, am I glad about that!

MY BOOK could not be a complete "God Talks," without you each knowing the importance of your own individual AWARENESS. AWARENESS, as a state of BE-ING, is you as Soul Self epitomizing your own ESSENCE. It does not mean that you have to walk around on tippy toes, afraid to make mistakes and expecting to be a *"perfected being."* Perfection cannot be found on the Earth, YET you are each "perfect" in every nanosecond of your life. True, some more so than others, but what the heck, I MySelf am not perfect either, you know. Or, perhaps you don't know.

Celest — OK, God, that is a very reasonable and non-logical explanation. This is what I wanted others to know also. Thank you, I will be back later in the chapter.

God — You are welcome and somehow I did think you had more to ask.

God (received by David) — In the greater cosmic realm, where all is known, there are many who believe that the universe was intended to unfold as it is, or was, or shall I say, "shall be." I prefer to look at everything with optimism and I relish in *seeing* the bigger picture, knowing that everything is as it "should be." One of the greatest truths of all is that Universal Events unfold as they should, in their own time, at their own pace. **The universe is always on time.** Now this does not make "all in perfection," this simply draws into the realm of possibilities that which is the never ending desire to reach that state of perfection. I, just as you, am at all times evolving to the best of My own abilities. I am dependent upon each Soul Cluster and every individual within that Cluster to achieve their own awareness, their own understanding of all that affects the whole of Creation. It is at that time which "knowledge" comes into practice. We who are the guardians of all the Universes have a great responsibility to those whom we watch over. It is not Our *chosen* desires to watch you stumble and fall, yet Our responsibility requires us to allow you the freedom of choice to permit yourself to fall backwards and pick yourself up in order to learn from the experience *without any outside interference.* What would you accomplish if we removed all obstacles (lessons) before you had the experience? *Nothing,* would be the correct response here. We applaud your efforts to continuously attempt to better yourselves by laughing at your mistakes and dusting yourselves off, after picking yourselves up after a fall and trying again. When the work is done at the end of the day, is it not the compilation of your good efforts and deeds that paves the way into tomorrow's enhancements?

I would like to share with you My thoughts on the **"awareness perspective."** When all you do at every moment affects the rest of your conscious moments, would it not be in your best interests to become "one with yourself"? If becoming one with yourselves includes all the different aspects of yourselves, then would it not be prudent to analyze all these different parts of you and discard those that are no longer relevant? Then you can go on and enhance those parts of you that clearly state the Godliness that you each are. Would it not be also in your best interests to share what you have learned with those who are seeking the truth, so that they may come into awareness as well? Following further down this line of reasoning, would this conduct not sweep into other areas of your world that need to be altered, corrected or discarded? Of course it would, and that is how *change* comes about, by one person making a difference and BE-ING a difference. *One step at a time, one Soul at a time when necessary, Our Work shall be done.* If you had available to you a tool, or device, that would greatly improve your understanding of what transpires around you, would you not use it? Of course you would. That tool is there for the asking, I gifted it to you, it is your intuition. That is what makes you "thinking, reasoning, sentient beings," instead of drones or clones.

Awareness is the "key." Those who are in awareness know that the "key" is there for everyone's enhancement and that you should never want to miss the opportunity to use a "key" that has been shown to you. Each "key" has a purpose; each unlocks a door of understanding to the next level of your ascension. The beginning of every moment in time begins with a purpose, one that is designated to be a catalyst which impacts on the whole. It is not I who steers your boat, that is something you do of your own free will. Since you and I are inseparable, then one might say, you steer **Our** boat.

Awareness of who you are and why you are here is again

another "key" to understanding the mission that you have been chosen for. *Or that which you have volunteered for.* Each person's mission is intertwined with all others, what is innocently thought of in one mind, attracts to itself all other similar thought forms. This in turn causes a ripple effect to all other life forms throughout the Universes, in all the different dimensional levels of Creation. This is part of the "Tapestry of Life" that you are weaving. Just as there are the Greater Weavings of the Universal Plan in action, there are also your own personal tapestries that you are Creating. Each individual's tapestry adds substance and color to the whole. When you try something new, when the urge strikes you to spend a moment in awesome splendor, when you embrace another, or when you take a moment to step outside of yourself and enjoy the beauty of the moment, you are then existing in that moment. Are you not also adding another thread to your tapestry?

From where I exist I am aware of all your frustrations, I also see the radiant beauty that shines from within the deepest reaches of your hearts. I, too, sense your anguish and disappointment when things do not turn out the way you envisioned they should. Yet when I see the spark of awareness, of partial or complete under-standing glowing within you, then I know you have awakened to the true meaning hidden behind the illusion. With each illusion cast away as a leaf in the wind, it becomes easier and easier for you to remove the veils that still lie before you. This is "awareness."

"Awareness" can also be a double-edged sword; it not only cuts through the illusions that have been created by others, it also cuts through the programming that you have nurtured and possess yourselves. When this occurs, the world becomes brighter and clearer to you, you see hope where before there was none. You see once again into the realm of possibilities, where all probabilities and limitless possibilities of joy, happiness and love unending exist. There is a time in everyone's life when the spark of awareness flares up and the beginnings of truth stir within them. This is the *Soul's Voice* calling out to you, urging you to find that peaceful place within your hearts, the place where you are One with The Creator, One with Creation, One with **yourself**, not to mention, one with Myself. The peace you find which can only be found <u>within</u>

is joy for My Eyes to behold. I wish that all of you could truly understand how blessed you are.

Just as I see your anguish, I also feel your joy. When the light within you glows brightly, it touches deep into the Heart of Creation. This light radiates outward and touches all who are around you. That moment then can be shared by many, yet its beauty is held within the bearer of the light, as a jeweled treasure that money can never buy. The time of manifestation is upon you, yet many of you are unaware of that which is needed. You need *Soul Food*, you need to renew your Spiritual Connection with your universal families, with all universal truths, to reacquaint yourselves with Universal Laws.

You think of Creating or manifesting what will make you happy; you dream of riches without knowing the most simplistic of truths. That truth is, "all you need, you already have; all that is desired is within your reach; all that would make your corner of the world seem much brighter is already there." All that is required is understanding that it is. Visualize it, see it, feel it, touch it, call it to you and like a warm, gentle breeze, it shall be yours. So many of your insecurities are self-created, yet many others have been force fed to you throughout the ages. It is up to each of you to see through those veils of illusions and quite adamantly state out loud, *"no more, I see clearly now, I am de-programmed!"*

David — God, I am sure you remember when I myself stated out loud, "I am de-programmed," what peace I felt and the weight that was instantaneously lifted from my shoulders. OK, so how does stress affect one's awareness?

God — David, I remember it well, I thought I was going to have to send you a lifeline to keep you from floating upwards into the ionosphere. I am also well aware of the stressful times you are all living in, and that stress is the great destroyer of common sense and any sentient responses. Stress removes the sentient awareness of the realities of any situation. Stress is a subchapter in the world of fear. Fear itself is the unraveling of all senses. Fear is created; it is not natural, never has been and never will be. Fear gets in the way of living; it holds you Earthbound and captures your ability to soar without limits. When entering any given situation, whether it was self-created or some situation that requires your presence, always remember to surround yourself in *"The White Light, The Christed Light,"* and always remember that I, too, am there with you. I promised you I would never leave you alone, remember? And promises made are promises kept.

Stress is a self-inflicted disease; it causes great damage to the physical vehicle. Think of the word dis-ease, does it not make you uncomfortable just thinking about it? Stress is the catalyst for many diseases because it affects the body's natural immune system. I would like to reiterate the messages that My Children have been sending to you for as long as you have been; *"there is no disease that is natural to this planet and/or to the human race."* All diseases were created and inflicted upon the human race for the sole purpose of making you <u>reliant on others</u> for your well being. The dark ages of your planet, of My planet, are rapidly coming to an end. With this final conclusion will be the end of all diseases and dis-eases. There will be no more need for psychiatrists, insane asylums and old folks' homes. Those do not exist in the higher frequencies to which you are all traversing, well, OK... that many of you are now journeying to. In time you will come to recognize your own power, you will wield it as the **"Sword of Truth"** that it is. There is a time in everyone's life when each Soul will come to understand that all they want to be for themselves, all they need to accomplish, they already are/have. All they need do now is to start remembering that which has been forgotten.

So take a look around you, don't stop reading your newspapers, don't stop listening to the news, do not stop becoming involved and certainly do not stop caring about others. BUT read and listen with great *discernment.* You have no idea of the amount of light that thoughts, understanding, caring and compassion generate that Creates change. It is true on the other side of the spectrum as well, if you feed fear, if you nurture doubts and insecurities, then that also is Created. Now please, do not become over infatuated with what you see or hear, simple acknowledgment that there are injustices everywhere that need to be corrected will do for starters.

Closing your eyes, turning your backs, or ignoring a problem will not make it go away, nor does it correct it. Look, if I wanted you to go around sticking your head in the sand all the time, I would have made you all ostriches. Now mind you, the ostrich is a wondrous creature that is vastly misunderstood by most, it saddens me the labels that are given to certain Aspects of My Creation by those with ignorant belief systems.

Did you know that your planet, which is My planet, has some of the most diverse life forms anywhere in the Universe? Did you know that Earth offers more of a variety of terrains than anywhere else? Did you know that the vast varieties of plant and animal life, I believe now would be a good time to include each of you, all that inhabits the Earth Star planet came from other areas of the universe? That's right, you are amongst the most diversified life forms ever assembled on one orb. Now you may ask about the dinosaurs, animal, plant, etc., life that has been believed to be extinct. *Nothing goes extinct.* I have had My children save a certain number from your different species and relocate them to an environment somewhere that is especially suited to their well being and evolutionary status. Now many of the species on the Earth will evolve into a new form of themselves, this is within the natural order of any life form's existence, just as you will evolve from physical beings into wondrous beings of pure light. I felt it pertinent to point that little detail out to you at this time because so many things are taken for granted. Too many of My Children rationalize everything and never stop to absorb the splendor of all the magnificent treasures that exist on and within Eden.

While we are on the subject of awareness, let me suggest a practice for you that the indigenous people of Earth have long known and passed on to all their succeeding generations. Watch the animals, become one with them, watch how they behave and where they go, for they instinctively know what to do, what is right and what is in their best interests. They require no teachings in this area. Also please listen to the children, give them credit where credit is due, many of them are acting on their natural instincts. The innocence that you were born with exists in the purity and love of All That Is. That innocence is the closest you will ever feel while living in a physical existence to The Creator. Innocence is a natural response, awareness of the lack of it is the first step to moving into the direction of your Soul's urgings. The Soul Voice will do all that it can to steer you back on the path that leads you into the Unity of The One. The purity of a child can most easily be seen during the time of birth. This is the most wondrous expression of unconditional love, that which exists between an infant and its mother at the moment of birth. Those of you who remember your innocence, which existed before you became aware of the physical realm, will understand what I am speaking of when it comes to the innocence of children.

The defensive posture that so many of you assume is not a natural occurrence in the higher dimensions. This reaction is a self-defense mechanism that you have nurtured along with all your other conditioned responses. You see, in the higher frequencies all is known, the thoughts, intentions and actions of others are not concealed or hidden, there is no need of this. All communications are accomplished through the use of telepathy, so there can be no confusion as to the actual intent of anyone's actions. On Earth in the current times of now, if you were to pay attention to even the most seemingly insignificant of happenings, you would learn much from their interactions with all other currently transpiring events. One event is not separate, yet one event can act independently on its own behalf. When spending that moment in splendor and awe while contemplating what you are now *"in awareness"* of, observing and understanding the interplay of occurrences, always remember to give thanks to all of The Creation as well as to The Creator for bringing these blessings into your lives. I, too, fall into the category of **All of Creation.**

One thing is for certain in the times ahead; those of you who are left to witness the unfolding of *The Golden Age* will become much more aware of their surroundings. You will take pleasure in the simplest of things. You will watch a weed grow and know that it too has the potential to become an object of extreme beauty. Do not discard in the times of continuing your "becoming awareness" all the wondrous life forms that exist below the surface of the Earth's crust. Each mineral, each drop of fossil, every particle of seemingly insignificant matter is connected to the rest of Creation through its frequency vibrations and its purpose of be-ing. Within the oceans you will find "new old" life forms reappearing, you will soon understand the necessity for extremely long incubation periods of many life forms.

You will find out more about the cities that exist under the ocean's surface as well as those life forms who live inside of the planet and the necessity of their being there. For they are your brothers and sisters, those you will once again be united with, not only in Spirit, though. You will be working hand-in-hand with them to build a better world as well as a better more universal version of yourself. The wonders that lie before you are indeed so momentous, it would be hard to know where to begin to bring you up to date, your segregated races have been living in the grasp of darkness for so long. Suffice it to say that the future before you will be nothing like the past you are leaving behind once and for all. The past will serve as guidelines, as teaching tools to all future generations on "WHAT NOT TO DO!"

David — Spiritual Warriors are birthed by Spiritual Awareness. Thank you, God, for bringing awareness to the forefront.

God — Spiritual Warriors are what you each are, it is the refining of these attributes that makes you Great Teachers.

Suzy — It's me, God — hello! As I was reading what you said about awareness — it's so much more than our common concept and use of the word — I kept thinking about the problems caused by poor communication. Often words are interpreted differently by the listener than the speaker meant, and that's when both speak the same language! Especially in vitally important international issues, meanings need to be clearly understood. But are they? There can be unintended — or deliberate — distortion when a third party interprets what the first is saying to the second, who doesn't understand those others' native language. So it seems that for all of us to live together harmoniously and cooperatively, clear communication is essential. How are we going to handle this with so many languages, dialects and slang expressions in addition to lack of education in one's own language?

God — Well, Suzy, I wish I didn't have to say that I'm stumped here, but in a way I am because you want a solution to this dicey situation right now. Since I don't have an "umbrella" solution for making the near countless words in all languages and their derivatives understandable to everyone on Earth, I'm relying on GOOD WILL — actually, *GOD* WILL, because you're all god or goddess parts of me — to handle this temporarily by BEing in your hearts more so than in your minds. I think that will do it until the translation system that converts all languages in the universe into a common language is operating, and it will be so for all of you who go along with Earth to her high plane of origin. That system is an ingredient of every soul, so that part toward the clear communication you want is already handled. And when all telepathic connections are open between Earth and wherever else, you won't have to rely on words being heard exactly as they're spoken because the *intention* is clear in your feelings, and in telepathy, there's no way to hide those, you know.

So, is that a satisfactory answer for the moment, until you're actually into it?

Suzy — It sounds promising. Thank you.

God — You're not feeling altogether good about this, are you?

Suzy — It just seems that our current communication, which is often miscommunication, is a really big obstacle to get past so we can do what you said, "BEing in our hearts more so than our minds." Some of us are doing this, or at least trying our best — I guess not enough of us to turn things around quickly, though.

God — Now, now then, my impatient child! Yes, things would change in the wink of an eye if all my soul parts were doing it, but since they're not, the next best thing with those slower parts is to let things take their legal course with them. Denying them their legal rights would undermine the system you want to recover, wouldn't it, and where would your world be then? In anarchy, chaos, pandemonium — a huge mess, that's where. As more of you remember and *use* your AWARENESS, things will speed up. The inpouring of LIGHT with the outpouring of LOVE is the bottom line — that combination is the ultimate solution to everyone living in the magnificent abundance and beauty of my beloved Gaia, your Earth homeland. You know this, my child — you do have that awareness!

Suzy — OK, God. I'll work on that more so I stop being part of the problem and BE a better part of the solution.

God — I'd say "atta girl" but you'd argue about typing it — see, just like I said! I'm here to help, little Suzy, remember that. I wish EVERYONE would remember that!

Suzy — We're working on it with this book! *Ciao* for now — you're holding up production here!

Celest — God, as I see it, it does not matter if a person's sole contribution to "being the difference" is merely a change that he or she is creating in their lives which will ultimately cause them to see life more clearly, or if it is a quantum leap in understanding Universal Laws. As long as there is an alteration in the individual's vibration/ frequency in an upscale movement, this enhances the person's illuminative matter and can cause the minutest matter to begin its ascension as that Soul evolves. So, to me, "being a part of the solution" does not necessarily mean that we should all move at the same accelerated pace as do many evolved Souls. Each Soul must move at Its own pace. That's it, that's all I wanted to add, God.

God — Thank you, Celest, for bringing up that point. No, no one needs to feel that they are not doing enough if they are doing all they are able to. Yes, each Soul must move at Its own pace, anything more would be deleterious to the Soul AND the physical vehicle It inhabits. This is what I term, "Soul Ascension."

Celest — God, I had another thought, perhaps it would be a good idea if you spoke a bit more on the in-pouring and outpouring of Light and Love. I personally believe that in order to have love, one must first have Light. Also, love itself is not enough. It also requires dedication, selflessness, empathy towards all others and a desire and ability to live life to the fullest.

God — Celest, as I have told you before, I KNOW I can always count on you for handing Me a "sticky wicket." Let Me see how I can explain this simply and understandably. Yes, love does require all those things that you wrote about above. Love is an emotion to some degree, but Love is an intangible energetic form in its own right. Love responds to the same energetic form that it itself is; yet love does not contain dross, it is not heavy, it is not tainted, it is not lust, it is not sex, it is a buoyancy of a state of being. You, yourself, Celest, have on occasion described it as *"part of a state of grace."* Love can be experienced through all the senses; the sense of touch is an important part of love. Love brings with itself a flowing, magnetic quality which attracts all others who have not been conditioned to "hate." Love is an integral aspect of the music of the ethers in a tangible sense. Without the Love vibration, the musical notes would be stale, listless and discordant.

Love, like Light, cannot exist in the dark; it cannot exist in tumultuous experiences, or in people who are heartless, vain, or deplorably arrogant. Light is the incandescent matter of MY Soul and yours. In this sense, it is the Voice of the Soul, which radiates with such beauty as Voice ascending the musical scale adds Its Voice to all Other Voices in this particular Tapestry. Light may be minuscule within the Soul Matter of many of My Children, but as long as there is a mere flicker there, there is hope for them. The Light of **ALL Lights is My everlasting Light, MY Love and My Passion** for Creating life and maintaining life everywhere in My universe. **My Light is also a Beacon of Light** which encompasses all life forms and calls to each Soul to ascend in majesty as each Soul moves progressively to return to Source.

It is when pure love co-joins with pure Light that miracles are birthed. Think of these two energetic qualities as "right hand, left hand." Neither will flourish and arrive at the **total** apex of itself without the energetic form of the other. It is not that one cannot exist without the other as the Soul arrives at Its Maturity level; it is that with each working in harmony with the other, it then becomes an unstoppable force. And that, dear Child, is as simple as I can make this explanation. You are satisfied?

Celest — Yes, I just wanted to hear YOU say it, God. I think I will just...leave temporarily now.

Chapter 5

The Psyche and Psychosis

God (*received by Celest*) — Hopefully this chapter will be of assistance in better understanding some of the misconceptions that have plagued all races of My Children, since forever it seems. The psyche is an important feature you have been given by the Creator and MySelf; that is not to imply that the other Gods of the other universes did not also have their input on this matter. I like to think of it as "the Divine Brain Child." What is the psyche? What does it do? Why can't I see it? These questions are the ones I sense would be uppermost in your minds if you gave it any time for thought. The psyche is a "place" where much knowledge is stored, yet it is also a "place" where minute areas can be "cracked," in a sense. If the personality housing the Soul Self acts and or reacts to unhealthy situations in an unhealthy manner, or if the circumstances surrounding the individual **cause** that person to become so overwrought with unhappiness and deep despair, then those microcosms within the psyche become weak **and/or unstable.**

The psyche also has a pivotal role in the levels, stages and evolutionary nature of a being's Spiritual Status; this monumental "hub" of Creativity can of course become tainted through misuse, neglect and dis-information. Although this hub is sadly overlooked in practical everyday life, there it sits, waiting and waiting to be put to good use CONSCIOUSLY for the evolution of a person and for the expansion of itself. In one sense, the psyche cannot be "seen," but it most certainly can be felt; this happens through great thrusts of "inspirations and previously unthought-of ideas." For one thing, it releases a subtle wave of non-emotional feelings, enhances sentience when it can, and helps to heighten a person's feeling of well being. The more evolved the Soul, the more heightened all the sensations shall be.

The **psyche** is sometimes referred to as "the hidden chamber" because of its unique ability to act in conjunction with each person as a much needed, unseen "counterpart." However, the psyche itself can also be hurt, as I stated previously, by the emotions, thought forms and deeds of a person. The psyche harbors no "ill-will" towards the person who I shall say is its "caretaker," it has no **practical feelings**, yet it can instigate sense and sensibility in many ways.

It is the practical level of "shaping thoughts" that reflects how a personality makes choices that have "defining life moments," which then reverberate back to the psyche. The psyche then assimilates those decisions and must act accordingly to the choices that have been made. I am not trying to make this sound complicated, but some things just sound so when speaking about parts of yourself that have been unnecessarily shrouded in mystery. See, if you lift your left arm up in the air, you know consciously that you are doing this; you know this because you can see and feel it. But the psyche reacts in the manner of "cause and effect," you cause a thought form to be Created and the psyche reacts to that form as well as to "implanted thought forms."

So practically speaking, that unseen part of yourself is in constant movement, even if you are not consciously speaking with it. Yes, of course you can talk to it. After all, you are speaking with Me, aren't you? I would have to say if you are aware that you are speaking with Me, then you should be aware that you can speak with anybody and anything at any time. If what you are planning, thinking and doing are following healthy pursuits in life, then of course the part of your psyche that deals with the practical is as healthy as your thoughts, words and deeds. You are actually dealing with the "id Factor," where the practical can be **over-governed** by the ego, views life as an everyday, routine, pattern that you have each chosen. To some degree most people do not like to have their patterns broken or changed, heaven forbid that better ways may be pursued in life! I will speak of *"the change factor"* at a later date.

The ego waiting to protect the personality of the individual always tries to understand all "incoming" information received by the person and observe the data filtering into the mind. Then ego, in a well-balanced person, attempts to either adapt a more neutral role or has learned to share communion with the Spiritual part of the individual, which is also a part of the psyche. Thinking of the "id" as a big house perhaps will help. One room adjoining the next room is delegated for "protection of the person," that is how healthy ego manifests itself. The adjoining room is where the Spiritual Part of the psyche is freely roaming **in a balanced, Spiritually sound person**. Your "brain center" is in another room, awaiting all the necessary inputs and reflexes in order to best serve you. BUT, all the rooms in your house... and remember, you ARE the house... can do is act and react accordingly to the stimuli you are sending/receiving to these parts of your mind. The brain will think on any given situation and analyze it just as any good computer will do. Yet it is still you yourself who has **"room control."**

On the Spiritual level, all that you are *in the present life experience* is housed within the Spirit Room of your psyche. The Soul and the Spirit Room walk hand-in hand, in a manner of speaking. All that you have ever been is, of course, within the Soul, BUT the Spirit Room must deal with all that you are today. Whether you are evolving or in a "standstill" position, it is still all reflected in that room. Let's just say, hypothetically of course, that in a previous life existence you were a Benedictine monk. Today you are a "new ager." Please now, that is not nearly as farfetched as you may think. Using just that one previous life experience here, all that you believed as your primary life's structure at *that time* radiates from the knowledge of Soul to the Spirit Room as a **"used-to-be-energetic** form."

Your "id" Spirit Room is then in AWARENESS that the previous life existence may or may not color your belief system now; it also knows that if it does, the Spirit Room knows to what degree it is, but it cannot know how long it will last. Only you as your primary self will be able to answer that... in your own time. Because you are a product of your own beliefs, you have the innate and CONSCIOUS opportunity to alter them at any given moment. When and IF this occurs, then obviously there is an alteration in the rooms as well. What you believe today, at this very moment in fact, can be changed if any of your preconceived ideas are now seen as "without merit." Or perhaps they served you well through your Spiritual Puberty and now you are ready to mature.

Each belief system of each person is relative to their previous lives AND their present experience. Some experiences have been too painful and **non-fruitful** in this lifetime. When you start questioning your former beliefs without any knowledge **consciously** of your previous lives, then the door you open for the new, better belief structure automatically replaces the former "grounded" beliefs housed within your Spirit Room. Please, I am not advocating any "revolving doors" here. I do not want you to think that you must change your beliefs from moment to moment without your understanding WHY, without JUST CAUSE!

You see, the biggest problems that so many of My Children have thought are insurmountable occur when the Spirit Room receives invasive attacks; this usually occurs from outside forces, but not always. Again, when the person is well-balanced mentally, Spiritually, emotionally and physically, these invasive procedures known as"psychic attacks"... although the correct term is "psyche attacks"... can be repelled, can be destroyed. I am not suggesting that it is always easy to do so; I am stating "for the record" that it CAN be controlled by you.

On the other side of the coin are those who are emotionally unstable, or perhaps they have physical deformities or illnesses that impact on them emotionally. Unless those children are of incredible Spiritual strengths, it will be easy for the dark, un-empathetic energies to assault them again and again and again, until such time that the "cracks" develop in the Children's psyches. The "cracks" represent a loss of Spiritual Energy, an aberration in the person's belief structure, an anomaly that is not healthy. If this continues unabated, then the probability factor comes into play; this just means that it is highly probable that the downward spiral that the person has begun shall continue as more cracks develop, or as the cracks present elongate. This is when "psychosis" rears its viperous head.

NOT the type of labels placed upon true visionaries, true Speakers for Ascended Masters or any of My own Speakers, of which there are many! I speak of those poor Souls who suffer terrible torments heaped upon them by the Spirit-sucking beasts who are controlled by My other Children, those Children who have become tainted with darkness, illusions, deep phobias, gross levels of disillusionments and pains that no doctor can cure assail those suffering people. Many feel torments that defy "logical" description. Very seldom can any of these assaulted ones revive themselves Spiritually if the cracks have transformed into crevices. Most spend what is left of their lifetime in another kind of "holding pattern," one that seems to them "without end."

You should not have to ask why the psyche is such a target of the dark energies when you understand what it can do and what it represents as well. All the "rooms" of the house receive devastating blows when this type of personal holocaust takes place. The very foundation of the house can be ripped apart. The person then oscillates between various realities, and some people just can never recover. Ego may try to assume a supreme control while trying to protect the person without really understanding what is going on. The brain may just "shut down" because it no longer can compute the things taking place. Each case is slightly different, yet each case is the same.

Celest — God, does the psyche heal itself after a person has passed over from physical life?

God — Celest, think of the psyche as an off-world version of "the energizer rabbit." Throughout every life experience, it just "keeps going and going." Of course Soul knowledge would never share those traumatic times with the personality on a conscious level, as you know. But the point is, the being (the one who was incarnated) learns from the experiences of how it happened and what the true causation was. Soul can remedy the situation so that it need not occur again... that is, with the willingness and the determination of the personality It will inhabit. Yet although the experiences may have far exceeded what the individual would have expected as "worst case scenario," the individual Soul, as well as Its Soul Cluster, cherish all that was learned in order to continuously expand Their own consciousness for Soul Growth.

David — So in essence what you are saying here is that all the experiences an individual has impact on all of his/her Soul Cluster?

God — Yes, David. Each mote of energy, whether it be of a positive experience or from a less positive one, the entirety of the Soul's Congregation, so to speak, benefits from the experiences of the one. If you remember what I have taught you through the teachings of all of My Messengers throughout the ages, you will see that "all is one." Being so, what one does in this lifetime alters the perspectives and realities of your other life experiences. The same goes for the interactions between all other Members of a particular Soul Cluster. On a subconscious level you always stay in touch or communicate with one another; it is done for the purpose of either learning from one another, or to keep tabs on the others' progression. The one aspect many of you are yet to realize is that all you experience, all the "revelations" you make on your own, all your emotions and the impacts of those emotions that arise while dealing with your psyche, I learn from also. For you are also an aspect of Myself, remember? One may say that I am an *honorable member* of all of your Soul Clusters.

David, you know as well as anyone, and no one on Earth is perfect, of the crack you can create within your own psyches while visiting or Creating other "rooms" in your mind's eye that are not healthy. Now your case was different; for you wished to experience all that you could in this lifetime in order to better inform and educate yourself of current realities that were present for the trying times that are presently at hand. One cannot reach out and teach another a better way of living, of expressing themselves, without first having walked in their shoes. Now I must admit, you are not the only one to do this, yet all of My Children who chose this role of experience in this lifetime will know that it is not always easy to remain detached from "living in the moment" and becoming part of that which you are here to combat. Being a Spiritual Warrior, you must first learn what you are dealing with in order to come up with alternative ways to combat the Spiritually inept.

However, once you send the "thought pattern" to your psyche, which informs all the other rooms of "your house" that you have learned from this lesson, that you have found a better way, and that you no longer wish to pursue this course of action or chain of events, the Soul Voice is then being heard and the rest of your options become available to you. Now it is those who become ensnared by life's erotic tendencies, be it from alcohol, drugs, lustful endeavors, ego-based or **power-based** ambitions, etc., etc., who will find it most trying to extricate themselves from the current situations. These Souls are not only "living their life for the enjoyment of these tendencies," but these inclinations are not dictating to the Souls what is acceptable and what is not. "Acceptability" is <u>allowing</u> one's emotions and feelings to be caught up in the moment. Emotions, although not a human trait alone, can misguide you in your quest for truth and en-light-enment. When faced with the most trying of times, a moment's peaceful pondering will bring knowing and recognition to the present tense, and thus your reactions will be precise and accurate instead of erratic and harmful.

David — So why is it that we are not permitted to remember more of our past life experiences in order to better prepare ourselves for the present one, and is it in anyone's best interest to go into past life regression to find out more?

God — David, you know as well as do I the answer to those questions, yet there are many who do not. Let me paraphrase this here or we could be working on a whole other book. Previous lifetimes held for you experiences that were necessary at the time to overcome some aspect of self that, say, needed a tune-up, or in some cases, a major overhauling of perceptions that were jaundiced. Each lifetime holds treasures for each individual in the guise of the lessons to be learned and/or learned from. In many instances the next lifetime may be to counter an action that manifested itself during a previous one. If you were wronged in a way, or if it was you who erred against another, then there always must be a balancing for the cycle to reach a conclusion. Now if you were to remember these experiences, would you then be willing or able to perform whatever you needed to do, to undo these actions from the previous lifetime, or perhaps multiple incarnations? In most cases the answer would be "No," for it may have been your turn to be the "bad" guy that time around. You may pause and inadvertently miss the window of opportunity that presented itself, which by the way, you wrote into this life's script to assist in balancing out the past.

In all instances it would be in your best interest to live a good life, be helpful and courteous and trust that by being wherever you are at any time, it is where you should be in order to anchor the Light necessary to help heal the planet. Earth has given so much of herself for you in order for you to complete your lessons. Many feel a need to go into past life regression, or find other ways to find out more about their previous lives. In most cases it is a nudging that Soul gives you, to help guide you in the correct direction to find satisfaction, or completion of a cycle. Now, not all people benefit from this, there are many amongst you who find no need for this as they already feel balance in their life. Their willingness to *"stay in the flow"* keeps all doors and windows open for the next moment that is presenting itself. Now I will not say that at that stage of evolvement that things become easier; in fact, many tests become much harder, for if it was easy or a non-event, what would you garner from it?

The Soul Voice and your Spirit Guides will always give you as much information as is necessary for you to understand the "present" and act accordingly. They will never give you too much of the picture, yet at the same time, when there is an event that requires your presence, you will be there... one way or another. You may liken it to a movie script, one that you wrote, that is unfolding as should be and you are now there to play your roles in the blockbuster movie *"So this is my life."*

Suzy — Well, God, it's my turn to get into this. But between your explanation of the psyche and your answers to Celest's and David's thoughtful questions, this is the most comprehensive information I can imagine about the extent to which our psyches profoundly influence our lives, so all I can say here is *"Thank you!"*

God — And I say back to you, Suzy, that is quite a commendation! Since you are me and I am you, both of us know that usually your mind is afloat with questions and, on occasion, a hefty argument or two with what I tell you. What you don't know is that your arguing with me always gives me a good chuckle, and that's a good thing. What do you think about that?

Suzy — I think it's good. If laughter is good for our souls, then it's good for yours too, right, God?

God — Right! So then we're in agreement and now can move on.

Celest — God, I wanted to say how appreciative I am that you chose to discuss this matter in Your Book. Far too many people have not understood the illusions that can be attributed to psychosis and why it occurs. The more people know, the greater their understanding shall be. I personally believe your Words here this day will be especially helpful to people trying to evolve and trying to better understand the madness that can capture one's mind. That is all.

God — Celest, I think you said a mouthful! Good job.

Chapter 6

Emissaries

God (*received by Celest*) — Well, Celest, I know you have been chomping at the bit to hear what I have to say on this topic, so with no further ado let's go for it! Besides MySelf, the other Gods and Goddesses of each Universe have chosen or asked certain Beings to speak on Our Behalf at certain times, in certain places. This, of course, can only take place on planets (Universes) that we each are the *"Care Takers"* of. In My Universe I am the Overseer or Care Taker and have the freedom of asking some of My Other Selves to participate in the transformation of Earth. They accomplish this through their un-selfless acts of sharing wisdom, inspiration and guidance with all of My Earth Children. All of these emissaries are Souls from civilizations in My Universe. I AM the Supreme Being of this universe. In other words, another of the Gods or Goddesses may not enter into this plane I watch over and decided what is best for the planets in My domain. That is not to say We do not listen to ideas We each may have that may, or may not, be of use to Us in Our continuous expansion of Ourselves as One Entity. The term "One Entity" simply means that you who are here as humans, who coalesce into a group acceptance or mass consciousness, that has MySelf and the Creator as the Central Hub of your beliefs, merge slowly sometimes, yet merge nonetheless, into an expansion of Myself as well as into an intangible Aspect of the Creator.

So, since I am not permitted to intervene nor interfere in humanity's affairs, those others who I have asked to Speak for Me can and do visit here. Some for just a short span of a time, others for a lifetime. It may vary depending on not only the missions of the individuals selected, but on the desires and capabilities of those individuals. Yes, many of the Beings have been asked by Me to repeatedly journey here since the Earth was Created. All are free to say, "no," but to My recollection none have. *"Emissaries"* are *"ambassadors-at-arms"* of a sort; they are all peacekeepers, they all are "in tune" with the *"Universal Plan of Growth through Diversity."* That term reflects back to the "reincarnational themes."

Some have stumbled during their missions in the past, and as a result are always seeking the ways and means to expand their consciousness through the learning process of which "a walk on the wild side of the galaxy" has been ever present here on My planet Earth. All of My Emissaries are from various Soul Clusters, most of them have worked together here countless times. Here on Earth they may share the memories of the joy as well as the tears remembered that each human has shed or rejoiced in since forever. These Beings share a commonality with My human Children; often I have asked them to yet again rejoin those Children with whom they have walked, shared lives with and loved long ago on Earth.

My reasons are multipurpose; it has always been that love as the main concept for all of My Children to share, can and is strengthened by the further sharing of love with all others receptive to love, and by the integration of energies that the Emissaries and My other Children emit. "Love" as a beacon cannot be extinguished when more and more love energies are attracted to that Light. My Ambassadors "come with instructions." Not that they will remember them consciously, but their individual Soul Voices are "in awareness" and heightened by the knowingness that so many others of their same vibrations and energetic fields are close by. "Close by" means "somewhere on the planet."

Celest, if all My Children would think of themselves as "Emissaries," and stop trying to separate themselves from Me by believing that they are somehow beneath Me, rather than walking hand-in-hand at My Side, how simple this would all be! Well, of course I must have more evolved Children here to assist, but that does not in any manner detract from the fact that as more and more of My Children become aware of the reality of who and what they are, they will know there truly is no "favoritism" at work here. Each Aspect of MySelf I sent and am still sending here *"speaks for Me and with Me,"* just as it was intended that all other of My Children should. Emotional entanglements that are experienced here, along with physical problems and loss of Spirituality, are not "new news" to these ambassadors.

Many of them have walked in all peoples' footsteps long ago. Because they quickly, at least some of them, learned what not to do here and they learned the lessons well, who better to **STAND** and lead the way while shining My Light, yet simultaneously, teaching others how to lead the way. It has been said that *"step by step, one by one, God's Work shall be done."* All right, bearing that statement in mind, doesn't it make sense that someone must take the giant steps and teach those taking baby steps how to increase their stride? Well, it does to Me.

I know, I know, so many people want Me to *"come down and fix everything for them."* Well, Children, that will not happen. I am providing the best teachers, the quickest and easiest venues and all the "rah, rah, rahing" I can muster. This is as good as it gets. Because I MySelf am experiencing life here on Earth through you, I can and do understand your vexation, your frustration and, for most of you, your earnest desire to "ascend." My ambassadors are teaching all peoples who are receptive that you each may *"ascend"* in every moment of your life here. They teach "how to" and "why to" and then "cut you loose," so that you do something on your own with the knowledge you have been given.

Great teachers know when to *"back off"* and when *"to enter another's life."* They also knew prior to descent here only on a FULLY AWARE level back then, that many of My other Children would not understand when certain increments of time, birthing segments of "future present tenses" relative to a person's forward momentum, would Create the designation **"on your own time-lines."** Many of My Children are not aware that these "timelines" or "gridlines," do intersect in every individual's life. It is when this occurs that the Child or group of Children must move forward alone, but never *"in alone-ness."*

Remember, I love you each as I love MySelf because we **share** one another! I love you enough to let you go, trusting that "in the end it will be fine." I remind you again that from My point of observation I see what you do, what you feel and what you think. I see the varied means, sometimes convoluted, that My Ambassadors have had to take in order to teach you **"to BE the difference."** I have smiled at your antics and theirs as well, as you each share willingness to move forward in your personal evolution, while attempting to show to others <u>that which you know, but cannot prove</u>. Those of My Earthbound Children who seek the pivotal point of personal evolution do not take the Emissaries for granted, nor are they unaware of how the sweeping forces of consciousness affects the Earth herself.

Children, have you never stopped to consider that you may have been a selected Emissary at some previous time? Have you never stopped to consider that perhaps you have forgone that role in order to be an active participant in diverse life experiences now? It can happen, you know, I have never prevented any of My Children from exchanging the roles they have chosen to play. I cannot do that, I am only God, not the Creator, and I know He will not do it either. But I am permitted to send the *"Special Forces"* to be among you, and they readily accept the assignments regardless of how often they are called upon. Although they do not refuse, I have suspicions that a few times I heard some mutter, *"oh no, there they go again,"* when referring to many of My Earthbound Children. Oddly enough, I have heard some mind-thoughts from some of My Children here on Earth, wishing they could identify, or "know," when they are being approached by the ambassadors.

Perhaps they expect the Emissaries to wear a big sign on their backs, or maybe to hear drums and trumpets heralding their arrivals. I think not! What possible purpose would it serve if you knew beforehand the "who" and the "where" and the "when"? The probability is that everyone would be on their best behavior, whatever that may be. What would that accomplish? I can't say *"God only knows,"* because I don't. I can hypothesize, however; My Children would be eager to be seen as "okay," you know, *"nothing's wrong in my world."* My Children would be acting a bit "out of character," I think.

So it is that My Emissaries enter on the wind, subtly in most cases, bringing their auras of peace, grace and humility with them which complements their golden Light. This is why so many of My other Children, those who have "lost their way for now," cannot abide the Emissaries' presence. On a Super Conscious level, these lost ones are reminded of who they are, they are reminded of their own true origins, they are reminded of MYSELF and ALL of DIVINITY. Consciously those Children cannot bear My Light, at least not for now, not in the condition they are in. They cannot abide the "brightness" of the Emissaries who radiate and reflect all which the lost Souls now find to be the antithesis of who they themselves are.

What those Children cannot anymore understand, what they refute as non-truths, they then despise and hate. So even if it is not known consciously the "who," and the "what," when I walk among you in the forms of My Emissaries, My Presence is well-known, in one manner or another.

David — Why would anyone want to be an Emissary, especially during this chaotic time period in Earth's history?

God — Why would they *not?* My dearest Soul, you yourself jumped at the chance to be there now. Celestial, despite her father's (Blue Star the Pleiadian) urging her not to go, persisted in giving Me a headache until I agreed to let her join forces once again on Earth for the times you are now currently experiencing. Now mind you, I have heard a few grumbles and some muttering going on from time to time among My Emissaries. Not all remember their previous trials and tribulations, those ordeals that presented themselves to these emissaries in previous times while walking in the heavy density of the third-dimension. No, I did not call it a "third-world planet."

Not one of my children said, *"hell no, I won't go."* That is not in your nature, nor should it be. I am not sending out My children to become *Martyrs;* they all know better than that. The challenges ahead were well known to be treacherous, yet all knew full well not only of the rewards to be had, but the importance of **all** *their* chosen missions. You are all emissaries in My eyes. You courageously chose to partake in this Creation of a new race of beings and you agreed most whole- heartedly to be on the front line, to secure the future existence of the human race as a whole. You knew only too well that without your help and the help of all My Star Keepers, and those from the Spirit world, that Earth would have been doomed, she would not have been able to continue her evolvement, she would have perished. The Earth would have been no more.

Each one knew this would not be an easy task, yet you each, you who are the same ones who are there now as you have been so many times in the past, knew of the vital importance of this mission, of this timeline. OK, so some of you feel like *"well worn sages,"* big deal. You are making a difference, whether the results are apparent at the time or not. Many of you are there in your secluded locations, isolated from others that you can easily relate to, in order to anchor the incoming Light where it is needed most. I believe My Son Jesus the Christ said it well when He stated, *"I never said it would be easy, I only said it would be worth it."* You will have plenty of time to recuperate before your next life experience, wherever one that may lead you.

All Children who walk the Earth, those who are presently lost to the darkness, and those whose auras radiate the purest expressions of *The Christ Consciousness*, are all there to do their parts to save my beloved Gaia from Her total descent into darkness, well, Her planetary body anyhow, Her Spirit still resides in the higher dimensions. I want to encourage all of you to not look for someone to follow, look for someone you can learn from instead. There is a difference. I do realize, however, that not all are yet ready to become leaders. So it would be better, perhaps, to find where the truth is most prevalent and learn what you can from all of these fine teachers. When you have moved past that particular stage of development, the next teacher will appear.

Always remember to call upon your Master Teachers, your chosen Spirit Guides, and do not forget about Myself. I am always walking beside you when you have questions that need clarification. We will always be there with you, whether you are aware of it or not. We are not willing to do the work for you; We are there to guide you. The best guide, the best mentor, you have available at every given moment is yourself. Have you ever heard the expression *"Me, Myself and I?"* Trust in the accumulated knowledge and wisdom that resides within you. *Trust in, believe in, you.* Start listening to

your song of life, that which is "you" as your Highest Self.

And then when all else fails, or perhaps do not wait that long, call upon Us and We will show you the way through signs, visitations during your dream state, telepathic communications or a simple casual response from a passerby. Do not discard any given information; **there are no "coincidences."** That sign on the highway you passed a million times may change its wording, just for you, just for a fleeting moment. All you need to do is be aware. There are those who were chosen to be My public speakers, there are those who are to be My eyes and ears, there are those who are to be on the front line, and there are those who are to be working behind the scenes, to enact the much needed changes. None are more important than another. You, My Child, are as important to Me as I Am to Myself. I do not play any favoritism, as the saying goes, *"All are equal in God's Eyes."*

Suzy — Hi, God, it's Suzy. Throughout the ten years we've been talking, and even with all your long explanations about "who you are," what you said about wishing that all of us would think of ourselves as your emissaries is the first time I've ever thought of myself like that. But it does make sense because I know that every one of us not only chose to be here now, but were selected, because many other souls also wanted to come. However, since most people here don't consciously know that each of us is a part of you, so they think of themselves as "alone" and you as a totally separate all-powerful and all-knowing being, how can we who know that ALL of us are ONE tell those others?

God — Well, my dear little Suzy, for one thing, your BEing is getting this awareness across to some people subconsciously. The energy frequency of all who are aware of the truth reaches others at soul level, where it ignites a spark of conscious remembrance and starts the questioning juices flowing. You often refer to this as "soul-searching," and that's a good term for it — the conscious mind is seeking the truths that the soul knows. When the truths come out about the false religious teachings, the job of all who recognize yourselves as my emissaries will dramatically extend from BEing

83

the truth to also actively teaching it. *Teaching* the truth of who I am and who you all are will replace the *preaching* of the falsehoods rooted in the religious dogma concocted many centuries ago by church-and-state leaders who did that to control the populace.

You and a number of my other children are teaching this now through writings and speaking, but as you know, you're reaching only the receptive folks, the ones who are seeking the knowingness that spiritual truths impart. That's why you feel your mission is easy — well, you do think of it as extremely time-consuming, but without any hardships — and at this point, it is. This soon will change to "challenges" as the truths come to light more publicly and the resoluteness of my "hardcore" religious children, in defense of their beliefs, will increase accordingly. You teachers will experience a lot of resistance until their minds and hearts either open to the truths or they will choose to hold firm to their beliefs, leave this physical lifetime, and once in spirit, realize that their decision means reincarnating in another third density world and another chance to accept the truths. Most of my children on Earth have done this again and again and again because of the pernicious hold religions have over them. Since they are parts of me, I know the souls' disappointment that so many opportunities have come and gone because they weren't recognized during the incarnate lifetimes, but once back in the spirit world you call "heaven," they welcome the chance to choose in their pre-birth agreements still another chance "to get it right" the next time around.

Suzy — I'm thankful that this time I've finally learned what's true and what isn't, so I don't have to go through all this third density stuff again! But from what you said about souls volunteering to be "ambassadors" to worlds like this — I might do that sometime?

God — Suzy, my dear little soul, you did that THIS time — you've just not consciously known it.

Suzy — Well, probably that's why I feel my "spiritual information service" is easy — I've had a LOT of times around in third density because I screwed it up more times than I want to know.

God — Oh come on, you know better than to think you screwed up — what you did was learn from your "times around" and that's why you're back there! A few of my ambassadors know the role they're playing, but most are like you, accomplishing their missions by following their inner guidance.

Suzy — I see. I have a question about what you told David, about remembering to call on master teachers and chosen spirit guides for help and not to forget about you, too. It's my understanding that we don't have to call on anyone because you know all our thoughts and feelings about the help we need and you send the emissary that can give us that.

God — That is so for the people who know it, Suzy. But remember this — everything I'm saying in this book may be a refresher course for some, but it's an Aha! for the folks who don't have a clue and confirmation to those who have been wishing that's the way it is. It IS the way it IS!

David — I would like to introduce a guest presenter to this "God's Book." Her name is Melena, Her origins are from Arcturus. She is my Master Teacher and Spiritual advisor. I reunited with Melena some five to six years ago, and She has been one of my most valued and treasured mentors as I struggled to start remembering my purpose for being here on the planet Earth once again. Melena asked me if she could briefly share with you her awareness on what she considers issues of importance.

Melena (*received by David*) — Good day to you, my Earth cousins, I am Melena. I am of Arcturian descent as is David, and I am here to share a message with you from our home world of Arcturus. Long ago, when the *great* human experiment began, the Creation of a race of Beings that were to be half-man/half God, it was decided that there would also be a consortium of Beings from all parts of this universe that would oversee God's planet from its inception to its eventual oneness with **All That Is**. Eventually you, the human race, would join all of us in your rightful place as members of the Galactic Federation. We, the Arcturians, have been a part of that consortium for as long as Earth has been. Although we are not alone in this, we, like so many other races, have sent our emissaries, our master teachers and our Spiritual warriors to the Earth Star planet to assist in any way possible, *without* interfering in your own personal and planetary destinies. As you know, from the infancy stage through the later years of life, when that crucial point, the "awareness of truth" state, when wisdom has been reached, there is much to be learned during the in-between times. We are a race of healers, we are a race of teachers, we are a race of philosophers, just as our cousins the Pleiadians are. We work in harmony with the Great Spirit that you choose to call "God." His true name — vibration — is impossible to speak of within the confines of the human language. Suffice it to say, "He is All that shall ever be."

The language of light, which you know of as telepathy, is a far more advanced (natural) way of communicating with one another than you may realize. Even when using telepathy, we are somewhat limited in expressing ourselves, due to the evolvement level of the intended receivers and also their educational background. David knows this well, he has struggled many times trying to grasp a word that we are trying to relay to him and finds that it is one he never, or very occasionally, chooses to use. Now I would like to emphasize that there are two ways of telepathically communicating, two basic ways, that is. One has to do with thought-to-mind basic telepathy; the other is a Soul Voice-to-Soul Voice connection, which is how these three scribes choose to receive their communiqués. It is much more efficient, it requires less effort, but a stronger connection between the two beings involved is accomplished. As I said earlier, we are teachers, and in that capacity we have long played an active part in Earth's development. We are also an active part of the forces, "the peacekeeping forces," that have volunteered to help protect Earth and its citizens from those who are intent on using you for their own betterment and amusement.

I am going to make a point about something that very few people seem to realize, although David and Celest understand this well. The less evolved children **need** you. *You **do not** need them.*

The lesser evolved children need you much more than yo
consciously acknowledge to yourself. They require your ability to
procreate to serve their needs. More so, they need your ability to
"Create, to manifest." You see, a long time ago, when they first fell
from the light, perhaps withdrawn from the light is a more efficient
use of the term, they gave up their abilities to manifest and Create
things anew. They are limited because of the fact that they can only
keep re-creating all their originally preconceived ways of dominating
others and fulfilling their own needs. *We, My Brethren and I*, have
spoken at length with many of you about your natural abilities to
use thoughts to Create what you require in your lives. We have also
spoken at length of how all like-minded thought forms come together,
they merge, when another similar thought is put forth. That
thought attracts others, like a moth to a beacon of light; it attracts
those similar ones that are floating in the universal pool of
knowledge. What this means is that if you think of peace, you call
to yourself other similar thoughts and that is what starts balancing
the scales in that direction. If you think there is something drastic or
bad that is going to happen, you attract the energies from that
energetic form and you find that it is materializing just as, or
similarly, to what you conceived it to be. As the omni-versal beings
that you each are, you have the abilities to bring into manifestation
either the good or the not so good. Those children of the lesser light
have chosen their paths; their only viable option from this point on
is to move into *The Light of God* for their own salvation. Earth is
being continuously sent the *Light of All Lights* to infuse this planet
with new life healing and creative energies.

Those that have controlled you for so long can no longer
survive in this abundance of in-pouring light being generated by
your distant cousins. Those unilluminated ones have known for as
long as the Earth Star planet has existed that in order to control
you and get you to do their bidding, they would need to keep you in
the dark about universal truths such as these. They have known
that by eliminating your true connection with the God of this
universe and by manipulating and coercing the way that you think,
and altering what you term as your *"dream states"* in order to
better confuse you, they could essentially control you. And it has

worked far too well. For far too long technologies have been withheld from you that we have shared with your governments to enhance life there on Earth. Those who hide behind the scenes have manipulated your every thought, your very existence for far too long. Their wastefulness and their subliminal coercion of your races to follow suit has stretched Earth's natural resources to the brink of extinction. They have convinced you to drain the very lifeblood of your planet (oil) to the point of destroying Her existence, which no doubt by now you know would also end yours. And — you have allowed it. Their arrogance and the redundancy of their actions have brought you to the brink of physical and mental exhaustion and, interestingly enough, has also made you **aware** of what they fear the most from you. They fear your awakening and remembering of who and what you truly are.

The sages of the past are the same sages of today who have been chosen and who have *chosen or been selected* to come to Earth repeatedly to do what they could to help bring en-light-enment to the peoples of Earth. They, my dear cousins, are what you would now term as **well-worn sages**. They have been the ones who have always stood up for right when only wrong was prevailing. They have fought the battle against The Beast from within and managed to hold their ground. They stand in truth for they know no other way. You are slowly being able to recognize the fruits of their labors in every vestige of your societal structures. They know far too well that this time, this time long awaited, is *for all the marbles*. There will be no second chance, no other time quite like this will again occur in Earth history. They will not fail. There have been timelines in the past when and if Earth's populations had joined in harmony as a mighty force of one, that you all could have released yourselves and Her from their bonds. This time they, those well-worn sages, and you, shall succeed.

With love in your hearts and light-heart-edness in your everyday attitudes, you can overcome the imprisonment that you have been in. Those that will not survive Earth's journey into the higher dimensions are those who **choose** not to see that anything is amiss. They feel very comfortable in their lifestyles and addictions and the rest; well, that is just the way it is for them for now. I am

here to tell you that this is not how it has to be. They have need
you to survive; you only needed them to learn from, in order to not
let future generations repeat this experience ever again. Earth has
lived far too long in the dark ages. Now those days are about to end
once and for all. Focus your thoughts on good. Focus them on the
positive. Focus them on change and **be specific** when doing this.
Do not be judgmental of others. Send out thoughts of love and
peace. Focus your thoughts on how you envision Earth can and will
be when She is restored to Her vibrant health. Imagine the flora
with its succulent scents flowing everywhere and the unlimited
vibrant colors that will soon surround you. Imagine the crystal
clear waters and the constant beauty that can be a part of you in
every breathtaking moment of your lives. Imagine a world where
all of its life forms live in harmony. A world where no one would go
without the basic fundamental needs that all of you require to be
healthy and those that enable you to have a fulfilling life. These are
all within your grasp. Be the person you always knew you could be.
There is nothing holding you back anymore. Only you can do this,
only you can rise above the moral turpitude of the masses.

Understand the words that you have or will read in the pages
of this, **"God's Book,"** and search your hearts to see the truth and
wisdom that has been shared with you. We, your neighbors from
afar, are as much a part of you as God is Himself. For we are all
one. You are half-human, half-God, you are "God I AM" living life
in a physical universe. Be aware that you are The Children of God,
that you are **one race of beings**. He needs you to be stronger now
than you have ever been before. Stand in Truth and defend your
truths to no one. Let them, your truths, STAND on their own.
Teach those whom you can, what you can, only when they are
ready, and then let them choose their own path. Do not prostitute
yourselves any longer. You are far more than that. With that I wish
to bid you a fond farewell, and I thank you for letting me share
these moments with you. I am always just a thought away as are
all the rest of your universal families. We await your call, your
request for our assistance. We cannot offer this without first being
asked by you to help. That would go against everything we believe in
and against **"The Universal Law of Noninterference."** Of late

you have been hearing much about *"The Law of Attraction."* Mind you, there are many other Universal Laws that you must learn about and adhere to and bring forth into your everyday lives as well. Good day, I am Melena, your cousin, your sister, from the planet of Arcturus.

David — Melena, I appreciate you taking the time out from your busy schedule to share with us your views and insights to the times we are all living in.

Melena — David, these times are the greatest of times. It is the time you have all been waiting for, with bated breath, I might add. The future is unfolding as it should and I might add *"the universe is always on time."*

Suzy — Melena, hello! I'm very pleased to have this chance to thank you directly for the loving assistance your people are giving us. Some of us know that you can do this only if we invite you, and believe me, we *are* inviting you! We know, too, that we have to do our part to rid our world of the long-time darkness. But considering the entire population, it's only relatively few of us who are aware of this — are we doing enough to bring peace in our world?

Melena — Dear friend Suzy, we know that some of you are doing everything within the powers of the mind and heart to accomplish your goal of peace, but others are not. Yet, the collective thoughts of the unaware that also are focused on peace added to the thoughts of you who are aware are enough. It will be necessary for the lingering darkness to run its energetic course, you understand, so it will be a while before we can join you on your planet and we can rejoice together as family. In the meantime, be assured that we are with you every step of the way toward our common goal of completely liberating Earth from her bondage due to the recalcitrant souls' influence. Their hold is waning by the moment, so stay in the enlightened thoughts about what is on the way for all lighted souls among your peoples and you will manifest the glory on Earth that we see already is complete in the heavens, in the continuum.

Suzy — Thank you for that assurance, Melena, and once again, for your great help to us.

Melena — On behalf of my people and myself, you are welcome, Suzy, our friend and sister.

Celest — Melena, I appreciate not only everything you have said, but I appreciate your reasons for wanting to participate in this book. Your wisdom is invaluable.

Melena — I appreciate your understanding how important I felt my words are for the people of the Earth Star.

Celest — A dear Soul who I have the utmost respect for has asked to participate in this book. His name vibration is "Tomás," he is a very ancient being who holds a prominent position on the High Council. His interaction with all Starkeepers in this universe and with those on Earth walking in human form is invaluable. Tomás has lived many, many lifetimes on many planets and his wisdom is impeccable. He has a sense of humor... at times... but is usually far too busy to enjoy many "days off" from his assignments.

Tomás (*received by Celest*) — I send you wondrous greetings from all members of High Council; they have all been awaiting the release of this book with bated breath. As Celestial has already stated, the council works with the constant integration of Star Keepers from all other planets in this universe. We do so for the purpose of not only promoting their worlds' evolvement, but also for the convergence of all life forms into one perfected *"ONE with God"* level of awareness. My assignments range from incorporating the everyday tasks of managing and overseeing the Star Fleets' protocol for defending all the worlds in this universe from the invasive attacks initiated by dark beings, to the care and protection of each Soul who has been assigned to a planet, in this particular case the Earth Star, for the purpose of initiating the Jesus the Christ Consciousness and maintaining this energetic wave. At times many of the Souls selected to be on the Earth Star have experienced great periods of frustration as they eagerly seek to move ahead more quickly than is in their best interest.

Most of these Souls know only on a conscious level that they need to slow down, they do not know *consciously,* on another level or state of knowing, that maintaining specific paces are necessary in order to adhere to certain gridlines of "time." Many Master Teachers seek my advice when dealing with a "charge" that is being recalcitrant or inordinately obtuse. It is then that I scope the energy fields of the charges and see if I can persuade them to listen to my advice. Sometimes I can, sometimes I cannot. I am an elder and preside over many disputes that Star Keepers have about certain protocols, for example, which they would like to have changed. I, along with the rest of the High Council, also answer the petitions that inhabitants of planets send us.

The Earth races have been sending far more petitions for sanctions and protection than any other planet. Rightly so, I might add. I also assist many of the Star Keeper forces here and in the Crystal City when they themselves seek sage advice. High Council meetings are convened on a "per need basis" for the most part. Because the "need" is so great now, especially when the topics and the Souls are from the Earth Star, that we are in a continuous mode of daily and nightly "conventions." Council members are composed of a specific number of Souls representing all the planets in this universe. Each incoming petitioner Soul is seen and listened to in accordance with our bylaws. **None are turned away.** Our "priority Souls and priority topics" are set in motion by us as soon as we read the agendas and the declarations from each planet/inhabitant.

I have chosen many, many times not to reincarnate on the Earth or on another orb, for I believe my assistance here in the dimension I reside in is needed far more than "Star-Walking." I have "been here" to see the "beginnings of the beginnings" and observed far more bloodshed occur than seems possible. We, the God of this Universe, and the rest of the Ubiquitous Worldizens from other planets, are each in our own manner doing all which we can do to provide the aid and wisdom that your planet's inhabitants require. I revel in each wondrous endeavor you succeed in, regardless of the fact that it may seem "insignificant or trivial to you." In Celestial's case, I <u>very</u> often must visit with her with great hopes that I can manage to convince her to slow herself down a bit. I will not tell you my success rate in this matter!

So many Souls, whether they are from other planets or are "natural" inhabitants of the Earth Star, are in fact quite anxious to be a difference in the little time remaining here. Unfortunately, at times they feel impotent if they are not always moving at an accelerated pace. Yes, yes, they all do know that everything is happening on a specific gridline; they also know "they came with instructions." However, I understand their plight when I see them surrounded by "the black hats" and vastly outnumbered to boot. The point here is that I do want to **impress** upon you the reader, that we ARE watching over you; we are alerting you to upcoming personal collisions with dark energies prior to the event taking place, as one example of how we are best aiding you! I love you each, as do all my brethren, you are not "forgotten," we shall not **leave you behind as Earth continues to transcend the filth and despair surrounding her and moves in great dignity to her APPOINTED destination.** I can only hope that you do not leave yourself behind.

The God of this Universe will not allow you to be left **without your consent,** nor shall I. Your consent can be construed as: acceptance of personal defeat, unwillingness to change, or not caring enough to change. I must allow you to each either "remember" or "continue to forget to remember" why you are here and what your assignment is. As one example, a **Celestial** being who is Star-Walking on Earth, was reminded by me, rather forcefully I might add, that she needs to continue to allow herself a respite from Spiritual-Walking and ALLOW herself to simply be pragmatic when she is able to do so; that means when certain conditions are prevailing, so that she can regenerate, recharge her batteries and RELAX for a while. I will not mention any names here; suffice it to say that she not only has been known to give God a headache, but Blue Star and myself as well.

I share this knowledge with you so that you can see how dedicated so many Souls on this planet are. If you are reading this book and keeping an open mind and a receptive thought for all that is said in the book, then you are **expressing dedication** as well. Too many Earth peoples think that everything they do must be grand and a stupendous "work of Spirit." This is untrue. Think on the little things, those everyday moments that you can infuse with laughter, with joy for living, and consider the incontrovertible fact that each time you smile, sing, freely and honestly express yourselves, you are loosening the bondage that has held you in its grip for so long.

From where I "hover" here in another dimension, each time one of you does this, your energy streamers alter their coloration and your own personal musical note is heard by all. **You are each part of the music of the ethers; you have just forgotten this truth.** The dark energies abhor these actions, these good uplifting patterns of actions and deeds that mean so much more than you realize. Am I asking too much of you? I think not. You need to better understand that I see what you hear and I hear what you see. This is not by any means a trivial statement, I assure you. This is my "meter"; it is how I can correctly ascertain what is going on with you as individuals and why it is occurring. I have great need to know these things; otherwise I cannot render assistance properly. As the "whirlwind of spatial time" continues to move forward, ever bringing to all planets, but especially to the Earth Star, the flux necessary to insure that changes will occur here in spite of many of the peoples' complacency about these matters, I will continue to do whatever I can and whatever I deem necessary for the good of the Earth and for furthering the manifestation of God and the Creator's wishes. I can do no less. By the way, as I prepare to take my leave now, I would suggest that the Earth peoples cease their silly terming of all other planets' inhabitants as "Extraterrestrials" or "aliens." All life, whether humanoid or not, are "Star Keepers." By the way again... since you are inhabiting a planet, what does that make you? You are "alien" yourselves!

I thank you for your time, I salute you each and all... Tomás

Celest — Tomás, you and I have had such glorious times together; it is such a personal pleasure for me to have you address the readers. There is so much more I could say, but I will simply say... "I salute you."

Tomás — Celest, we shall speak in private shortly, you know my heart well. "Salude."

David — Greetings, Tomás. Above you said, and I quote, *"It is then that I scope the energy fields of the charges and see if I can persuade them to listen to my advice."* Tomás, I know this communiqué is not normally done while people are awake in their everyday lives, so I believe what you are referring to here is done at Soul level, where you are speaking with each individual Soul that requires your assistance. Why is it that a Soul would go against its own best interests? Is this not a form of Spiritual suicide? Also, you referred to the Crystal City; most people do not know what this is or where it is. Could you expound upon this as well? Thank you for the wisdom you have shared with all Earthizens. I do hope your occasional "headaches" do not cause you to change your mind about remaining on the Council. I know you are much needed just where you are.

Tomás — David, I know how your fertile mind works, for we do indeed know each other well, even though you are consciously unaware of this. In answer to your question, and yes, it does need to be addressed; we shall proceed to see if we can bring to it some clarification. Each Soul has a Higher Self, the aspect which **IS** *Soul Voice*. Most Higher Selves have many other splinter personages experiencing life somewhere. An example of a personage's Higher Self is the One you know as Jesus, who now wears the Mantel of Greatness and whose name vibration is known to you also as Sananda. At the time He was there as Jesus, his Higher Self was Sananda. Sananda now has a new Higher Self as well.

Each Soul has a need to expand upon Itself, however at times it may become jaded by Its own success and allow Itself to cease Its progression, no longer understanding or assimilating knowledge through the chosen experience. And yes, this is a form of **Spiritual Suicide,** a term that not many may be aware of. *Spiritual Suicide occurs* when a Soul loses interest in the body that It is occupying and the life that It is living, also when the individual does not respect and care for their physical vehicle as it should and the Soul deliberately causes or allows the body to die. The consequences for this can be most debilitating. Refreshment of basic **Ascension 101** classes must then be undertaken before these Souls can proceed on to their next incarnation.

Now *Spiritual Suicide* is not the same as a suicide caused from a physical infliction. Suicide is a premeditated act of release from some issue that people are either unable or unwilling to face. None are judged by us for committing this act, this is something which they themselves must come to terms with. Death is another form of rebirth; it is the completion of a cycle. A *symbolic* death and rebirth is termed as a **transition**. Transitions are a means of acknowledging accomplishments and moving ever steadily forward up the Spiritual ladder. For a Soul who throws in the towel and wishes for a different experience, this choice is completely up to them and for some it is an option they have added into their individual soul contract. However, the random suicides are the ones which are never an easy sight for us to *bear witness* to. However, what most people do not understand is that if a lesson is not completed to the satisfaction of the Over-Soul who chose the experience, then that Soul must repeat the lesson that was left incomplete.

I, We, reach out to those that are in need of our assistance. It is The Creator's gift of Free Expression that causes many self-inflicted heartaches along the way. This wondrous gift has been abused by far too many for personal glory and gratification without understanding the reverberating consequences to all others. We cannot tell someone what they must do, we can only try to relay our personal perceptions to them and point out the reasons for us bringing this to their attention. The choice is ultimately as it should be, up to them. I cannot persuade someone who has mental or physical reservations to proceed with what they as Soul originally chose for an experience to be had, this is something they them-selves must come to terms with. This is where practicing **passionate detachment** is a must, just as you should when watching others who are playing out their own dramas. *Spiritual Suicide* is a Soul level drama that needs to be addressed in order for individuals to move forward on their own personal evolutionary path. Currently there are many personal and planetary dramas that need to happen and will be played out in the days ahead, in order to transmute the baser energies of these long overdrawn scenarios.

Now as to the Crystal City, David, you have been there many times; you have remembered this from your night visions and meditative states. The Crystal City was a grand experiment much like the Akashic library. Each of these places keeps growing and expanding as more information and different levels of awareness are infused within them. No one ever knows exactly how big the Akashic library is, this is where your *"Books of Life"* are, for it changes from moment to moment and this in itself is a spectacular sight in its own right. It is a supreme example of Divine Inspiration, Creation and expansion. The Crystal City is more in a dimension rather than a place; it is where people go to congregate, where they come to rest from everyday life. It is also where many council meetings are held. I could go on and on about this wondrous place, however that, too, would require the writing of another book which I am well aware the three of you simply do not have time for. Suffice it to say, each of you has been there at one time or another, in time you, too, will remember this as well.

"Headaches," no, they are more like "intense long lasting debates," actually. David, your desire to question everything in your quests for truth and understanding only fuels the fires of my passion to continue to be of service. I enjoy a constructive dispute or debate; much is to be learned from the bantering about of emotion-filled expressions. Some, however, derive far too much pleasure from this and I feel it pertinent here to remind you that much may also be learned from listening. With that having been stated, I again say my adieu.

David — Thank you, Tomás, I have paid my dues where ignorance and arrogance is concerned, and I only wished to add clarity for others so that they may glean some truth from your words of wisdom.

Tomás — Ignorance is no excuse, for some people it can be a way of life. I appreciate the fact that you understand better than most the pitfalls awaiting people who do not use discernment and have no desire to learn from their mistakes. No one knows everything. Experience is the KEY to understanding, and those that do not question issues are destined to follow, instead of LEAD.

Suzy — Hello, Tomás! This is Suzy Ward greeting you with heartfelt thankfulness for your dedication and attentiveness to Earth and her residents. I think all of us need to learn, or be reminded, about the constant loving assistance others in the universe are showering upon this planet and us. You know our minds and hearts, so you know that it takes enormous patience for us to keep waiting for our efforts, which are united with yours and all other light being helpers, to bear the fruit of peace on Earth. But our trust that together we will be triumphant does not waver!

Incidentally, Celest may not always follow your instructions to slow down, but she tells me to do that, so in this way, she is paying attention to you and I am paying attention to her.

Tomás — Ah, Suzy, thank you for your thanks, but you needn't introduce yourself to me. How could I and many others not know of you and your beloved son Matthew? I assure you, we do, and I heartily commend you on your part of the grand alliance of your souls that began in your term "light years" before this lifetime.

Suzy — Well then, probably you know that I trust in this "alliance" without understanding how it works. I've been told that someday I will understand, but for now, my not knowing is purposeful — others who don't consciously know either can relate to me and be more receptive to the information I receive and pass on.

Tomás — And that, my dear Star Keeper friend, is exactly according to your service agreement. I say, "Keep it up, you're doing well!" and for that, I thank you. To all readers who relate to Suzy's awaiting the emergence of full en-LIGHT-enment, I say to you, you too are performing well within your agreement to trust the voice of guidance that is your soul speaking. And with that, I take my leave.

(Serapis Bey, the ascended master known primarily for his lifetimes in Egypt as a light warrior and an architect pharaoh, is now in that region only etherically. He came from higher realms to be a guardian of Earth's evolution, and in recent times has telepathically given loving instructions for souls' disciplined living to aid in their spiritual evolution.)

Serapis Bey (*received by Suzy*) — A good day, dear ones, from Serapis Bey, and a very fine day it is! You may associate my name with ancient architecture, and rightly so, yet a builder of much more importance to you than of pyramids and such, ah yes! Most notably in your history as a designer and builder by talent and trade, I shy away from returning in a body for more construction. Instead I am lending my energy, or perhaps "infusing" my energy is more apt, to receptive ones who may or may not realize that their motivation and inspiration are in part in cooperation with me. It does not matter if they do not know. All that matters is that they beautifully express their talents in inspired ways.

But return I do in this manner to whet your appetite to the self-realization and self-actualization of your individual building, *your soul evolution,* by way of LOVE in all undertakings to restore Earth to her former health and beauty. Your homeland is greatly beloved by me and countless others whose great desire never diminished to be of service to her and to all who live upon her.

At one time Earth, when she was known as Gaia or Terra, was one of the most magnificent of all celestial bodies, a paradise without blemish, and God's favored creation. That was before civilizations came and brought some of their baseness along with their grand intellect. Through the eons since then, the degree of intelligence and spirituality of the populations has fluctuated and with that, her well being and pristine beauteousness faded.

During the past many millennia, with the few exceptions of God's chosen messengers and other believers in their Oneness, the peoples' beginnings were totally lost to memory and they spiraled into an abyss of love-lessness. Love without reservation or condition or expectation; love that acknowledges soul-self's connection with

God and all other souls in this universe; love that sees and is thankful for blessings; love, the highest of all vibrations and enables each soul, each god and goddess self, to be a divine powerhouse beyond your wildest imagining, went missing.

Darkness took its place. The absence of that kind of love is why Earth plunged from her high placement in the universe into so-called third density, a thriving hotbed of low vibrations where the basest aspects of what you call "human nature" let havoc abound in every conceivable manner. In other lifetimes, some of you participated in the terrible destructiveness that cost Earth such severe blows that her blood-soaked, light-depleted body was near death and her soul was in deep despair.

Maybe you have memories of those times and know that you returned to mend Earth, to shower your love upon her and ALL her life forms, not only those with special appeal to you, but most of all, those considered despicable, because they are the ones in greatest need of love. Just as God honored Earth's request for light so she could rise out of the low dimensions and countless members of your family, as yet unknown to you, responded, so do we also honor your souls' requests for light to aid your emergence from non-remembrance into full conscious knowing.

One expression of love is light beams and their healing effects. Therefore, love and light may be used synonymously in language as they are indeed one and the same, with only their expressions differing. When there is no light, there is its opposite, darkness, and "darkness" and "dark forces" aptly describe energy streamers carrying dark thought forms that weak ones invite, and those fortify the weak ones' ideas of atrocious motives and actions.

Let me tell you how this happens. You may think that the opposite of love is hatred, but it is not. The opposite of love is its *absence*, a most painful void in the heart space. Into that void can flow the streamer attachments of fear, brutality, greed, deceit and all other manner of low vibrational ideas and behavior, but if that void can be filled with love, there is no room for any darkness to enter. When love is in the heart space, no soul is weak.

And love is flowing again in great abundance on Earth! Your love for her — and a most loving, compassionate, nurturing, long-suffering

soul she is! — for each other, for all fauna and flora, and for yourselv
Yes, for yourselves, and rightly so! How greatly we respect you who
asked for and were granted this lifetime to help restore your homeland! Ah, the joy of seeing Earth rejoice as souls fill with love! We
yearn for the same in your brothers and sisters who do not remember
that they chose to help Earth regain her glory, and thus their own.
Yet, we take solace in knowing that if not this time, they may help
some other troubled world rise out of its travails and, in so doing, will
rise out of forgetfulness and know the heights of glory.

And so, beloveds, as architects who step-by-step design and
build your destiny on this unique stage of your eternal life, do so
with the assurance that I, Serapis Bey, and heavenly hosts without
number are with you, adding our light to yours. Keep smiling — ah,
the radiance of love in a smile!

David — Serapis Bey, your excellent examples of what Love
is and what *it is not* should be inspiring to all. I for one thank you.

Serapis Bey — Each of you should know that love is the
guiding Light that separates each of us from our primitive instincts
to becoming beings of love filled, love enriched, love enhanced,
and light of immeasurable proportions. As such you should also
know that universes are sensual in nature, it is where love defines
and love expounds darkness and brings to all of us harmony and
peace. With that I bid you farewell, for now, at least.

Mother Mary (*received by Suzy*) — I greet you in loving
tenderness, the energy of the gentle but strong goddess aspect in
every soul. For eons the masculine warrior temperament has ruled
beloved Gaia, your homeland planet Earth. Now a remarkable new
era is unfolding. The feminine counterpart is rising within souls and
heralding the dawn of peace and harmony throughout the lands. I
am within these new vibrations that are embracing Earth, saying to
all who will hear my words: *Make peace within and your peacefulness
will flow throughout this world. Love one another and you will
transform this world. Know that you are a part of God as surely as
is my son whom you call Jesus. Within the eternal divinity of I AM*

THAT I AM, my blessings are with you always.

Suzy — Thank you, Mother Mary, for your beautiful message and your loving energy.

Mother Mary — You are welcome, Suzy. You and I share maternal feelings for all of God's sons and daughters.

David — Hello, Mary, been a few days since we last spoke, I trust you are busy as ever?

Mother Mary — David, I, too, have enjoyed our conversations of late. These conversations, as you know, are not the first time we have spoken, for we do indeed know each other quite well. I, like the rest of the universe, anxiously await the responses from this, God's book.

David — Thank you, Mary, all my Love until we meet up again.

Mother Mary — And the same to you my, dear soul, our time together is not nearly at an end yet, we both have much work to do before the "cock crows."

Celest — God, I always impress upon people the need to maintain contact with their Master Teachers, their Spirit Guides and of course their "off-world families." I have my reasons for doing so. Yes, I want people to learn or relearn their abilities as Co-creators in any life experience, BUT I noticed that so often some people will become so engrossed with their own manifestations that they forget to seek guidance about what they are doing and can make many terrible "errors of judgment." I attribute most of this to the fact that they sometimes forget to *"walk with one foot in each world."* Just because all of You who are "off-world" know all our thoughts, etc., does not mean we cannot make errors and not know it until it is too late. Too many people take things like this for granted and that really bothers me. Well, I think that statement is my comment/question, God.

God — I had a feeling this chapter was not at an end. Yes, the way to Earth-walk, to best Star-walk, is to *walk with one foot in each world.* I know your heart well, Celest, so I do indeed understand your genuine concerns for those who are co-dependent upon Us and those other Children who fail to seek Our guidance because *"nobody told them they should."* Children, I want you to ask Us for help when you are unsure of what to do, I want you to ask Us for guidance when you are facing dilemmas, or perplexing problems that cause you to be unsure of which avenue to take. However, under no circumstances do We want any of My Children to develop a co-dependency on Us, thereby relinquishing "personal responsibility" in any serious matters. Call upon all of Us **as you need to,** but do not become redundant in your questions/issues, and do not think for a nanosecond that We will allow you to "skimp" on your own responsibility.

Also, before My charming daughter, Celest, has another moment to think, I will add this part as well: From time to time throughout My book, I have repeated certain information, just as have the Ascended Voices who have graced My book with their information. This was done to further instill the repeated information into your consciousness. Remember, calling upon Us for guidance is one thing, but not listening to the answers we give you is another matter. As Celest tells people very often, "don't ask me if you don't want to know." Use right action in your lives, ask, **listen** and then do whatever it is that is necessary to Create change in your lives and stop recreating your past errors. In this manner, "you are walking the talk." Well, Celest, are you satisfied now?

Celest — Yes, I am, and again thank you for expounding on these matters.

Celest — I wish to give a giant hug to each of our Ascended Voices of Spirit who have willingly and unselfishly spent this time with us in this chapter. Never stop believing in our co-joined quest for harmony and evolution. We do all know that we shall not fail ourselves.

Chapter 7

There is a Valley

God (*received by David*) — Good morning, afternoon or evening to all, whichever the case may be. I am reaching out to you this day to en-light-en as many of you as I possibly can about the far reaching problems that lie deeply embedded within your societal structures. The beginning of any good treatise and the understanding of the writing is dependent on the format in which it is presented. As such I shall be sharing with each of you, in the *most simplest* of terms I can muster, important information in spite of the limitations of the many human languages. As many of you know, *everywhere else* except for My Earth Star planet the spoken language is of light and sound, harmonics or frequencies that vibrate at different rates and in different ranges. Telepathic communication leaves no room for error because the recipient receives every mote of information first hand. This is, of course, providing the recipient is a "clear channel." Also much communication is accomplished through the use of imagery much in the same manner as the functioning of your cameras of this day. All is done at Soul level so there can be no misunderstanding or miscommunication.

Now there are two main arenas of distinction to be discussed this day, one which is Spiritual Essence and one which is religious in nature. Each in its proper place holds the key to understanding one another. In the religious realm there exists the imposed and self-imposed belief systems that are structured and relentless in their masking of the truth. The original teachings have been altered to such a degree that it is no wonder so many of you are confused as to who actually said what. It increases your natural puzzlement as to what really was the truth, which was originally intended to be given to the people. Religion allows for only so much leeway in your quests for understanding of the greater truths. Truths which are not constrained are misconstrued as "beliefs" which are inconceivable, not to mention unbelievable by many people. There are parts of the human anatomy, for instance, that only allow for shortsightedness, it allows only for what can be felt, smelt, touched, all that is tangible only. On the other hand, the intangible religions teach that there must be faith. Faith in oneself, faith to reach beyond and look for a higher power. "Today" I shall be *your* higher power; on a future day, one that will be of your own choosing, **you** will once again be that **higher power.** You have always had Creative ability within you; it was never necessary for you to rely on another's belief systems to structure your lives. I Am the Overseer of this universe, yet this universe could not exist without our working in harmony. Remember as I have stated before, "I am you as you are I," you see.

Religion walks hand in hand with politics as a "twosome." Together they both breed the need for power which leads to greed. In every society on My planet there are those who would contort the truth in order for them to keep My other Children in bondage. There is no middle ground there, it is "all or nothing," and unfortunately what most of you have ended up with is "no-thing-ness." Now is the time to reclaim what is rightfully yours. I know your thoughts and your desires for peace, yet peace can only be procured by peaceful means. Are you aware of how many wars have been fought in My name? Do you know that I did not sanction ANY of them? Do not think for one moment that I was asked if I thought that some of My Children should kill, murder or enslave another of My races of My Children. Have you not yet understood that you are all the same, that the only obvious difference is the color of your skin? Do you not yet remember that you have all at one time or another been "the other person," that you have worn the other shoe? Do you not see the connection between reincarnation and this concept? How can you really understand what another Soul is enduring until you have experienced this for yourself?

I told you all before entering into the Earth star walk that it would be difficult at times, that your convictions would be CONSTANT-ly put to the test, that many of you would fall prey to the illusions being cast upon you. The illusions that exist within the lower dimensions can be magnetized and directed at anyone at any time, if the individuals have "weak spots" within their psyches, for instance. Dimensions are like sunglasses, each one designed to filter out evidence of the other. I also told you that as long as you walked upon My planet you would never be alone. Again I tell you, *"promises made by Me are promises kept."* As you traveled further and further into the depths of the illusions of "Time," you began to understand less and less of your own Godliness. You forgot the truth of your origins; you masqueraded and danced to the beat of a different drummer, one which was most certainly not of *My* choosing. Time was created so that you would have a means of governing yourselves. In the days ahead, as time completely evaporates, you will each start living in the NOW. There will be no more constraints that time imposes upon you.

You let yourselves be led into a realm of confusion, a realm of long term forgetfulness. My intention these days is to reunite you with your *forgotten* memories so you may once again participate *without constraint*, both as individuals and in like-intentioned groups with the further evolvement of the Human race at the forefront of your every thought and action. For those who do not understand this, "Hu-man" is the universal word for god-less-ness, "Human" is the term for those of My Children who "walk the walk and talk the talk." In effect, the Humans are "walking the talk" at long last and it is now in this present time more so than during any previous Earth epoch, of paramount importance. They are *The True Human Beings*, all that is *Half Man-Half God*. This is how it was always meant to be and *By God* it shall be again.

Religion and politics play upon your fears, further feeding the "fear" frenzy and creating insatiable desires. There is no difference between the two; both are money based, power thirsty and greed induced. Both create a sense of inferiority within many of My Children. Religions and politics know no master; both have become enslaved unto themselves. They **do** know what they are doing, "naïve" they are **not**.

Now on the other hand there is the path of the Spiritual people, individuals who are constrained by nothing and no-thing. They are the ones who understand that there is no separation between themselves and another being, regardless if other beings walk upright or whether they swim in the sea. *It is the Spiritual person who sees the beauty in all things,* yet acknowledges that not all things are beautiful. This type of person relishes "the knowing" that "all for one and one for all" is the better way to live life. These people KNOW that the truth is the way to the Light. The Spiritual person requires no solid evidence, no proof is needed to be seen to tell them that what they feel inside of themselves and what they sense and intuitively know is **ALL** part of *All That Is.* Their connections with Me is not taken lightly by them, yet they find no need to always seek My guidance. They search within themselves, using their own innate understanding to find the answers they are seeking. They go within to understand the true meaning of life.

I and all the other Gods and Goddesses of all the other universes work hand in hand with one another. We understand that what is occurring in one dimension, in one universe or another, always and in All Ways affects the others. Our concern for humanity's survival as a species has not been unfounded. We see the larger picture of what is and what is yet to be. What you may consider as "hidden secrets" kept in your mind like a closed closet has been a problem you share with many other of My Children. In truth, those "secrets" do not really exist. Somewhere within the depths of your own Souls all is known. There now, *do you not feel better?* You no longer need to keep anything hidden within you, nothing that causes you to keep looking over your shoulder. *Ah*, what a weight that should be off your shoulders, to know and UNDER-STAND that anything you are not proud of doing in this life, regardless of what it is you have done, can be undone and balance brought to it. Anything you have failed to do can at some future time be dealt with. **Deal with first things first, please**. You now have the freedom to be as you are, you can now be free to experience life without regard to how another may react to your choices. You are now as you always have been, "perfect" in every moment.

However, do not forget the fine print, anything that you may direct at another person for your own personal pleasure or gain which is not in accordance with Universal Law, you shall be held accountable for. You may be wondering at this moment, "how do I know, if I am not in a state of 'knowing,' what Universal law constitutes?" Well, as an easy reference point, you could remember this: *"If one person treats another as they themselves would like to be treated, if each person honors all life as sacred while taking nothing for granted, if each person believes in their own power to create rather than to destroy, if each one loves without conditions imposed, if each truly believes that 'a life well lived is its own reward,' if each Soul believes in their own immortality and that heaven and hell only exist within their own minds,* **then** *you are each on the path of the Spiritual Warrior. This is the path where peace, love, humility and understanding are not a 'learned response.' Rather, it is a way of life."*

The true Spiritual Warriors are the ones who can at times be identified by an unusual sparkle in their eyes. Their true natures are also evident by the manner in which they move; they do not walk in the same way as do other people, rather they tend to gently glide from place to place while giving the **appearance of walking.** These Souls are at peace with themselves, they are well-loved by themselves, they are supreme examples of all that is good. When Souls accomplish this type of "ascension," then and only then can they be a true friend to another. Then and only then can they truly love another.

Love comes from within the individual and it cannot be bought, sold, traded or used as barter, otherwise it becomes a perverted parody of the Love Essence rather than the real thing. *Love is priceless yet it costs nothing.* Love is the universal language; love breaches unseen barriers of non-existence. It is harmony in action, it is poetry in motion. When an individual arrives at this level of understanding, then the person sees that all is possible, that "impossible" does not and could not exist. By empowering your perceptions of the impossible with thought-provoking possible realities, you bring into manifestation what you once may have thought of as "the unbelievable," thereby making that also, "possible." You live in a world that dreams are made of yet many of you do not know this. You exist *TO BE*, yet you may see yourself as nothing more than the physical vehicle which your Soul resides in, that vehicle which looks back at you as you gaze thoughtfully into the looking glass. You are all immortal be-ings with a purpose and a reason for be-ing and that reason is to "BE." You are everything, yet you are nothing, ponder on that one for a bit.

In the current moments of NOW I encourage you to reside in a world where many of your fellow Earthizens are now learning to exist. They too are learning that "living" is part of "existence" rather than "living **just to** exist." This is continuing to change in every nanosecond as more and more of My Children arrive at this understanding. And as I have said before, it is change that is constant. "Change" is an art in itself and it is also a work in progress. You are each painting the picture which is "you," can you not see that? I suggest that you exist **now** by living in the *NOW* moment; don't live **for** the moment. It is **IN** the moment where all is probable and possibilities may be transformed into "probabilities" and "certainties."

I have seen your troubled hearts surge from disbelief to joy as what you may have once fathomed as impossible dreams become realities. I have watched your hearts become laden with despair as "unthinkable situations and events in your lives" occur. I have watched as your frail bodies become heavy with despair over the loss of a loved one. I have also watched seemingly ordinary people transform themselves into heroes by doing what they instinctively know to be right. Yet I wonder, do you not see in yourself all that I see in you? Can you not understand that what is good in this world is the good you have made it to be? Can you not see that what still needs to be changed was also initially *created* by you? Can you not understand that it was your lack of convictions that created the imbalances in the first place? Can you not see that without the influence of the "less positive, less industrious Souls" around you, that you would not know what "positive" truly is? I ask you these questions because I can tell many of you still do not believe enough in yourselves to rise up to the challenge of facing the truth, of facing your selves. The truth is, you *ALL* Create the world that you live in, it is not I, it is all of you as separate but equal aspects of MySelf.

There is a valley of wondrous splendor, one that is a visual sight to behold, a valley that is a matrix of all Creativity existing in a different dimension. Here in this "place" lies the center of

Creation. It is here where all those who recognize truths, understand these truths and use them not as a crutch but as a tool with which to better themselves, will find the peace and fulfillment that all are longing for. On both sides of this valley, rising high up above the stratosphere, are two enormous mountains that have been Created as a separation between that which is Spiritual and that which is termed "religion." On one side stand those whose spiritual attributes and accomplishments have led them to be the teachers and guides to all My lost *but not forgotten* Children, as well as to those others seeking to further evolve.

On the other side sits many of My Earthbound Children who still hold firmly to the beliefs which their peers and religious teachers have passed on to them. For some of these Souls, their present beliefs have occurred repeatedly throughout their many lifetimes. They have not yet seen the illusion, they have not yet seen through the "veils." Much of this happened as a result of ignorance, much was also a direct result of the person(s)' state of "un-awareness." Yet where does the true fault lie? In part, it occurred because of the people who willingly and forcefully imposed false ideas and ideals on innocent and trusting children. I ask you, though, could it also be because of those whose desires for power and greed had led them to be the initiators of all those who would enslave many others in their quest for power and glory? Who really betrayed whom? Was it I who Created you in My own image, or was it those who were unsure of their own inner strengths and weaknesses? I allow you each free expression in order to venture onto both sides of the path you can best learn from. It is you who must choose which path to take next. All paths lead to the same place, yet not all paths are created equal. One is the path of the Spiritual Warrior, the other is the path of the "spirituality challenged." Which path are you on now? Which path will you choose for your journey tomorrow?

It is here, high in the mountains above this valley, where the final separation between those Souls shall be witnessed by ALL of Creation. This is where those Souls who are deeply rooted in their religious beliefs and those other Souls who walk in Spiritual clarity and understanding shall make their final stand, just as it is taking place on Earth now, *"as above so below."* It is also here where "in time" all shall come together as one. No, mind you, this does not in any way mean that those whose beliefs are deeply rooted in religious dogma will allow themselves to have an easy transition into this (their) higher state of be-ing. Many are of good heart and good character, yet they have been sadly misled. It is here in this valley where both sides stand in readiness to defend their truths. It is here where all of My children who are in The Valley currently rest while preparing themselves for this epic time. It is the battle for your Soul's salvation, for your own immortality. It is in the center of this valley where both sides shall meet and become as "one" again. This is an arena where all will become known, a venue of epic proportions. It is here where you will be reunited with your "Highest Selves" and with all your other selves in order to become one complete be-ing. It is both the beginning of an end and the beginning of a beginning. It is the circle of completion. It is here that The Creator, Myself and all others of Creation exist. It is to be the union of self with Soul Voice, it is to be the infusion of love and peace and the final removal of all your lower based desires. For it is then you shall find that nothing less than perfection shall be desired. It will be *"the day without end."*

I am but one of many who will greet all of you here on that day. All that is required is for you to raise yourself upwards into the love filled, light be-ing that you are and reunite with yourself first. Then realign with the rest of your patient, loving and awaiting family. They all reside in and as **part of** the higher frequencies. It is where Love is the universal language and where ALL IS ONE. It is your destiny; it is also your birthright. I and so many others await your arrival, for it shall be the feast without end. I love you all individually and collectively much more than you can possibly fathom. Could a parent love their child less? Would you have me play favoritism to one over the other? Would you have me fix your worldly problems Myself and rob you of your chance at bettering yourselves? I think not. You did not reincarnate all these many times, further testing yourself and improving yourself and bettering yourself, to have it all swept away in your moment of glory. You are all Gods and Goddesses, whether you realize it or not.

David — Why does *"dance to beat of a different drummer"* suddenly come to mind?

God — Because you all are. The times of dancing to the beat of someone else's tom-tom is almost over, and you shall all soon begin, if you have not yet, singing your own song and dancing to the beat of a universe in peace and harmony.

Celest — God, for a long time now I have tried to teach people about the meaning of "Higher Self" without too much success. Although I do understand why it is a phrase that I personally consider to be very misunderstood, would you please see what you can do to broaden people's perspectives of this important term? Please also explain how "Higher Self" is an integral part of the "valley."

God — Well, Celest, I did know that you would be asking that question because I am "in awareness" of your pet peeves. I do agree with you that this "State of Being" should be discussed. Not only because of its relativity to the stages of evolvement and the levels and progressions of ascensions, but also because everyone should know how important Self is to that progressive movement. OK, here I go, my "little firecracker Child." Although there was not any reason to use the terms "Higher Self" or "lower self" until the planet became inundated with dark ill-intentioned energies, it was during those earlier times that many who were My Speakers, *at that time,* sought words and terms that would delineate low based frequencies from the Higher World frequencies.

You see, the term "devil" was already far too much in use and the term "God" was already far too much in disuse. The term "devil" equated then, as it still does today, with evil, nefarious, perverted and other such terms coined for further impacting upon the mass consciousness of the times with the tried and true "fear modality." The name "God" was attributed to the early religious factions who always had to have a deadly god, one that seemed to walk around with a flaming sword and all that. It was always a god of hate, a god of despair, a god of vehemence that people were taught to believe in back then. Hmmm, it doesn't seem to have changed that much over the centuries, does it?

The sad irony here, and the serious implications of how both "devil" and God" were cloaked in lies and diabolical teachings, is that My Children... well, at least most of them, did not know how to tell the difference between those two manufactured entities BECAUSE both entities possessed the same attributes. This was a primal example of a very twisted, very dark energetic force bent on the destruction of the Souls of the peoples by playing a dark game against the masses. Those forces knew full well that most of the people would not be aware of what was really afoot. You see, in both cases they "imaged" these two entities to the captive populations as deadly and malignant forces. It was easy enough to accomplish this despicable act. The "brainwashing" techniques conducted today on hapless people are nothing compared to the ones that have been conducted on people in centuries past.

It was only a matter of a short time before each religion was "given" at least one god to follow and one devil with its army to be afraid of as well. So if "god" didn't get you, the "devil" would. This is one reason why I caution all of My Children not to be callous or cruel when thinking of the "failures" of past generations' abilities to discern truth. After all, **you were there too!** It was then, during the first purges of Spiritual mind clusters by the dark forces, that My Speakers of those times decided to use the terms "Higher Self" and "lower self." They did so when quietly teaching the populace of the truths of the Soul Ascension process. They taught also of the various ways that people could or would fall prey to moral turpitude by believing in the lesser truths. The Speakers further warned the people that this could happen if they had "lesser **states** of mind and lower mind "consciousness." Although the language of the times was slightly different then, one thing you can be sure of is the Speakers who were able to break through the cords of uncertainty experienced by the people, and some distrust by the same people, did certainly make a difference in the individual and group "mind cluster thought forms."

The Speakers patiently explained that "the Higher Self" was Soul and the "lower self" was the thought processing of what we today call the "intellect." It was easier for the people listening who had the intent of understanding the teachings, to grasp the concept of the two different "selves" this way. It was then that the most studious ones among the "students" during those ages began to silently repeat the words, *"I Am my Higher Self."* You could think of it as a type of "mantra," for it gave the individuals the opportunity to believe in something other than what was being foisted upon them, yet the words themselves sparked a heightened sense of awareness within the person uttering the words. It is true that their "awareness factors" were quite different than the ones of today, yet it still functioned as a small step up the spiral staircase. Then, just as now, it is the small steps that cause a Soul to travel further and further upward in individual and group ascension. This is the desired "choice of action" for each Soul to aspire to.

So although Higher Self came to be acknowledged as a term for Soul Self, it was not a good idea back then to explain much more fully the true nature of the two selves to the people. It would only have contributed to the confusion of the masses. If that had occurred, then all the good My Speakers were accomplishing would have been for naught. As time "evolved" into more progressive manners of thinking and more civilized ways of living and learning, many of My Children returned to Earth again and were once more playing the roles of "teachers" to the people who wanted more detailed information, as well as to those who were ready for more expanded manners of thought processing. So, progressively, the **true reality of Higher Self and lower self** was revealed. All right, as simply as possible I am stating that there is only a "Higher Self." "Lower self" as an entity independent from the Higher Self does not really exist. There truly is only one Self. The times are long gone when people needed a more primitive understanding of what Soul is and is not. Soul is composed of all aspects of the individual, even though the individual may be wearing a human guise. You see, it is not about the physical vehicle the Soul is inhabiting, it is about the Essence of the Soul, which is the very heart of the **Matrix of the Soul.** In today's present time, you can think of the term "lower self" as one that denotes the less evolved yet still important aspect of your cumulative Soul. It is simply a way of seeing how your steps to personal evolvement went from step #1 to # 3 and so forth. Think of it as the steps a baby must take before it can learn to walk, if that will help you to understand this. However, please remember that the term "lower self" does not exist except as a distant Soul Memory for the *Spiritually* progressive person. In other words, "Higher Self and lower self" are **one entity.** This is why in the "Valley" Higher Self is always present in one form or another Be it as an individual prism of beauteous Light, or as a star flashing its radiance for all to enjoy. The Valley is where *all come together and rejoin as one massive cluster of breathtakingly beautiful evolved Illuminative substance.* It is a place that is a "Spiritual Compass," it is where "east meets west" in this sense. Well, Celest, how did I do?

Celest — Thank you, God, you did well (smile now, God!). Seriously, God, I appreciate very much the full explanation you have given. My fondest hope is that the people will now begin to live as "their Highest Self."

David — Undoubtedly, someone is going to ask if this "Valley" exists in the physical world, i.e., something that is tangible and fits into some people's somewhat limited views of dimensional realities. What do you say about this, God?

God — Oh my, I believe you are correct in that assumption, as you are with most of those ideas or thought forms which swirl around inside of that inquisitive/expansive mind of yours, David. OK, here we go. David, as you know most of what people perceive to be the truth lies in areas or arenas that exist only within the limitations of their physical senses. By "physical senses" I mean everything they can see, hear, smell or touch. Most people have not yet reached beyond those senses to **remember** their true connection to *All That Is.* Nor do they yet remember their other *God-given* abilities. In other words, what a person can perceive as real is, in many cases, an illusion disguised as truth. The physical vehicle perceives the basic five senses while the Spiritual part of that person, which resides as Soul Voice, perceives everything as a reality or a "possibility" of a reality. The "possibility" reality then may have the option of turning into "probability," depending upon the amount of energy focused at the time. The physical universe exists via thought forms, yet when it is viewed in the higher frequencies, all which appears solid to you is seen by those in the higher stations as fluctuating frequencies of light and energy. Nothing is solid, yet it can be, by *thinking* it is.

Thoughts are vastly misunderstood. Thoughts create realities. Thoughts can build new worlds or destroy existing ones. The power which you perceive evil having over good is the amount of energy that each of you give to it. Without your fears and insecurities, etc., to feed upon, the dark or lower based energies could not exist. In other words, the dark exists because *you allow it to*. There is a time and a place for everything. Now is the right time and you are most certainly in the right place for you to release all of those self-induced doubts and fears. Allow them to fade away into nothingness. They are holding you back from your *own* immortality. They are weighing you down with unnecessary burdens that keep you constrained as though you were in bondage; in truth many of you are. I cannot stress enough the importance of opening your hearts and your minds and reviewing your current belief systems so that you can allow yourself to be free from the constraints of a physical universe, or at least one perception of said universe. I am not going to venture into dimensions at this time, but suffice it to say that although what you perceive as true from a 3rd dimensional reality, others who are in a higher dimensional reality will see the same events from a totally different perspective.

Which brings us to parallel universes and those alternate realities, both of which I am also not going to venture into at this time. Perhaps in the next book, We will see. What I will tell you is that all of these different scenarios are running simultaneously, and what you do in the present here and now most certainly has an effect on all of the other realities in alternate/parallel universes. Mind boggling is it not, David? You yourself were just thinking this morning about how you could help all your other selves, all those existing in different locations, all of their/your playing out realities at the same time. You see, dear readers, David has discovered something that very few ever bother to fathom, contemplate or even conceptualize. David has found that by offering his assistance (in the here and now) to all the other aspects of himself, he is, in effect, helping himself much the same as if he were personally teaching someone else. Which brings us back to "Higher Self." In doing this, he is uniting all aspects of himself as one completed Be-ing working in harmony with self to improve self. Quite a concept, if I do say so myself. This is an example of a true Multi-versal Be-ing epitomizing the true meaning of **walking with one foot in both worlds**. You may liken it to shape-shifting into something else while still being present and active in your current reality. Remember, dear Souls, as I have said before, *the only limitation is your imagination.*

Now back to the original question, does "The Valley" exist in the physical or only in the Spiritual? Both are true, depending on which realm the possibilities you currently believe in are occurring. Scientists know of the different dimensions, they also know of the existence of the micro-verse and the macro-verse, yet they do not speak of them. Governments have known for a great many years of the presence of extraterrestrial life, yet they keep it to themselves. Why do they do this? They do this for their own personal gain and control. I know, *as well as should you,* that this world which you currently call home has and is a Soul entity Herself. She feels, She thinks, She evolves just as do you. So please be kind to Her. She has given so much of Herself to allow you the various venues you can utilize to expand yourself and also which you each can learn and evolve from.

David — Thank you, God, now I have another question. What would be the quickest way to breach the differences between these mountains and bring this Valley together as one?

God — By examining your belief systems. Toss out all that does not resonate any longer with you and believe in "You being your Higher Self." Allow the *Light of All Lights,* which is *The Christed Light,* to consciously enter into your total Self unabated. Love all with all parts of your heart and mind. Love each Soul without imposing conditions and, as always, allow love to be ever expansive. Spirituality is quite simple if you allow it to be. You do not need to read hundreds of books, sit upon a mountain for a decade, give away all your earthly possessions, become celibate or learn all the current *cliquish* or new age terminologies. You are each an aspect of Myself, yet you are all individuals with the capacity to expand upon Self with no limitations imposed. You are all also a part of *All That Is*, remember that. You could not be in better company, if I do say so Myself. **Love *is* the one** common denominator that unites All of Us together as one, yet it is sadly misunderstood by many.

David — Love I feel, for most part, has become a commodity that influences individual life choices.

God — That, too, is about at an end.

Suzy — Hi, God, it's me, Suzy. I'm glad you said something about "not forgetting the fine print." What I've often thought of as the "fine print" that goes with what we've been told about asking within for answers and trusting what comes via our intuition is, "And use the common sense God gave you." Is that what you would say — that is, are we really born with common sense or do we have to develop it?

God — My dear little soul-self Suzy, let me give this a moment of thought. Very well. When the word "common" is used as an adjective, generally it is understood to mean something that is usual and widespread, is it not? OK, then we can conclude that "common sense" is most people *usually* thinking or acting sensibly, right? And "common sense" comes from the intellect?

Suzy — Well, I'd think so.

God — Then consider how often you've thought that if you had used common sense in some situation, the outcome would have been much more favorable. In tandem with that, you've "beat yourself up" for not trusting your intuition when you realized that if you had paid attention to your instantaneous reaction — that's what

118

intuition is — you could have avoided what did happen as result of your thinking, thinking, thinking how to handle the situation. So, isn't it likely that you aren't unique, that probably ALL of my soul-selves — whether or not they have those same thoughts that you do — fail at times to use what at least some of them also consider "common sense" and that rather than acting on their intuition, they also analyze it to death?

What I'm getting at is, "*common* sense" as it's understood, is a misnomer. Thinking and behaving "sensibly" — isn't that what most rational beings regard as sane thought and behavior? — is NOT common because it's not usual or widespread, just as trusting intuition is not. NOT trusting intuition is ignoring the "sensible" answers that the person has asked for, and those come from the soul — these aren't two separate aspects or functions, they're one and the same.

Think about this: Is it using common sense/heeding intuition when transparent lies are accepted as truth and wars are fought repeatedly to attain peace? When a few people have vast fortunes while billions live at bare subsistence level? When generations of national leaders act in the best interests only of themselves and their supporters and ignore the obvious needs of the masses of people? When laws meant to protect ones from injustice aren't applied justly? When the trivialities that are intended to distract your attention from significant matters are successful in achieving their purpose? Those are but a few examples of people NOT using "common sense," which is the same as not behaving "sensibly" in accordance with their intuition. And I'm not even going to get into the whole religion thing that for millennia has controlled thinking and actions or that EVERY life in this universe is inseparable from all others and whatever anyone does affects all others! Even without knowing those truths, if the "common sense" that is an integral part of "intuition" were widespread, the huge majority that are subjected to the tiny minority's greed, injustices and war-faring would act in unison, and the light in their desire for a peaceful, fair and harmonious world would have created it.

Suzy, since we are one and the same, of course I know your thought that this is coming about, and blessedly so! The light that for so long was lamentably sparse in your planetary world is coming in such profusion that it is awakening the consciousness and connecting it with the soul. My children are beginning to act from their hearts, which is the "sensing" of their soul-selves, and no longer blindly accepting what they've been taught is "the truth" or "just the way human nature is."

To answer your questions succinctly, my dear little one, "common sense" is the *sensing* ingredient of the soul, so yes, you are born with it. And contrary to ones "developing it," it's a LACK of their using this aspect of their BEing that lets it atrophy and results in their apathy. This has helped form the high mountains on two sides of the Valley.

Suzy — That's a good explanation, God, thank you. I have some other questions. Do you mean that all *light*-receptive souls here will meet in the Valley as our next step in spiritual evolution, and is that the same as entering Earth's Golden Age, where all people and animals will live peaceably together? Or will all souls in the *universe* meet there sometime? If so, it would seem that some civilizations will get to the Valley way ahead of others — or are they waiting for the rest to "catch up before anyone goes there?" Will we all look the same as now, just younger like Earth folks do in Nirvana, and will animals still be animals — or won't this meet-up be in physical bodies? When all souls are "eligible," will that be because all have attained perfect balance, and if so, is that reintegration with you? I know you love each soul-self equally and don't judge any of us for our choices, but it's my understanding that not all souls are equally evolved, so I don't see how the lesser evolved can meet with the higher evolved anywhere — aren't their respective vibrations too different for all to be in the same plane? Or am I confusing the souls with their personages' experiences? But then, aren't the souls the cumulative result of all their personages?

God — I'm going to add to what I said about listening to your souls instead of thinking, thinking, thinking: It is a *joy* to see ones thinking DEEPLY! A thorough reply to all your questions could require another book, Suzy, and I'm not sure that that would be any more understandable anyway than short and simple answers. "At the top," so to say, things ARE simple. It's in the lower layers of conscious comprehension where, by dark design, things deliberately were made complex and confusing. That's so you would have no framework for understanding the factual simplicity of you, my god and goddess selves, letting me "experience" through what you do yourselves. I've told all of you that many times, but few have listened because they've been told, *"If you hear a 'voice,' it's Satan talking."* That's another story — well, it's the same old story.

So then, I'll tell you about my soul selves. Every one is an identical, equal spark of the love-light energy that is the essence of Creator, in which ALL life throughout the cosmos has — and IS! — its Beginnings. A soul is the composite of all its independent yet interconnected parts, or personages, and that includes those that choose to experience as animals and any other manifested form, all of which have a level of consciousness. All of these individual parts are evolving or DEvolving in accordance with lifetime choices, and the experiencing of each contributes to every other. As thought forms of dark nature kept diluting the light in our universe, knowledge of the Beginnings likewise dimmed in the density of the physical forms that the souls desired for the specific experiencing those offered. The souls' purpose in multiple lifetimes is to give all of their parts the opportunity to consciously REdiscover their Beginnings. Life is eternal and so is change, otherwise there could be no learning, no conscious *remembering* of the Oneness of All That Is.

The Valley is our universe's *soul* equivalent of Earth's magnificent Eden, and the coming Golden Age — in the continuum it already IS! — is Earth and her light-receptive peoples' return *in body* to that plane of spiritual awareness and radiance as the *souls* rejoice in seeing their personages move closer and closer to the Full Understanding in the Valley. Because there is no separation of soul energy, none waits on any other, but rather each assists all others to reach the Valley, where BEing our Beginnings is the reintegration of my god and goddess selves in soul ONENESS. Will that do, Suzy?

Suzy — I understand your words, God, and thank you, but the concept is hard to grasp.

God — You mean *"Thank you for trying, but no cigar."* I know it's hard to grasp, Suzy, and it's hard to explain, too, because few on Earth can relate to what they have no memory of once knowing. Let's wrap this up with my promise that one day, and it's not too far off, all of this will be clear to my children who want it to be.

Celest — We are ending this chapter with a well known quote from my father, it is a briefly stated message that is meant for all peoples.

"There is a Valley where the Spiritual stands on one side and the religious stand on the other side. In the middle walks the Creator and the Creation. In time, all shall be as One. I shall meet you there."

Blue Star the Pleiadian

Chapter 8

An Act of God

God (*received by David*) — Good afternoon, My dear Soul David, I believe We shall shatter some belief systems with this one, and nary a moment too soon, if I say so Myself. There are far too many misconceptions going on about what is and what is not Created by My children. For example: please realize that those who seek to control you have been altering the weather for quite some time now, under the guise of humanitarian reasons, i.e., global warming and better communication advancements. An "Act of God" can be described as "anything that is **not** created by man and is an unforeseeable act of events that lead up to perceived catastrophic accidents or unforeseeable death and/or destruction." Those of the Illuminati families and their easily coerced human counterparts have long sought out ways of better controlling you. It has not been all that long since the advent of *weather warfare* entered into their minds. Although not the only reason behind the strange weather patterns that are currently assailing this planet, it is a determining factor in many instances. Remember now, there are still far too many who believe that the human race is the only intelligent life in this universe.

Your insurance companies like to bandy about those words, "an Act of God," whenever they see that it is in their best interests. In other words, it removes them from any financial liabilities, and let's face it, it is all about money and power to them, is it not? They are not alone, the governments and the shadow governments behind the governments also like to play with the "hands of god" when it, too, suits their purpose. There is nothing and no-thing on Earth that they will not use, manipulate and corrupt to keep control of this planet. I am happy to say, however, that their time is about at an end. Now your religious representatives will also use this term to explain the unexplainable and hide behind this veil that keeps them comfortably safe. You cannot fault all of them, however; they are simply relying on what they have been taught. This also prevents them from having to take any personal responsibility and they encourage you to do so also. How far from the truth can that be? Each of you has to, at all times, be held accountable for either the actions you have done or those you have failed to do. This goes for the dearly departed as well. I do not always know the exact timing of the departure of any of My Children from their chosen physical existences. Suicide is a prime example of this. Many times there are chains of events happening that have led up to an unforeseeable action which prematurely ends their existence through the method of suicide. In any case, the main idea to focus on here is what did this experience, yours, and theirs, teach you? After all, this is a "Schoolhouse planet," lest you have forgotten.

Now, as you may have just noticed, I had David insert the previous quote, the "hands of god," without capitalizing the letters. Why? There is always a polarity at work here of positives and negatives. For example, there are the loving benevolent Gods and Goddesses who are the Overseers in all of the universes, and there are also the illusions and the holograms which are sent to confuse you and alter your way of believing and discerning the truth. This is how it is, "truth versus perceived realities." There are the false gods that the *Illuminati* has created for you to worship. They are also the same ones who birthed the false prophets which are currently running amuck, and they are being very blatant about it, if I do say so Myself. Each has their assigned role to play in these unprecedented times. Those children of the lesser gods will eventually succumb to the preponderance of the Christed energy/light, or they will die physical deaths. That choice is and always has been theirs to make. Those who refuse change by not acknowledging the truth will not be able to withstand the current *in-pouring of light* which is causing the somewhat subtle changes in your physical vehicles, your bodies, so that they can survive in the higher frequencies where Earth is destined to be. They, too, shall leave this life experience to move on to their next one, leaving many current lessons unlearned. There is nothing neither you nor I can do about this. This is their right of "free expression."

Now let me remind you yet again, are you not all Gods and Goddesses? Were you not made in My Image? That being the case, are you not responsible for your own actions? Was it not *you* who chose to start altering or accepting that which did not resonate with your Soul Voice, thus going against all which you knew to be truth, in order to take the path of least resistance? Many started worshiping and paying homage to false gods in order to keep from *rocking the boat,* in order to keep from upsetting their now fairly predictable and comfortable way of living. Have you forgotten how to **take a STAND?** I certainly did not create these idols, nor did I encourage you to worship or bow down to those "gods" whom you have **allowed** to exist by giving your power away to them.

Simply stated, there are many of My other Children who would have you believe that My Hands and the intent of My Actions is always involved in the worst of all common occurrences. This simply is not true. I, as the Overseer of this universe, did not/would not orchestrate these disasters. Some are natural *cleansing* occurrences, and others are the direst results of your combined actions or thoughts that are pulling together from other similar thought forms. It then Creates whatever energy you feed the most. There are many pockets of negativity held within this planet that must from time to time be released. There are also those who like to play with nature, to alter DNA or, as I said, change the weather. Oh yes, I have heard some of their thoughts, a predominant one is, *"would it not be the ultimate weapon?"* Of course it would. I ask you now, who can stop a raging storm? I'll give you a hint, to a great degree, *you can.* You can do this by the intent and purity of your thoughts. The more you dwell on unproductive ideas and lines of reasoning, the more you empower those particular thoughts. Each thought carries an energy signature that draws to it all similar energies, thus bringing whatever thought is predominantly in the mass consciousness *energy pool,* into manifestation. You vastly underestimate yourselves and the personal power that each of you holds within your Souls. You knew this before you first incarnated; you have simply forgotten who and what you are, and it is time to reclaim that which is yours.

The word "God" has been tossed around to and fro as if it were a Band-Aid to be applied to every moment of stress induced panic or fear. How often do you hear My Name offered up for all the goodness that goes on in your lives? Give that some thought for a moment. I am The Creator of this universe, with that I admit comes both the good and the not so good. This stems from your own free will choices or freedom to express yourselves as you see fit. As aspects of Myself you have *the choice* to Create peace, harmony, abundant love and beauty in all aspects of your lives, and you also have within you the ability to cause havoc and malcontent within the proximity of your own personal worlds. The world which you are living in has a duality of roles which you can play out. Each must choose for themselves which side to be on and which role to play. For many people right now, it is a balancing of the karmic scales from previous lifetimes. Far too many people have given up their right to *choose*. Rather they remain living an uncompromising life of compliance and seeming comfort, and let *Us* not forget... servitude. They do this by believing in the illusion that "all is right in their world" without questioning the realities of the situations. You each can do this by believing that all which is considered the "status quo" is for your betterment, without questioning the validity of these statements from those supposedly "in the know."

It was never a thought of Mine when I Created the human race that they should suffer from disease, poverty, malnutrition and suffer from wars, much less the brutal inhumane killings of others, in order to evolve as a species. Remember, this was to be a type of Nirvana, a place where all who reside in the higher realms could come to experience and enjoy another *paradise*. The world you live in has grown vastly out of proportion. "Proportion," interesting word, is it not? How evenly do you think things are divided up now? Would you say that you have all that you deserve and all that you have earned? Who sets the standards for that? You, or what is commonly termed the "powers that be?" As a true "Act of God" I declared that on My Earth Star planet all would be divided equally amongst the masses, none would do without, that all would have plenty of food and a warm place to rest their heads at the end of the day. I gave you all the tools to not only survive, but to flourish and expand and enhance your consciousness. Can you not see the harm

126

that is done by genetically modifying a grain of wheat or a kernel of corn? Can you even imagine a planet with more diversity of flora and fauna life forms, not to mention climates and terrains? This planet was Created to be "Eden." *It was your thoughts and actions that lowered your individual and planetary frequency into the 2nd and 3rd dimensions. It will be your thoughts and actions that raise it back up into its pristine state once again,* **with or without you.**

Never did I say that you should have to toil and work yourselves to the bone to try to make ends meet. Never did I once say, "please send Me a tithing so that you can feel closer to Me." "Whoa," you say, "God's got attitude today." Not so, I am merely making a point, one that is long overdue. You gave over your powers of manifestation to those children of the lesser gods. I might add, with little resistance. That was your own choice, not one you would have made had you not been spoon fed conditioning to teach you to respond out of fear and desperation in order to survive. I, too, feel your sorrow and I feel your pain. I feel your anguish and I feel your disappointments when a "prophesized" event fails to unfold as foretold. Have you ever checked the source of that prophecy? How many of you know how to check the sources? How many of you still **hear Me not!** Have you considered the variables that must occur in order for a prophecy to come into manifestation? Hopefully by now you realize that *change* is the only Constant in the universe. Change is what brings about evolution and quantum leaps in anyone's consciousness. Change is what is happening here in the NOW. Change is sweeping across this planet like a sandstorm from the driest of Spiritual deserts, by the way, that sandstorm is not too far away. Many of My Children will soon be frantically searching and thirsting for the last drops of Spiritual water for their sustenance, knowing full well that they tarried too long before **choosing** which side to be on.

So many people, for so many different reasons, were draining the very *life blood* of this planet without thinking to replace or say thanks to Her for that which was taken. As I have stated before, She was dying. In Her dying gasps She asked for all assistance so She could remain alive and in orbit and flourishing, as She was originally Created to be. She gave Her very life blood for you to all learn from, yet *far too many* still take Her for granted. Change is sweeping through your minds and hearts as this current massive wave of Spiritual energy reaches enormous crescendos. My Energy, My Son Jesus The Christ's Energy, Our Energy that is composed of The Christ Consciousness, is bringing Spiritual awareness and sustenance to the vast desolated pockets of the Spiritually devoid. Religions have beat Spirituality out of you. Again I tell you it is time to reclaim that which is your God given right.

I watch as My beloved *Terra* releases Her long suppressed tensions from within. I do have My other *off world* children lessening the impact of this released negativity by doing what they can, when they are permitted to. This does not mean that there will not be many trials and some devastation. All remaining lower based energies must be **transmuted** before you will all settle in the higher frequencies that exist as pure *love energy*. That is what happens when two forces of gigantic proportions "face off." You can liken it to the *battle of the titans* if you choose to. All the negativity that has built up within My beloved Terra must be released in one form or another. When this happens, there will be damage to structures and properties alike. There will also sadly be loss of life. Now I do not think to myself, "let Me see what I can do today to make their lives more miserable." That is not what I do, nor is it My desire to see any of you suffer any more than any other loving parent would want their children to suffer. Yet there are lessons to be learned here and learn them you will, one way or the other.

There are many avenues for you to choose to release tension, aggression, insecurities and self-doubt. So, why do you suppose so many need to do this by demeaning another person? How long will it take for you all to realize that you are all connected, that you are all brothers and sisters, that you are all related? An "Act of God" is a term made by man to explain the unexplainable. If you had not drifted so far off course from your intended paths, you would all know what so many of the *indigenous peoples* and *others of like-mind* already know. They have never forgotten their true origins or their connections with the many Star Keepers. They have never forgotten their off world families and those of the Spirit World, not to mention Myself.

These typhoons, tsunamis, etc., that you are currently experiencing were designed and intended to cleanse the planet. However, some are manmade and designed to be destructive forces, to create mayhem and fear among My Children. Can you tell the difference? Can you think of a better way to keep you off balance? Personally, I see these environmental disturbances as another means for bringing more and more of you together, working as "one unit" for the betterment of all. Hurricanes, large storms, and wild fires are all a natural way to balance the scales and align planetary and human energies. They balance out, or should I say, they cleanse those areas that have pockets of less positive energy, and those pockets do exist all over this planet. All these energies must be transmuted as well. These natural phenomenons were designed to do so. Do you think there is anything My Children, anything at all, that The Creator and I left to chance when it came to the well-being of all My life forms? Humans are not the only sentient life forms on this planet. Some of the greatest "light anchoring be-ings" on this planet are from the animal kingdom.

I want to stress the importance of changing your belief systems and allowing yourself to see beyond the physical so that you may see all that is right in front of your eyes. Listen to those intuitive urgings you get from within. I want you to explore all that you *believe you know* and question the validity of all which you have been taught since your earliest days. Become Children at heart. Laugh, sing, dance and be merry. No, I did not say go out and cavort and drink yourself into a stupor. Ignoring situations does not *put them on hold until tomorrow*. Start educating yourselves and research "weather warfare" amongst so many other things. Leave no stone unturned. Then, take a STAND and issue the call for changes to be made. You can make a difference. I know this, I chose all of you who are the "movers and shakers" currently residing on Earth, for your abilities to rise up to these challenges. Make a difference by Be-ing the difference.

Another misconception prevalent among My Children is that if someone dies of cancer, or if a child passes over before their parents, people call this an "Act of God." Are you willing to understand that sometimes things just happen? There is no disease on this planet that was not created for selfish, self serving reasons. There is no disease or dis-ease that cannot be **cured by positive thought.** All forms of dis-ease occur when you allow them entry. You all have within you the abilities to heal yourselves. There are vast fortunes being made by those other Children of Mine, whose greed and desire for power has allowed the rampant destruction of your health and well being. Please make note here, *they never do anything in **your** best interests.* I ask you to now please "wake up." Wake up and see that there is something not right in Oz. I can make all your pains go away. "Really" you say, well of course I can, by giving you the strength to reclaim your own power. Call upon Me at any time for assistance, I am always here for you. You have such little understanding of what you are all capable of. If you only used but a fraction of what you as Soul carries within you, there would be no boundaries that could not be breached.

I am aware of all the connotations that are related to the term an "Act of God." I am also aware that for so many of you these implied meanings are only implanted thoughts in your heads. I would like to remind you ones that there are always multiple sides to every situation. Yes, I Am the God of this universe, therefore the responsibility may be presented to Me for all actions that each of you makes as personal choices. However, We do each of us share in this responsibility. I must do My part and you must do yours. The Creator granted you free expression to choose the path of least resistance, if that is your desire. However, **the other path** is *the one most of you are now currently exploring.* I never said it would be a "bed of roses" for any of you. This other path also leads to change, change from dis-organized chaos to organized chaos. So in that frame of reference, if you are "bucking the system," then you are indeed on the right path. I caution you to do what you do PEACEFULLY. I am now reminding you that I will always be available for you, should you want to consult with Me. That **consultation** is an "Act of God," in the greatest sense of the term, if I do say so Myself.

Walking in third-dimensional, physical existences can be try- ing for even the most evolved of Souls. When you lose a loved one in the days ahead, please know that it was not an "Act of God," it was most likely part of their individual Soul Contract. Whether the individual Contract was amended to fit the occasion because of current circumstances that the Soul could not, or was not willing to deal with, or simply because that is what they wrote into the original Contract, does not really matter. What does matter is "individual choice." We do not have time in this book to go into all the "ins and outs" of Soul Contract preparation. So I urge you for the future to "feel" with your hearts and discern if this was indeed their own choice. I would never willfully wish any of you harm or discomfort, that would be like injuring Myself. And please to remember, I never asked any of you to become martyrs for "the cause," this would be against all universal laws.

The current weather pattern changes occurring all over this planet are predestined occurrences. Remember what I have told you before; they are a means of cleansing and purifying this planet, once and for all. Some alterations will be more dramatic than others, yet they all have a purpose. A wise man once said, *"do not build your house upon the sand,"* and still so many of you find it necessary to live in areas that are below sea level. If you feel a relentless nudging from deep within you in the days to come, please know that I am urging you to relocate to the area that is more correct for you. For many people, when their individual Soul Contracts are written, it is stated that they need to be in a specific place at a specific time, to be part of, or to bear witness to, these ongoing changes and events. In the times ahead you will see many other life forms, animal, mammal, birds, etc., that will be acting out of character. They are being set off balance by the magnetic shifts currently taking place. Their built-in sonar will be off-key. You will find birds running into things that normally they would soar around. You will see some erratic behavior. Know that this is not an "Act of God," it is the gently shifting of frequencies and the diverse infusions of light coming into the planet.

Many of the animals and plant life will become extinct for a while. Some will evolve as nature intended them to do. Please know that We have left nothing to chance, all has been accounted for. As a true "Act of God" occurs, and yes you will know it is an Act of Mine, it will be for the betterment of all life on My planet. These are the times you have all been waiting for all these many lifetimes. It is what you prepared for. Rise and shine as the true *Spiritual Warriors* you each are. Send Love out to others, just as you would offer another candy. Embrace your fellow human beings. Whether they are black, yellow, green or blue, makes no difference. They are all one and the same; they are all part of Me as they are a part of You.

David — By saying, "it is what you prepared for," I believe you are referring to accumulated knowledge that all our past lives have held for us and our abilities to draw from these experiences, whether they be conscious or unconscious memories?

God — Yes, David. You were each chosen for your respective roles in this current adventure called life. You left nothing to chance when preparing for this lifetime, all the tools you needed to succeed in your missions are at your disposal. It is up to each of you to recognize them (these tools) when they present themselves, and lest you not forget, then and only then, does the responsibility fall on you to follow through with what you have been given and acquired, and put these tools into practical use.

Celest — God, here are some of the situations that both David and I have witnessed far too many times. When teaching people of either the "why" certain events occur in their personal lives, or the "why" certain other events will transpire, predicated upon the individual's response and "response time" to certain events/issues, is that people lack the **tangible** understanding that things can and do go awry in their lives, **when** they are either not in control of a situation, or fail to see the illusions of truth surrounding the situations.

What we observe is that regardless of how much work we do/have done with people about these things, ultimately it is not until they find themselves faced with a dilemma of epidemic proportions, perceived or otherwise, before they realize that **without undergoing the experience** they cannot truly relate to it, or understand it. It remains nebulous to them until "some **thing**" has grasped them by... the "short hairs." What can You say to people that we have not said, that may help them to better understand that all "Acts of

132

God," are birthed in Love; no Act of God is desultory in nature nor are true Acts of God sent to anyone without a pure purpose?

God — Whew! Although I saw those thoughts swirling around in your mind, Celest, I too feel that these are important issues you are bringing into the conversation. All right, I do understand the frustration that I have seen and felt emanating from both you and David over the years when you are **being the difference**, while helping others of My Children. I also understand your other point here, you know, the one you did not verbalize, Celest. I agree your concerns are well justified, it is the "human" part of each Child here to want to believe in Greater truths, BUT wanting **tangible** assurance at the same time about what is being taught to them about their roles in their lives, the probable outcomes and their "secret" wishes to remain apart from anything that is "out of the ordinary."

My Children have, for the most part, adapted to all the conditioning implanted within their minds, thus altering their free expression without their conscious knowledge. As you know, when this occurs it does not matter how much work you have invested with the person or group of people, it all "goes down the cosmic drain" until such time that someone or something rocks their personal world. The term "experience" is vastly overlooked and misunderstood by millions of people all across this planet. An "experience" is a "happening moment — one that is a **defining** life moment." It may be a trivial occurrence or a monumental one, BUT the impact of the expressed action that has taken place resides in Soul Memory.

Because the experience has taken up residence in Soul Memory, the individual or group of people then have the choices to make of whether to repeat that exacting time or LEARN from it. There is no "gray" here. It is one or the other. To people who demand "tangibility" with an experience... I promise you, *you will receive it and you just may not like it!* Celest, you once told someone who was trying to understand "what" I am, that I am a "pumpkin pie." Unbeknownst to you at that time, pumpkin pie was that man's all time favorite dessert. The man was shocked and swore off eating his favorite pie, pumpkin pie, for life. I knew why you did that, you were showing him something that he could relate to, something that was ordinary, good, wholesome and tasty. You were essentially bringing the intangible into tangibility. Well, considering he never spoke to you again after that **life defining moment**, I can tell you that, to this day, he will not eat pumpkin pie. He has learned to like apple pie, though. You affected his perceptions in an "ordinary" way, giving him something "common" and without logic to deal with. Although he still cannot "deal" with it, eventually he will "get the point." The **experience** he had formed a tiny thought, "what if God is ordinary?" Had you smacked him across the head, the impact would not have been as intense as the loss of his favorite pie. You see, Celest, this man, along with millions of My other Children, cannot relate to Me unless they "image" the thought patterns they have been raised with; they cannot see an Act of God as anything other than "a performance of pain and/or vengeance." Too bad, they could learn a lot from a pumpkin pie.

As to the other point, what all of My Children need to understand is that each of them as *individual entities are indeed in control of their own lives, their own destinies. It is what they do with that knowledge and how they understand it that can Create new visions of life for each of them.* Each Child can alter for good or evil all that occurs in their personal world, BUT only if that individual does not need to rely, or be dependent, on another person. Each of My Children IS an Act of God. Each Child enacts Acts of God each day. The levels of the Acts may differ just as the stages of growth of each Act may be variable. But that does not mean that the action taken is less important than the Acts I MySelf perform each day. There is more to the meaning "all for one and one for all" than most people are ready to "understand." When the level of "knowing" is achieved, then all experiences will be cherished for what they have given to the individual and to their Soul Cluster. Hmmmm, Children, think of "experience" as a pie, perhaps that will help.

Celest — I had not thought about that... little incident... in years! OK, God, now that I am done squirming in my chair about that man's "food experience," I thank you for your enhanced explanation. My hope is that all people will achieve that level of "knowing."

God — No real need to thank Me, Celest, but please, if you are going to thank Me, thank yourself as well.

Suzy — God, it's Suzy — hello! As I was reading what you told David and Celest, I was thinking, *"Boy, God, you're really saying a mouthful here!"* Then I got to Celest's pumpkin pie and laughed at *her* mouthful. What a perfect analogy she gave that man — all the ingredients in both you and a pumpkin pie are inseparable, and what a great way to explain that simple truth!

The reason I was thinking of the mouthful thing is, what you were saying struck a chord with something that's nagged at me ever since someone told me years ago, *"Everything is in divine order,"* and I've heard this many times since then. Well, I admit that when I first heard it, I didn't really give it much thought, but I did soon afterwards and I still don't understand why I can't agree with it. What you've just said about "acts of God" is the answer — at least I think it is, but maybe I have a skewed perception of what is "divine order" and what isn't. What does it mean to you?

God — First, it was lovely to feel you laughing, and I wish more of my children would do that. I like your popular expression, *"Laughter is good for the soul,"* because it's true — laughing lightens the heart, which is the "seat of the soul" — and the expression that's bothersome to you — *"Everything is in divine order"* — is a bugaboo for me too. I'm all of the people who subscribe to that philosophy, you know, so I can tell you what it means to me by telling you what it means to them. It absolves some of my children from taking responsibility for their actions and accepting accountability for the consequences. Some find comfort in believing that's just how it is as they go about doing whatever good they can, while others are simply resigned to "that's how it is" and lose the will to try to make any changes. Some try to mask their actions that actually are sly manipulations, and others try to hide their desire to control others' thinking by convincing them that whatever is happening is "in divine order."

I'd LIKE it to be, that's for certain, but as long as free will to do what you want is your birthright, how could those who use it to treat others in ways that aren't in either of their soul contracts be in "divine order"? It goes back to the ages-old karmic merry-go-round that your souls are tired of riding and Earth herself is totally weary of it. Well, the reason that ride is over is so your world can get back to a state where much more IS in divine order than at any time most of you have any memory of. Yes, you have the choice, like always, to help or hinder your own progress, and the purpose of this book is to let you know how you're doing, either way. I highly recommend that you pay attention!

And now, my dear child Suzy, you know why *"Everything is in divine order"* hasn't ever sat well with you.

Suzy — Yes, and I thank you, but I feel like such a late bloomer in not realizing that myself.

God — You're big on trying to see things from others' perspectives, Suzy, so here's mine on "late bloomer." If your consciousness hadn't been attuned to your soul all along, either you would have bought that expression at "face value" or you'd never have given it another thought. I know that doesn't rate a laugh like Celest's pie got, but you're smiling a lot, and I'm happy to share your sunny feeling.

Celest — God, I thank you for the consideration you have given to this subject, it is very important material as well. My question has to do with various quotes that people make that I know are not true. The ones that disturb me the most are, *"If I am meant to be there I will be there." "Those who should be there will be, if they are not there then it was not meant to be."* Although many metaphysicians are adept at repeating this misinformation, I have noticed that "mainstream people" are also now saying this, and the worst part is **people are believing it!** Would you please offer your wisdom to everyone on this subject, I would appreciate it very much.

God — All right, Celest, I agree with both you and Miss Suzy that certain phrases, certain quotes, that seem to be on the lips and in the minds of so many people are not only erroneous, they are dangerous. Celest, I know well what you are thinking about the words you have written. You are concerned because people are accepting those phrases at face value. They are either unaware or do not realize that **interference** plays a huge role in these matters. The interference I speak of is a coldly calculated, diabolical impediment craftily designed to confuse everyone of the true nature of why they are not attending certain gatherings that would ultimately be of great assistance to them. It is a "counter-measure" enacted by dark energy as a means of further manipulating people and keeping the "unknowing" people in "a holding chamber." This type of chamber is part of where the unilluminated energetic movements lie. No, I did not say the chamber is a physical one. If it were, it would be much easier for people to see what illusion is being foisted upon them.

I have asked My Children repeatedly to use discretion about what they accept as truth. I have asked My Speakers to convey this message to all people as many times as they feel they must. Now THIS IS an Act of God. I truly understand the frustration that My Speakers feel when they see that their words are falling on deaf ears. There is a lack of personal reasonability when people do not practice the discernment that is so vitally important to their well being. I hear Children think, *"Must I question everything?"* My answer to that old question is, "to a degree, YES, you must." If you have thought of phrases, or heard words spoken by others, that seem to cause you to feel complacent, indolent, fearful, or if you are accepting what you have been told without looking to see if it is an illusion or if it is truth, then THAT is the degree of separation where personal responsibility must supersede what others say.

If you are going to question what I say, surely you can do the same with others, do you not agree? You have no idea of how many millions of "mainstream people" would be PART of Our Soul Odyssey rather than APART from it, if they have been able to override the illusions of truth, and attend Soul Gatherings geared to dissipate the veils of illusions. If people would spend a quarter of the time they devote on deciding what clothes, makeup and hairstyle is right for them, using that quarter time to react to dangerous rhetoric instead, by seeking the core SOURCE of the information, Our Mission here on Earth would become so much easier. If you wonder why My 3 Scribes in this book react so aggressively to the situations and words which people have become inveigled in, it is <u>because they should</u>.

Although We, My other Children off-world as well as Myself, must operate under the universal law of "non-interference," the unilluminated beings and the energy streamers they spawn have no such law. Therefore, they use every resource they can to confuse, abuse and dissuade people from learning truths. This then prevents the people from moving forward through the act of living the Greater Truths. The words, phrases and subject matter that Suzy, David and Celest bring to My attention are crucial to *"unveiling the beast."* I strongly suggest that you, Children, *stop believing what others are saying unless you are willing to conduct an investigation for yourselves.* I will not do it for you. My job is to inform, teach and Oversee what I can and patiently await each Soul's willingness and ability to overcome the last of the dark vestiges by using their God given discernment factor. Look beyond words, phrases and implanted ideas, THEN decide what is real and what is illusion.

Celest — God, perhaps what You have just stated will cause, at least some people, to better understand how and why deception occurs. Thank You, it is a pleasure to work with You.

God — I thank you as well, Celest, it is a pleasure for Me to work with Me too.

David — God, a thought occurred to me the other day while pondering evolution, levels of evolvement, the process of "moving forward" and other related issues. I understand that at any level of evolvement we each have a *Higher Self* that works with us and guides us on our path of choices. I have found over the years that I can speak at *Soul level* with many Beings who are presently above my own (perceived) personal level of evolvement (as I know it), such as Archangel Michael, Sananda and even at times wonderful conversations with The Creator Him/Herself. In Your message above, you were saying that each of us enacts Acts of God each and every day, which I understood perfectly. The question is, do you, the Archangels, etc., evolve and move up to higher levels as We *your Children* do?

God — My, David, your mind travels to areas that most fear to tread. It is, however, a God (good) question. Let me see how I can phrase this without confusing everyone. I Am the Overseer of this universe and as such *every one* and *every thing* that was Created by Myself and My Children is also My Creation. There are many Gods overlooking many different universes and as such We each have many Children in our "fold." Many, well most, of those Children also choose life experiences in other universes as well. This process allows for their own personal growth and expansion of ideas and concepts, while gaining knowledge from each undertaken endeavor. Each of Us in the *Highest Realms* was birthed into conception by *The Creator*, and as such We were each born into "perfection." We are also an **Aspect of Creation** as are each of you. That does not mean that any of Our Children are always in a state of perfection, although they can be "perfect" in any minute of their mortality. They are, however, "in perfection" when first conceived. Then the learning process begins and, because of their own free expressive choices, each one ventures into areas that ***call out*** to them for learning experiences; such as I touched upon with Celest in the previous paragraphs above this.

We each, the Gods of all the universes as well as the Archangels, evolve as you evolve, it is a *Nirvana-ly* example of "group progression." We are each a part of you as you are of Us. Planets, spheres and other inhabited areas evolve as their life forms evolve, and We in turn move up another rung on the ladder, to becoming more completed Be-ings. Each Archangel has *"sowed their seed,"* so to speak, in all of Divinity. This is one way that The Creation process continuously moves in forward motion, and keeps from becoming static energy. It is the same momentum that you each possess when you Create or birth into this world a new child, a new idea, or a new "thought concept." Each time you do these things, you add another *Jewel into Our Individual Crowns,* just as you add them to your own crowns. The most simple answer I can give you is that We do evolve in every moment due to our own conscious awareness rising, by being a part of your experiences, just as you evolve from having those experiences. The same goes for all the others of your Soul Cluster who benefit from the experiences each of you is independently having. Yet it should be clarified that it was and is Our **choice** to remain where We currently are in Our present existence. In other words, we do not wish to segregate Ourselves from you; so We are all "aligned at the evolvement hip." So yes, in answer to the next question stirring in your mind, Our final destination and Our destiny is the same as yours, to reunite as one with **The Creator.** You may say, it is Our own **"Act of God."**

David, would you please take a moment and insert here one of our brief conversations of a few months ago, so that others may glean some understanding from it? You know which one.

David — OK, here it is.

David — *I had said,* "Thank you God."

God — "For what?"

David — "For being you."

God — (pause) "Well, thank **you**, David, for being **Me**."

David — It makes perfect sense to me why you wished me to include this now. Let's see how many other people get the point. Another question, if you don't mind. I know this may be a little off the subject, however I feel it is an important issue to address. The energy associated with pornography is drawing people into a type of cesspool that seems to be without end. I see that it has tentacles that reach into all facets of life. Any comments on this?

God — David, how wrong you are. It is not "off the subject" in the least. Pornography and all that it is associated with has drawn many a good hearted Soul off their scheduled path, their Path of Destiny. Temptations of the flesh is not any easy hurdle for anyone to overcome once the *pleasure-my-self* thoughts have formed in people's minds. In time it turns into a conditioned response that is very hard to let go of. These behaviors are drawing people's energy fields down into a much lower dimensional understanding of "what you are," and "why you are here." As such it is a vice which is best not experienced, or dealt with immediately. Each sexually addicted person willingly becomes enthralled by the experience, wanting to sample the waters, and then finds out the hard way, they cannot swim with the sharks. As prey, these people discover it is easy to enter into the murky waters, but difficult to extricate themselves from them. Many of these people, however, do not have the desire to leave. It happens to many a good Soul and there is very little neither I nor you can do about it. It will continue unabated until such time the "sexual prey" is ready to see the "Light" as the saying goes, or to see and understand the error of their ways.

I have had to bear witness to this type of behavior in its many perverted forms for centuries upon end. With each century sexual depravity, like so many other things, becomes more refined in its perversion and more morally acceptable. These energies are then passed on to the younger generations as well, at far too young of an age for these Children in their emotional, mental and Spiritual stages of development. They are trying desperately to grasp an understanding of what life in the physical universe is like and are rapidly being torn off course by sexual "imperfections." Their choices are being eliminated for them **without their conscious knowledge**. Look at what is currently considered acceptable in children's attires. What does this really say to anyone? It says, "Please look only at the physical me, this is all that I am, forget what is inside of me." Physical attraction is highly overrated. It is another hurdle to overcome and, trust Me, people have plenty of other obstacles that are far more important to conquer than how outwardly pretty or handsome a person is. Now please understand, physical appearance, colors, thoughts and dreams and the way you present yourselves are all a part of your energy field. Colors also accent your aura, bringing you into a more refined state of Be-ing.

Child pornography is more widely accepted than most would care to acknowledge. Turning a deaf ear to what you do not, or are not willing to understand, is not helping in the least.

Understanding ("I understand, I get it") is the **Key** to overcoming All obstacles, All perversions. The younger generation is force fed sexuality, but not taught about "sensuality." Promiscuous sexuality is as far removed from true Spirituality as one can get. Younger people's bodies and minds require a type of maturity to handle this type of "sexuality" pressure. Parents, I encourage you to look at how your children are dressed. Is this attire attracting others for the inner beauty and innocence of the child, or is it speaking loudly of lustful desires and provoking indecent intentions? You agreed to bring them into this world and to teach them properly until their maturity allows them to make their own decisions. Are you truly acting in their best interests by not setting a good example for them to learn by? What does this say about you?

There is an attraction here to the baser energies that surround these lustful desires. In time those baser energies can begin to be a driving force within an individual's heart and mind. Then it leads to all forms of perversions and abuse, not to mention the need for dominance and power over others, and the unquenchable need to feed the flames of sexual misconduct. As you should all know, each thought pattern of similar density attracts to itself others of the same vibration. Unfortunately, many of the people on Earth know so little of the true essence of the love energies that were a gift to you all. It is sad but true. Far too many of you use the energies from your 2nd and 3rd Chakras to find a moment's pleasure This "pleasure" ultimately has lasting effects on those who pursue it and all of whom they come in contact with. Each time you, for instance, have a moment of lustful desire that is directed at some- one who is not receptive, or someone who does not even know of your mind-actions, you plant another seed within yourselves. A seed of decay, an invasive seed. At that time the presence of this seed must be acknowledged and dealt with before the Soul can move on.

The effects to the person that this type of thought was directed at can be disastrous. That person, or persons, will feel an infiltration into their auric field. When this occurs, the body recoils from it and the Chakras can close down as a means of protecting themselves. I am speaking here about unwilling recipients of your actions. There are, of course, those who willingly accept and invite those types of violations into their lives for the titillating experiences that they derive from them. These are, however, not in their best interests, yet they know it not, for these sensations are something that they have conditioned themselves to respond to. These individuals will remain in that "need for deviated behavior pattern" until they have **had enough of the experience.** What I am picking up from your collective thoughts is, "How does this constitute an Act of God?" Actually, it is an act of your "free expression," not one that I perpetuate. Ironically, as I stated before, anytime something goes wrong and it seems out of the control of, or against the direct wishes of the one(s) directly affected, they tend to label it as an "Act of God." But although I may not like the actions of some of My Children, would you really want Me to put limitations on your ability to exercise your gift of free expression? What would you learn from that? The correct answer is *"nothing."*

The invasive thoughts so many people have which causes them to engage in these deplorable **acts** are either manifested by the individual or are telepathically implanted. This is done for the direct purpose of causing harm and malcontent among all who are receptive and also targets those who have cracks in their psyches. None of you arrived at any malefic decisions to violate others' free expressions when first you chose to be part of the human race. You did not enter here to cause deliberate harm to others. This is a trained response, one that needs *immediate attention.* Each time you, or anyone, I am not saying here that it is everyone, sends out, or participates in, invasive thought forms like this, they add to the murky cesspool of energies that are currently running amuck around the planet. It is like a belt of swampy, rusty, contaminated energy. Each energy carries its own hue or coloration. Those that are high in vibration are soft, pleasant, vibrant hues, those that are of lower vibrations carry within them a murky, polluted, dull, dim, lifeless color. Each of these lower energies must be transmuted. This is accomplished by stopping their flow, by cutting off their source of food and sustenance. They cannot survive without some-thing to thrive upon. In these lower energy waves you will find the assimilation of all that resonates to the same frequencies. These can be from sex, alcohol or drug abuse, to name a few of the common ones. Feeding also into these is the misaligned energies from power, greed and the insatiable desire to control all things.

These are all energies that will not survive in the Higher frequencies and vibrational waves which Earth has already embarked upon. You may ask, "What will happen to those who *choose* not to change and not to ride the wave of true Spirituality that is currently enveloping the planet?" Quite simply, most who are stuck in these areas of addictions and are unable to break free from them, as well as those whose desire is solely for self-gratification and those others who lust after only power and greed to satisfy their ego genes, will be in for a shock. They will find themselves living out many lifetimes in a downward spiral. There is no parole from those life experiences until they have seen the errors of their ways and have re-absorbed enough *Light*, to be able to lift themselves up and once again begin the walk UP the spiral staircase. For a goodly number this could take many a millennium.

True sensuality is always based upon the single most powerful energy in Creation. *That energy is* **Love.** It is where your basest of beginnings came from and constitutes the entirety of your being. Intimate relations are meant to raise and meld your individual energies, bringing them together as one whole completed be-ing. When your desires are not of the highest standards, you pass those energies on to your partner, and then the partner has to deal with them as well as you yourself do. If you love your partner as you say you do, keep your thoughts clean of perversions and you will ascend high up into the "heavenly," where Love is not a word, it is everything. David, I know we could go into this much further, however I do not believe any of you have time to write another book at the present time. It would require another writing to go through all the intertwining details of the beauty of love, the sense of touch and the cause and effects of each corresponding action. As an Act of God I encourage each person to get out of their intellectual, conditioned mind thought and embrace each other with the unstoppable, powerful energies of *Unconditional Love.*

David — I am sure what you have shared will help some find the answers that they are seeking.

God — That is, as always, My intent.

Suzy — God, I'm back because David's questions and your replies raised a question in my mind. In one of our talks that you selected for a Matthew book, you said that the energy of "dark forces" entered this universe when it melded with another one.

God — Suzy, excuse me for jumping in here, but I see where you're going with this. Please copy that section, your questions and my replies, because what we talked about is an important addition here.

Suzy — Well, OK. Here it is.

S: *Did reptilian civilizations start as descendants of the Christed realm or did they start in this universe?*

GOD: So you're back to those. The *energy* of those souls who embody as reptilians — I mean those you call "bad," for simplicity's sake, because others are "good," you know — didn't originate in this universe. That energy came in through the portals created when universes melded. That was a provision of our gaining some advantages in the melding, but frankly, I didn't foresee just how much damage and for such duration this would cause. There, *that's* quite an admission, isn't it?

S: *And how! There goes omniscience right out the window!*

GOD: Which is exactly where it belongs, Suzy! Now then, it is so that some among the reptilians have long been oppressing human populations not only on Earth, but in many other places in the universe, too. They are the mutated descendants of the primeval force you call Lucifer, and have proliferated with what I can say is alarming powers and numbers. In this time of universal cleansing, not only your planet's, the direct and primary effort of this essential change is to permeate those reptilian souls with light. They are without conscience, due to the light eons past having been eroded from them. It also is so that some of the reptilian descendants, far more in number than the pure bloods, are a combination of human and reptilian genetic orders and are not to be penalized by their heritage, which in most cases is not within their awareness.

I should — no, *you* never should say "should"! — clarify what I mean by those souls are not to be "penalized." Penalty is not a harshness except in your language and effects. It is more so a neutralizing of the darkness by the light so that a state of equilibrium can be obtained. This balance is required before the light can start to become predominant within the soul. Therefore, I hasten to say that it's in this context that I use "penalty."

S: *I see. Since the inclination for evil started with Lucifer's free will choices and he was in Creator's First Expression and you were created later, do you still feel responsible for that energy in this universe?*

GOD: "Evil" — that's what you mean here, isn't it? — was initiated by the misuse of Creator's free will gift to all Its creations before I came into being, that's so. But when I came along in the line and was given this universe to manage, all that transpired after that is indeed my responsibility. So it isn't an assignment of responsibility for that energy pattern, as that was not of my making, but it is up to me for *correcting,* shall we say, and I do wish to banish it so that love and light from the Beginning can return.

Suzy — There you are, God, just as you asked. You may know — well, of course you do! — that Horiss, the reptilian commander who gave a presentation for a later book, told me about the dark ones of his civilization and how the rest of them feel about them.

God — Oh yes! And now I'd like you to copy what my Horiss Self said about this. Just a small part, Suzy — pull up that file and I'll tell you what I want you to copy.

Suzy — All right. OK, God, here's the file.

Horiss: It is known by some of your people that certain of my civilization are fearsome creatures that have been causing all manner of evil upon your world for endless time. We are not proud of that truth, and I have been requested to speak on behalf of our greater numbers who equally oppose the influence of those dark members. We, too, think of them as dark because of their actions, and we are in combat with them to rid their influence on your planet and all the rest of this part of the universe.

It is possible that of all who oppose their darkness, we are the most vehement because their actions reflect upon us as a total civilization. Those members are not in the majority and are not representative of the rest of us and it is not how we wish to be portrayed. Please let me advertise to your world the nature of the rest of us.

God — Thank you, my child, and now I'll answer that question in your head. Do the other rulers of their respective universes cooperate with me on "correcting that energy pattern," as I put it in our long-ago talk, and the answer is, yes, we absolutely do! Not only those souls, but ALL souls who are straying from their beginnings in perfection, and this goes back to what I told David about soul evolvement, and I'll repeat it: "Our final destination and our destiny is the same as yours, to reunite as one with *The Creator*. You may say it is our own *"Act of God."*

Suzy — Thank you, God. I think this chapter makes it SO clear that our responsibility to live in goodness — Godness — is not only for our soul evolution, but what we choose to do affects all souls throughout CREATION.

God — That's exactly how it goes, my little Suzy. That's why I instructed the three of you to cooperate on this book that's filled with vital information that ALL my children need to know! It's joyous for my "umbrella" God-self, as you think of me, to feel what you, David and Celest feel as you serve US ALL in this endeavor that is an "unconditional love Act of God."

David — Imagine for a moment that there is a world all
around you that you were "trained" not to see. I ask you now, in fact
implore you, to open your hearts and minds to our next presenter.
She has been with you through every waking moment of your
Earth Star Walks. And in many cases long before you ever arrived
here. So I ask you to please "lend her your ear."

Terra (*received by David*) — I speak with you this day on an
important matter. God has granted Me permission to do so. The
topic is "Illusions," illusions Create false realities, false realities
breed disharmony within the universal mind, that which is God.
One of the largest illusions foisted upon the human race is that I
am not a live sentient Being. David, in his experimentations with
telepathic communications, found himself hearing My response to
a praise of *"thankfulness for all that I provide,"* which he offered to
Me one day. He and so many others like him are reacquainting
themselves with My Soul Voice. Have you ever heard the term,
"listen to the wind?" It is there, carried within the wind, where
you will also hear My voice coming through to each of you. The
animals have long been in communication with My *Soul Voice* and
the messages I send to them about upcoming Earth changes. In the
times ahead you would all be wise to listen when the animals are
speaking to you. They are very much in tune with My planetary
vibrations.

I volunteered for this mission of being the receptacle for
humanity so many long, long years ago, that most people would
find My choice of experience disturbing. Most people could not
fathom committing themselves to an experience that would last for
what would appear to be an eternity. "Eternity" to some individuals
is really but a blink in God's Eyes. I am your Mother, I Am the
Earth. I have gone by many different names since My inception,
however since the name "Terra" is the one David prefers, I shall use
it for the purpose at hand. I have been known as Mother Earth, The
Earth Mother, as Gaia, as Terra and also as the Earth Star planet,
to name a few of **your** favorites. I would like you to know that this
planet, this Orb, which I Am the Soul inhabiting, is God's planet.
You are each citizens of His planet, you are each citizens of Myself,

you are also the chosen Caretakers in the **present** tense, as well as the multitudes of you in the **past tense** who have previously been the gardeners, those who have planted the seeds for the future generations to come. The fruition of your combined efforts is now fast under way.

I wish you to understand that I know each of you reading this narrative as I would know My own child, for indeed you each are. You are as much a part of Myself as I am currently of you. I know your strengths **and** I know your weaknesses. I know who is here currently to assist in elevating Me once and for all out of the denseness you have allowed, which is the third-dimension, where most of you have been held captive for so long. By eliminating the dramas that you each have found so meaningful in your lives, you insure your passage with Myself to My pre-destined place in the higher dimensions. This is a journey that I am most willing to make on My own, the choice is yours whether to join Me on this cosmic journey or move on. I am aware of those of you who are here to help others such as yourselves, those who would see that those events which been continuously **re**-creating themselves find their way to completion. I also know which ones among you whose purpose for being centers around self-gratification and greed. These are the ones who are here to work with those others who would like to continue to be a hindrance. They would hinder all the many good Souls whose goals are to ascend into The Golden Age of God for the advancement of the human race.

What most do not understand is that I have given **all of you** My best in order to allow you to rise above your current state of awareness. In order to allow you to see through the illusions that have been force fed to you and to bring **true Spirituality** back into your everyday lives. This has cost Me dearly. When My call went out to the God of this universe for either assistance or to allow My planetary body to cease to exist, His response was "My survival at all costs." You have no idea of the number of incursions and altercations with the Dark Worlded Ones that have taken place by your extended families of Star Keepers and those of the Spirit World who have chosen to defend Myself, and all of you, from being sucked into the nothingness which is devoid of LIGHT.

I feel your pains, I feel your pleasures, I feel your disappointments and I feel the intensity of love that emanates from within each of you. I know those of you who try so hard to work in harmony with Me and those who would have My many treasures scattered to the four winds without a second thought to the consequences. Most of you do not yet realize that in neglecting to work in harmony with Me, you have almost caused your own demise. There is nowhere else in the universe that another species such as **you** exists. There is not another orb in the universe quite like Me, that has the variety of land formations, varied terrains, and plant and animal life. I was once, and shall be again, "God's Paradise," "Eden" if you will. The illusions you have been casting before yourselves, your everyday bragging to each other about your accomplishments and then patting each other on the back for your ingenuities, has endangered Me dearly. You see, you forgot to look at the larger picture and consult with Me. Your desires for instant gratification have had far reaching consequences. The ego-based thoughts that you have each had has anchored them to My physical body and Created the times you are currently experiencing. This, fortunately *for all of us,* is at an end.

You have heard or read about all the wondrous Beings that *used* to inhabit My sphere. Those beings who currently reside in other realms and exist only to you as mythological memories from the past. The unicorns and some of the Ascended Masters from the Higher Dimensions, to name a few, have long been unable to return to My once pristine world because the energies that currently surround Me would have been devastating to their auras and their energetic fields. Their chakras would have closed down, as mine almost did, in an act of self-preservation. This time is about at an end and I, for one, am happy to see this chapter in our histories together come to a close.

You have lived lives of illusions for so many lifetimes that most of you are unaware of who you truly are and what this world of God's was intended to be for all who ventured here. Sure, this is a *schoolhouse planet* you are inhabiting, however I do know that many of you have taken your lessons to extremes. Being **active members of the procrastination club** is nothing any of you should be proud of, if you get My meaning here. As I said b̲ᵉ̲ know each of you, I sense your personal energetic fields, I know where you have been in previous lifetimes as well as your current residences. I am aware of your past deeds and accomplishments, I know your intentions, I know that what you say is not always what you mean. I know that most of you thrive on dramatic experiences; I also know your personal present levels of accomplishments and evolvement, when you yourself do not. While you are each here, you are an integral part of Me, please keep that in mind during your decision making and planning for OUR future.

I now look forward to the coming times when My ground shall be fertile once again and the populations are not exceeding My capacity to sustain life for all of them. My human populations have expanded considerably due to your own lack of convictions to find completion in your chosen lessons. Thus you return here time and time again to resolve what has been left unfinished in your life. My surface, My water, My precious skies have been polluted to the utter brink of suffocation and this too was not meant to be. I've made it through your wars with each other; I've made it through your abuse of My natural resources with no regard to replenishing what was taken. You have not learned moderation and your addictions have cost us **all** dearly. You have allowed others to come in and dictate your life choices. I stood by and watched as you so willingly and wholeheartedly complied and relinquished your personal power as you signed over that gift to them.

New days are at hand, the illusions your leaders have cast before you are dissolving (being revealed and transmuted) as we speak. Corrective measures have been enacted to right Myself to My original state of well being once again for future generations to live in harmony as was the original grand design. The timeline for this has finally been reached and those of you who lovingly give of yourself to anchor The Christed Light energies of Love to My physical body shall be rewarded with splendors only imagined by you in your dreams. This Act of God to restore Me has been heralded throughout the universes and rightly so. There is so much more to the various life forms that inhabit Me, these other life forms which many of you consider **below** you. Their purpose for being is greater than most of you are aware. There must always be balance in any ecological system. You are not looking at the bigger picture and to those who say they are, I would recommend you look a *tiny bit* closer.

There are other races of Beings that have lived beneath My surface which have lived in harmony with Me for as long as they have been there. They call inner Earth their home. Soon they too shall be able to return to My surface once again. New life forms are emerging every day as others make way for them. Some current species will adapt to the upcoming weather, the topical changes, while others will simply cease to exist here anymore. It is all a part of evolution. My oceans and lands will soon sustain life forms of such beauty and intelligence that all the days gone by shall pale in comparison. The Masters will once again descend here to work directly with the students; visitors will come to enjoy the diversity and beauty that I shall once again be able to offer to them. These are all things that each of you have to look forward to. I ask that each of you send your thoughts of love to all those incarnate and discarnate who are working so hard and so diligently to make this all become a reality.

As you have been told, in the continuum this has already been realized. What I ask of you is to each do your part in filling your hearts with love and thinking thoughts of peace and harmony to bring this swiftly into manifestation for all of us. If you think that just because it has already been visualized in the continuum that you have no further work or effort needed on your part to bring this into full manifestation, please think again. As I said, those who choose and those who are READY, and have done the necessary work, will join me on thisjourney. It is not a free ride.

I am well aware that many of you do not fully comprehend My messages of this day. Those of you that do not understand the frailty of My body, and how, like you, I need nourishing, replenishing and love. Liken what has happened to Me much in the manner as what happens to those who have become addicted to the drugs and alcohol and how their bodies are shutting down on them and ceasing to be. Those that are in awareness of this fact shall be collectively ascending along with Me. The truth that you are not now, nor have you ever been alone, will be fully realized as your extended families walk freely amongst you on this world you call "home." I am but one heavenly, inhabited sphere that exists in this part of the galaxy. You do not fully comprehend how what is done to upset the delicate balance of nature, whether here or somewhere else, has long lasting lingering side effects on all other forms of life everywhere. As an Act of God in all Its grandeur, I am grateful that My request for help was received and acknowledged with the utmost compassion for My situation, it was met with credible, unselfish desires to be of assistance. I have, I Am, a Soul, just as you are. My Soul is part of the greater Divine Soul which is the One you refer to as "God." We, God and I, speak fluently together about a myriad of different subjects all the time, just as you do, or should, yourself.

I have asked David to receive My message, because of the closeness I feel to him. He always takes the time to acknowledge My presence and regards our relationship as **Sacred**, which it is. The indigenous peoples knew this well, they never took more than they needed and always in some way gave offerings back to Me. I am your home, I am home to all that resides within and on My sphere. Would you cut the legs out from beneath the chair you are sitting on? Of course not, however that analogy should give you an inkling of how close you all were to causing your own extinction. As I have said before, I am a sentient being and I can speak with each of you just as you would speak with your Spirit Guides or to God. I have heard your cries of desperation for things to improve. Your lack of **unity** to achieve this has been greatly disappointing. It has taken an infusion of *new blood,* new thoughts and ideas, to make you aware of what is and has been happening in order to get your voluntary support for all that is yet left to be done.

As a decisive Act of God, it was decreed to keep My planetary body whole, healthy and intact. As an Act of God, all assistance required by you to remain on course with Me through this tenuous period was also granted, to those of you who would listen. Now it is your responsibility as **"God I Am,"** to enact your own Acts of God each and every day, no matter how insignificant they may seem. The Creation of the human race should ring loudly in your hearts and minds as the true Act of God that It was. You should feel honored to be a part of this human race of beings who, in all of its acute awareness and God given abilities, are but minute expressions of God in comparison to what you all shall become.

As a point of reference I would like to share some thoughts with you. You look outside and say, "what a beautiful day." I would like you to consider for a moment that this is Me that you are acknowledging as beautiful. There are those of you who speak to your plants and to the trees. They grow ever stronger and healthier with every praise and acknowledgement **performed out of love** that you offer to them. Would you not do the same for Me? Would you not do the same for a stranger walking down the street? What is that you like to say, David? *"A stranger is a friend you have not yet met."*

You require My precious minerals and fossil fuels to make your life more comfortable, do you understand that these too are important aspects of Myself that keep My body intact? You require water and the air that you breathe to survive, yet you treat both with such disregard. You require the Sun to bring to you its healing and life sustaining energies, yet how many of you acknowledge the Sun's precious gifts that it bestows upon you? The farmers of old knew instinctively to work with the land in order for it to better serve them. Today you use pesticides and poisons on My surface. These cancer causing agents are as harmful to Me as they are to your physical body. These chemicals then drain into the aquifers and poison more than just the pesky little mite that chews at your plants' leaves. Are you not aware of the harmful nature of these products? You allow nuclear detonations on and below My surface, you explode your bombs, fire your weapons, you even allow the use of EMP (electro magnetic pulse) weapons to be used. Are you not aware of the devastating effects this has on all of our energy fields, not just those whom they are targeted at? You watch your violent movies and are coerced into those trains of thought. This you probably relate to, however have you considered the impact on My planetary body during the filming of these flicks? These are just a few points I thought should be brought to your attention. The list of unacceptable behavior is indeed much longer than this that will require your attention in the days ahead. In the future generations to come, this will all be an example which you will use as teaching tools as to <u>what ought not be</u>.

If you look around, you will soon come to realize that there is so much more than meets the eye that needs to be addressed in order for you to be working in harmony with Me, instead of *using and abusing, Me.* I gift you with everything your hearts desire for sustenance, for experiencing and to ease your ways of life. Being resourceful and wise in your actions and consumptions invokes harmony between us. Nuclear wars of the past and fighting amongst the different clans of peoples these days breeds inconsistencies to *the way of life* for all of us. Wars can be settled by peaceful pursuits. Diplomacy can be used to settle any argument or grievance with another. Most of you would not kill your own brother, yet you heed the call to war by your chosen leaders, as a license to kill each other. How can destroying any of God's Creations be a wise choice? What egos you must be toting around to believe that some of you are the chosen ones above all others.

How can I, We, impress upon you that you are all one and the same; that each of you are "the chosen ones," that you are indeed **the ones you have been waiting for**? I implore each of you to search within you, deep down inside of you, and come to be one with the Creation aspect of your Soul for the answers to the questions that you seek. We will all benefit from your accumulated wisdom and experiences in the days ahead, by understanding *cause and effect*, so as to remedy the future. Atlantis and Lemuria failed as did many previous civilizations. Some may argue that it was because *their intellects far outpaced their humanity*. I urge you to not let this happen again. Our life forces are connected in a way that few can comprehend. The Creator and the God of this universe granted each of you the right of free expression. Use it for the betterment of all and you will soon understand the concept of ***what you sow, so shall you reap***. On the reverse side of the coin, they too shall reap what they have sown. I shall leave you with one more thought, although I know it has already been said, and that is *"to see the beauty in all things while acknowledging that all things are not beautiful."* Much of what you see is but an illusion, I, however, am as real as are you. Removing the layers of illusions the unilluminated have cast before you allows you to see what is real and what is not, to be able to discern truth from fiction or outright lies. Discernment, is as always, a must. I thank you for allowing Me to share with you some thoughts and ideas that may or may not hold merit with you. Good day, I am Terra, your home.

David — Terra, you shall soon be known as ***Terra Haute***. What a grand sight that will be. I wish that what you have shared this day will be imbedded deep within the hearts and minds of those who shall take to heart your words of wisdom. You have never steered me wrong and, for our personal closeness, I thank you. All My Love to you.

Terra — David, the three of you, like so many, many others, have most always done what you could, when you could, to make a difference and to instill sanity, clarity and understanding to situations where there was none to be had. This you did, many times at great cost to yourselves, when all odds were against you. For this, I am indebted to each of you.

David — God, you had something you wished to add?

God — Yes, David, *Spirituality is something that cannot be toyed with and pulled out of the closet only during a time of need, nor does it accept any form of tithing. It is what you are, it is who you are, it is all-encompassing and defines and delineates where you are on your personal path of enlightenment, your level of achievements, if you will. You live it, you breathe it, you are in fact Spiritual Beings. There is no halfway point of demarcation. You cannot stick your toes in its waters to see if it fits, you must embrace it with all that is you and all that you will ever be. There is to be no dabbling in the art of it. It is not a cult-thing. It is the entirety of your Being. It is you. If you choose not to embrace it, not to use it, you **will** lose it.*

David — Well put, God. Point and counterpoint.

Celest — Terra, I just want to tell you how much I applaud all that you have said. It is time for people everywhere to grasp a thorough understanding of who you are, how you survive, and to see clearly that without you there would be no habitat for the human race as a whole to expand experientially both Spiritually and personally. We should **all** have your patience. Kudos to you, Terra!

Terra — Celestial, I have known you for so many, many millennia. I have never forgotten your love for me or your tears for all the debasement, both physical and Spiritual, that has been cast upon me. As always, Celestial, I thank YOU.

Celest — As for you, God, I send you a great hug for all your efforts to further people's understanding, particularly on this chapter's subject matter.

God — I send you a great hug back for all your own efforts, Celest.

Suzy — Terra, your message touched me deeply, and I thank you for sharing "heart to heart," in the purest sense of that expression, your love, natural beauty and wisdom. I see your Eden self in these magnificent trees; the deer, rabbits, squirrels and birds that visit; and our dear dog family, and I thank you for this dimension of my life that I treasure. It will be a joy-filled day when your entire body is restored to this kind of paradise.

Terra — Dear Suzy, I know what is in your heart just as God does, and your feelings are helping to spur that day of my full restoration to health and pristine beauty. I thank you for the light that you radiate through your heartfelt appreciation of my Nature. Yes, as you are feeling in this moment, All is One.

Chapter 9

To Thine Own Self Be True

God (*received by Suzy*) — Good morning, Suzy! Yes, these days of rain are greatly needed in your area, and it's always a delight for me to see — to *feel!* — the gratitude of some for weather conditions that disgruntle others because their plans that call for a sunny day get shot down.

But to get on with what I want to speak about for this book, and now I'm speaking to all of you, think how often you have said, "*Thy* will be done on Earth as it is in heaven." That statement, which is deeply ingrained in the memory of many millions of my children, of course refers to me: *MY* will be done. Well, that's NOT the way it goes — it is YOUR will that is "done," and that's why I want to emphasize the importance of being true to yourselves. I wish this bit of "drama" wisdom were as well known as what you call the Lord's Prayer, because this has it right: "To thine own self be true."

I don't mean to sound trite by saying that Self is much more than the "person" — I think everyone reading this knows that, but admit it, even though you DO know better, you still tend to get bogged down in the illusion that the personality and actions define who each SOUL-SELF is — let's say Self for short. So please consider this a reminder: Every one of you came in to BE what your Self wants to experience this time around. Self chose specific life circumstances, like parents and culture, talents and partner relationships, and those along with many other choices are your contract that's part of the pre-birth agreement you make with all the other souls who want to share the same lifetime. All of you make these choices for a dual purpose: your own spiritual growth and to help provide the conditions that the others in the agreement need for theirs. You don't have to think about whether your actions are helping you or helping another — you can't separate this any more than you can separate the two sides of a coin.

OK, enough reminding. The thing is, many of you are moaning about not knowing if the course your life is taking is in line with your soul contract. Well, some of you are on the right course — the one your Self chose — and some of you aren't. It is your responsibility to know if your conscious choices — and ONLY yours! — are adding up to the life you chose. Don't expect others to agree with your convictions or approve of your decisions — and vice versa, my dear children! Your reason for BEing there is to experience the spectrum of your pre-birth choices, and when that's what you're doing, you are *"to thine own Self BEing true."*

So, how can you know if you are on course with that? Ask yourself: Am I living from my heart? Your heart is far more than the organ essential for physical viability; it is the *very essence of your Self.* "Wholeheartedly, heartfelt, with all my heart, heartbroken" — you may not know that those familiar expressions were devised for good reason, dear ones. Now, I'm not talking about romance here, but LOVE, the most powerful energy in the cosmos and the pure spark of Creator that is the composition of the Self that is YOU. Living from your heart lets that highest energy smoothly flow in and out to keep your body, mind and spirit in conscious awareness of your soul's Truth that guides your life. Digressing from "living your core essence" blocks the energy flow and that's when "detours" from your contracts start.

Which begs the question, how can you know when you're digressing? Well, are you paying attention to what you hear or feel or sense within? Those are "instructions" from Self, the unmistakable clues that let you know when you're heading in the right direction or going astray. By "astray," I don't mean when you aren't doing what *others* think you should, but when your conscience is telling you **"uh uh uh!"** Conscience is your neon sign, so to say, that points you in the right directions, to the right decisions — the ones that are aligned with your contract. And you don't have to say, "Conscience, I could use some help here — are you around? Believe me, it IS — it's on duty 24/7 on your behalf, but you have to USE it. If you haven't heard the expression "use it or lose it," let me introduce it to you because it applies here big time. If you consistently refuse to heed this guide that is the "voice of Self," gradually it becomes too feeble to function.

Working in tandem with conscience is intuition, that instant knee-jerk reaction to a situation. Paying attention to this is "being true to thine own self" and can be especially helpful in situations that can be considered "forks in the road." Ignoring Self's first response to "which fork" leads to analytical, logical thought processes, and maybe discussions with others that can further obscure Self's message, which was clearly the fork your soul signed up to take.

Now, I'm not saying that your mind is useless in charting your life course! If it were, I wouldn't have given you a mind, but I did, and I hoped you'd use it wisely. Self-awareness encompasses ancient wisdom, the universal truths, the Beginnings, the ONENESS, and an OPEN mind allows those realities to consciously flow into the kind of manifestations that BEing true to Self is all about. It is the shallow minds, or worse, the ones that are tightly closed, that invite all sorts of complications, not to mention disappointments and disillusionment.

You also have what you call "inspirations" or "aspirations." They may not be what your parents or teachers have in mind for your "career path" or what your peers consider the highway to "success in life," but these strong sensations are nudging you into the course your Self chose. If you listened to those who persuaded you that your ideas were foolhardy and so you buried them, I tell you it's not too late to "follow your heart" and take steps to let those nudgings come to fruition. In other words, if not before, start now BEing true to your Self!

OK, Suzy, go ahead and ask about that "red flag" I see in your mind.

Suzy — Well, God, millions are living in tragic situations and it's really hard to believe that all of them are doing this to "be true to themselves." How can we know if we're creating needless detours from our contracts or if it's what we chose so we could learn from the experience or help others do that?

God — All right, Suzy, let's talk about this. Can we agree that what appears to be "tragic" or "needless" to you may not be regarded that way by others?

Suzy — Maybe in some cases, but for example, how can we think of what's happening in Iraq as anything but tragic — all the deaths, suffering, and displacement of so many Iraqi people and the destruction of their country?

God — By understanding that the majority of SOUL-SELVES experiencing those conditions are evolving spiritually, which always is the aim of a lifetime, and *that is being true to Self.* My children who are responsible for the deaths and suffering are DEvolving if they are not being true to Self. Collectively, what's going on is the winding up of the third density balancing act and moving into a higher plane. I know you're not satisfied with that simplistic answer, my dear little Suzy, and I'm not either, because it is EACH soul and not the collective millions that is the issue. But to accurately answer your question, I would have to describe the results for EVERY individual who is impacted by the conditions in that country. I can do that, you know, because I AM each of those soul-selves, just as I AM every other soul throughout our universe, but there is not space here, nor do you have time for me to tell you one by one who is reaping great benefits in soul growth and who is not and the particulars of each. So I am telling you, in short form, that most are joyfully greeting the growth from their chosen situations that you and others see as "tragic," and those who are not being true to Self understand at soul level that the consequences will be dealing yet again with third density conditions.

Suzy — OK, God, I understand, but it's not easy to see things the way you do.

God — Tell me about it! As that "umbrella God" character you think of me, I feel exactly as you do, and that's multiplied by the numbers of all who have the same perspective! There is not a nanosecond of separation from your collective feelings and my feelings, not an iota of difference in what we feel as pain, whether from starvation, disease, grief or fear. Likewise, I feel every uplifting sensation of self-discovery, the joy of welcoming each newborn and every bit of the unconditional love that is flowing more abundantly than ever before on Earth.

Suzy — I can't imagine feeling all that, God. But we're not supposed to be able to, are we?

God — No, Suzy, you aren't, but you do need to know the WHO our inseparable souls IS. All life IS of Creator's Beginnings and each of the countless Selves throughout all the universes IS ONE. Knowing this Cosmic Truth is the ultimate in BEing to thine own Self true.

Suzy — I don't know what else to say except thank you, God.

God — And that, my dear child, is enough!

David — *"To thine own self be true."* It is a powerful statement in all its simplicity. My thought now goes back to another statement, one not all that many people recognize or would agree with. It is, *"We **are** the ones we have been waiting for."* You recognize this one, do you not?

God — You have said a mouthful there, and that is saying a lot, considering the minimal number of letters required to form that complete sentence. Of course you are right, as you more often than not are, David. First of all, I want to tell each person who is waiting for some kind of Divine Intervention or miracle to occur as a "sign" of things to come, these things have already taken place, they are currently still happening. "What? "Really," you say. Well, of course they have. You are reading this book of Mine, are you not? Have you ever heard the term, *"The Return of the Bird Tribes,"* whose time I might add is at hand? Well, there you go. The *Bird Tribes* have arrived *en masse* and most of you didn't even know it. The native peoples know this, their prophecies and their conscious awareness of the connectivity of all life reminds them repeatedly of this.

The Call was issued by My Beloved Earth approximately 50 of your Earth years ago, to find a solution to the density that was permeating, suppressing and compromising even *Her* own free will choice to survive. That Call was answered not only by Myself, but all of My Children, they are known to you as "Star Keepers, Star Seeds, aliens," or other forms of intelligent life. This call was answered by you, yourself, David, as well as by My "Celestial" daughter and Suzy Ward along with countless others who volunteered to be there now for this, *"The Greatest Show on Earth."* This Call was also answered by Beings from other universes and far distant galaxies that know that all which affects this part of this universe has domino effects on all the other universes. Most of you didn't know that, did you? Most do not realize that what is done in one microscopic part of this universe, whether it is on Earth, Pluto or Uranus, has overlapping effects on the other spheres and areas of space. Not to mention that same ripple effect has lasting impressions on all levels of what you commonly term *dimensions* or *higher realms*. Even The Creator Him/Her Self is not immune to events that take place in what some would see as a seemingly insignificant area of space. Suffice it to say, when a stone has been cast into calm waters, the ripples always and in all ways reach out to the farthest shores. I hope you understand My meaning here. There is no iota of Creation that must not be taken into consideration before dropping a huge boulder into the calm universal waters where Love and Peace reign supreme. This is one reason why it was Decreed that there would be **no** nuclear war on Earth, nor shall there be. The cosmic aftershocks would be disastrous.

Now back to your comment, David, "Are you all the ones you have been waiting for?" Yes, you are. Without "you," what would we have? We would have a bunch of "Me's" running amuck. Come to think about it, I believe that We already have that happening now, don't We? You all were waiting for this timeline to come about, the time when all lies and illusions would be unmasked, their energies would then be transmuted and the **truth** would be revealed to all of you. This lifetime for many of you is a culmination of all your previous ones, a long overdue completion of a cycle that has run full course.

Religious texts, almost any one you choose, say that a savior will come to Earth. As you should know by now, most of those texts were written by scribes who tried hard to detail with accuracy the events and words of those days, relying on *ring around the rosie* and *musical chairs* remembrances of what was originally said. I can tell you right now that most of those texts were scribed by those who were hearing gossip, well, most of the time. When they had nothing from which to draw upon, they simply made it up. I said, "most" of the texts. What they made up, the *church fathers* then rewrote or edited the material to best satisfy their own self-serving needs. *Ahh,* the un-illuminated, Illuminati mind can be quite crafty, if I do say so Myself. Feed the people fear, subjugate and segregate them and put them into different classifications. "Teach them to want," and place value on minerals that are plentiful and worth nothing more than the value of a copper penny of today. "Teach them to forget" what they intuitively knew as truth, "tell them they are less than they really are" and foist false gods and idols upon them to which they can bow and pay homage to. Does any of this ring any bells? If so, you are starting to remember, as I promised you that you would. If not, "wait a while!"

Was it right for the church elders, those who were or are controlled by the Illuminati, to do so? No. Was it fair? No. Was it supposed to be that way? No. Did your individual fears, doubts and insecurities play a big part in it? Yes. My Beloved Son Jesus would have quite the burden to carry if He was to indeed wash away and carry all of your sins. Would you really wish to burden Him with this? I believe this is a good time to tell you something else, although I am not sure how you will receive it; however, this must be said. Actually, I will know immediately your responses when you have them, but that is another point. Contrary to what you have been led to believe, *"Death bed confessions do not count."* Personally owning up to your mistakes, and what you term as "sins," is your responsibility. Sins are your burdens. You Created them, you nurtured them, you fed them and kept them alive. Sins can or be abolished by those who *first* believe in them and se cknowledge that **they** themselves have Created them. you have it, the cat is out of the proverbial bag. What you decide from here on out is as it always was, up to you.

Many of you may not know the amount of worshiping that goes on each and every moment, praying for forgiveness and salvation. Those who are the religiously devout are going to be by far the hardest hit as the real truths are revealed to them. The point here is that as long as you worship another, not only are you giving your power away, you anchor them to you with those invisible umbilical cords of light energy that attach from you to them by thought. Remember well the energy that thought carries. My Son *Jesus/Sananda* does not need to bear the strain of your sins, nor should He. Other en-light-ened Be-ings do not need to be anchored down by your worshiping them. So "worship" yourself, this means "Honor yourself." Pray to Me by talking with Me, thank Me for what you feel important, speak with Me of what is in your heart and mind, but give **honor to yourself** as the God/Goddess, Kings and Queens, teachers and students, that you each are. *"The Greater I Am"* is God walking in the physical. Do you see?

"To Thine Own Self Be True." Such powerful words. Such wise words. Simple, direct and to the point is always a sure answer.

Are you the ones you have been waiting for? Are you the ones who are going to save this planet from yourselves? Are you Divine? Yes to all of the above. I wish that if only for a moment, that you could see your true selves through My eyes. Put no other person above or below yourself. If you wish to honor those such as My Beloved Jesus and Others who have done the necessary homework for Themselves, treat Him and Them accordingly and speak with Him and Others as the inseparable brothers and sisters you are. Learn from and share with each other the knowledge and wisdom that each of you has accrued along your individual journeys. The Ascended Masters and others learn from you as you do from them. Respect each other for the truly wonderful Be-ings that you each are. Honor your body, mind and Spirit for all that they do for you and for all they *gift* you the freedom to do. Talk to your bodies, remove your negative attitudes, your doubts and fears, and replenish your Spirits with love, with Soul food. The body will react in kind. What do you think your body responds to? Is it outside stimuli? Only if you allow it to. More often than not, it responds to what com from within. Disease can only exist if you allow it to, that is why they call it "dis-ease." Fuel your mind, assimilate true information. Turn it over and over in your minds and then transform that into "knowledge." Once assimilated, knowledge turns into WISDOM. What greater gift can you ask for yourself? What greater gift can you give to yourself? The human body is a wondrous computer, what comes out of it is predicated upon what you put into it. Programmed correctly, there is nothing you cannot accomplish.

Know that most of the trials and tribulations that you are currently going through are what you requested. Follow My guidelines for understanding when this applies and when it does not.

"To Thine Own Self Be True." Know that I am here to guide you, walk with you and carry you, but I shall not carry you forever. *Promises made, promises kept.* I shall leave you with another thought to ponder on, not that you do not already have enough of them to consider at this point. The thought is, *"A life well lived is its own reward."*

David — Thank you, God, and All My Love.

God — Are you sure you wish to give Me *all* your love?

David — Of course, the more I give out, the more I receive in kind, you know that. It is the Universal Law governing "Giving and Receiving."

God — Finer words were never spoken. Good day to you and, as always, *All My Love* to you for all you are undertaking to Be the difference.

Celest — Well, there is much I could comment upon in this chapter, but I am turning over this segment to Blue Star.

Blue Star — Greetings to all my Earth cousins, to all Earthizens everywhere. I am Blue Star the Pleiadian. I am a humanitarian, a warrior and a warrior teacher. I am part of a peacekeeping force which had been issued a broad assignment by the God of this Universe. Part of our mission revolves around special responsibility for maintaining contact with our child who are living on Terra, and engaging in battles alongside of many others of our Star Keeper brethren who, too, are dedicated to combating the last of the dark energies and the energy streamers they spawn. In this manner *We* are doing what we can to continue to alleviate the devastating actions that the dark ones still project upon the Earth Star planet.

Now, unlike *Matthew* and others like him who are of the *Spirit World,* I and the others in my command inhabit a physical universe. We live, we love, we die and we reincarnate again, just as do many other ancient civilizations. In a manner of speaking, this type of life we live better enables us to understand and commiserate with you ones, because we have also experienced many devastating events and withstood countless forays into our civilizations by the dark hordes. Those among you ones who are familiar with my *"Blue Star Transmissions"* are aware that I telepath messages continuously to my daughter, *Celestial Blue Star.* I do so as part of a multi-purpose plan. One part is dedicated to the debunking of lies which have been foisted upon you ones as a whole and revealing Greater truths that have been "cloaked in illusions" here. This occurred as a result of the insidious ways that the dark ones have chosen to confuse and disarm the human race, through their dark arrogance and evil skill at manipulating people. Another part is to continuously train or retrain warriors here on the Earth Star planet, so that they may each battle without fear, when they are attacked by the infamous forces.

These 2 parts of this Divine Plan is quite enough to keep me quite busy in every nanosecond of life. However, I also have my daughter to protect to the best of my ability during these dangerous times. Now that I gave that part some thought... I realize that just watching over her is a full time job! *Some Pleiadian's work is just never done.*

'Tis not an easy time in most parts of this universe. Dis-organized chaos is now on an accelerated collision course with organized chaos. The dis-organized chaos is the culmination of the energetic forms composed of dismay, lack of discernment, hate, greed, "lust" for life and violent tendencies, to name just a few. In other words,

...erything that is dark and dastardly. The organized chaos is a multitudinous form of all that is the long-sought sweeping change encapsulated in the *Jesus The Christ Consciousness*. As these two energetic titans that are diametrically opposed move in forward progression, completely "on time" for their long-awaited conclusive battle, all parts of the universe respond, or reverberate, because of either the disruptive momentum of the dis-organized type or the Creative momentum which is birthed by the organized chaos. Now, this having been explained to you ones, albeit briefly, which is not my nature to be, I want for you each to better understand how it is that you each, as Soul personified, are either reinforcing the D.O.C, *"dis-organized chaos,"* or reinforcing O.C., *"organized chaos."* You as Soul have grave responsibilities here on Terra. If you ones could each stop thinking about what you can *"get out of life"* and start thinking about *"what you can give to life,"* then as a Soul taking sequential steps to individual personal evolvement, you can also assist the planetary evolvement necessary to sustain all life forms.

Now, if you wonder why this is so important, then I refer you back to the beginning of this chapter and suggest you read the first part that God transmitted. You see, God's Will **is** to a great degree predicated upon your own individual free expression choices. I cannot say to you ones, *"As you go, so does God."* That would not be true. BUT *"As you go, so do the future 'yous' wherever that may be."* Tell me Earthizens, is it so important to you ones to emulate others who are friends, enemies, peers or idols? Can you not simply *"Be yourself?"* What a concept! You see, it is when a Soul is living a life as a human here on Terra, that all possibilities, all probabilities, all Creative doorways can be opened by that particular Soul as a means of enhancing and expanding Its own true nature. In this manner, Soul as human learns, or remembers, that unless It is true to Itself, It cannot be true to another life form, regardless of that Soul's evolutionary level.

Now, if a Soul who is in the immature state desires to be all that It can, even though It cannot elevate Itself by taking a quantum leap in Its evolution, then that Soul is far greater than an evolved Soul that is not being true to Itself because It has become "complacent." So it is that the immature Soul is preparing Itself for

168

an *"upgrade"* in Its next reincarnation **while It is either consciously or unconsciously** assisting O.C. in the final battle, the battle to end "all known wars" here on Terra. Meanwhile, the evolved Soul who has become complacent in Its quest for Greater Understanding is NOT being true to Itself or to Its GodSelf. In this scenario, it is the evolved Soul who is unaware that It is contributing to D.O.C. This happens because of *"non-action"* on the part of that Soul. *You see?* If you ones bear in mind that Creativity is the mother of chaos, then perhaps you can see how "Creativity," just as any other *sentient* energy, can be used for either "the Greater Good" or for "counting coup by the lesser gods," those energy forms that originated as "The illuminati."

Now, I would personally suggest that you each understand that when being *"true to your own self,"* not only are you enhancing your Spirit but you are also *"in knowing"* God's Will. When in this state of *"knowing"* there is no longer a segregation between your will and God's, for there is **no** separation, period. This then, my beloved chelas, is when you and the God of this Universe are co-joined as the Creator intended. I thank you chelas for your time spent with me and, as always, please to know that you are in my mind, my heart and my Soul. You have the ability to *"enhance God greatly,"* you have the ability *"to enhance yourself greatly."* I suggest that you ones do so without delay... **while you still can**.

Salude... Blue Star the Pleiadian

Celest — Father, I thank you as always for your wisdom and for your support. With that said... I am signing off.

David — Well, since I cannot think of a single question, I am signing off, too.

Suzy — Blue Star, I have just a few words of gratitude — not only for your illuminating addition to this chapter and your civilization's great assistance to us, but for teaming up with Matthew a few years ago so your daughter Celest and I would meet. She and David are a beloved and valuable part of my life.

Blue Star — As you are to them, Suzy, and to me. You sparkle in ways you can't even conceive of in this moment, but you will, I promise. And now, with love to you and all Earthizens, I, too, am signing off.

Chapter 10

If You Could Only See What I Hear

God (*received by Celest*) — Seeing, hearing, knowing, feeling. All forms of sentience, whether evolved or not, are energetic forms of communications and the birthing chamber of energy streamers. On *My Earth Star Planet* the majority of My Children are taught from a very young age to use only the seeing and hearing abilities as a viable means of communicating with others. How many of you actually stop to wonder about what the new babes in your household, or those who live in other familial units, actually *"do"* before they are taught to speak in the "Verbalizing" sense of the word? I can tell you what they do, they speak with Me, they speak with their own *Spirit Guides* and at times some may speak with the Creator.

The babes interact with those of the Angelic Realm, with their Star Keeper families (extraterrestrial families) AND **with others within their Soul Clusters**. All babes, regardless of their race, culture, or their Earth families' creeds, communicate exceptionally well with all of Divinity, and with themselves. Many carry on long conversations with themselves, excitedly exploring all the new possibilities that await them in their physical embodiment. No, I am not implying that any of the new arrivals enter this dimension "in awareness" of their individual Soul Contracts. They are most content when left to their own devices, smiling and outright laughing, as I or others of Divinity touch their brow and play with them.

They see their own individual world as merely a playground of sorts. They watch gigantically proportioned people tending to them and worrying about every slightest movement the child makes. The new arrivals have their own manner of communicating to the "big people" when something is causing them to feel unhappy. Babies would be most content to simply continue on their merry way, communicating through basic telepathy with all others in the world. However, grownups have forgotten that ability, and would be horrified if they were raising a child who did not verbalize. I wish that, even if it were for but a nanosecond, each of you could look inside a baby's mind, heart and Soul and experience the wonderment of *living in a state of purity* and living with all telepathic communication intact.

As a child makes "progressive movement" into the puberty years, if he or she is speaking in the manner that is acceptable to adults, then the child is not dropped into the waiting arms of a speech therapist or *"God forbid,"* a psychiatrist. Prior to the puberty years, children tend to "act out" as a means of expressing their individuality, even though in most cases, it is considered unacceptable behavior by the children's caretakers. During what is described by adults here as "the formative years," so much is lost, sometimes for the duration of a child's life, of the truly *natural way* of living and communicating with Higher Forms of the child itself.

Children "Forget" the innate knowledge they arrived here with. Children "Forget" the Infinite worlds of probabilities and possibilities because they are forced to live a life of constrainment. We have watched this occur millions and millions of times since the conception of the human race. I, Myself, have observed the slow process a child begins, as he or she starts to emulate the human adult and forget about the individual gifts the child has in abundance. At times, during the *"Civilized momentum of becoming a true soon-to-be approved of adult,"* a child will either rebel on an unconscious level against the imposed restrictions or rebel loudly and consciously against what its perceptions are of *"NOT for my own good; not what I want."* It is especially during these trying periods that children of all ages, even through their adulthood, feel a freedom to express themselves **non-verbally.** They Create huge statements about themselves personally, and the world as they perceive it to be. At times this manner of communication is tainted by the effects of others' thoughts and affirmations.

The challenges posed, and many times imposed, by the inhabitants of this planet with their rigorous rules and stipulations can, **at times,** unbeknownst to any of the participants, cause a child of any age to look deeper and deeper into their own minds; their individual minds. This happens sometimes at a frantic pace, other times at a leisurely pace, but the more deeply they look, the more they find truths which are acceptable to them and illusions they instinctively recoil from. These situations are relevant to certain sets of circumstances occurring within the child's life. As I have said, it happens at any age. If a person is 80 years old and has retained the child-innocence so prevalent as the babe's foundation, then that person is still "A child," in the essential Soul Status that each Soul is *birthed into.* Although in the Greater Sense of the word, you are all *"Children."*

It is during the probing for truth, during the instinctive searching for answers that make sense, that an individual can some-times stumble across their Soul Voice. Although, I have seen others trip over their Soul Voices in shock and amazement. It is during this time that the individual inhabiting the physical vehicle feels the astounding connections of communicating with Voice through simple "Mind thought." This is also called by you, "Telepathy." It then comes to pass that people called *"Gifted People"* choose to consciously use their telepathic abilities with the assistance of their Soul Voice and with the endless aid from all other Aspects of Divinity. Some do so quietly, privately, not willing to share what they are doing with others. Many of these people, however, choose or "Live" part of their Soul Contract by being quite public about what they do. Although not all "Gifted People" discover that they are each their own Soul Voice, most of them *do* in time, realize this.

It can be disconcerting for many of My Children to walk the walk here while listening to a bevy of voices in their heads. They must do this while carrying on many mundane conversations with *"Ordinary people,"* the ones who would have all the *"Voice Hearers"* locked up if they knew what was really going on. I am speaking here only about the Children who are not only gifted but quite sane as well. As a Soul progresses further into a *"State of Grace,"* the Voices then can become the ally that an individual cannot find in abundance among human people. So the individual or group of individuals set upon a trek to find others "of their kind." This is an anomaly of sorts; from the perspective of the mainstream people who are repelled by the actions of anyone who dares to be different, this type of behavior is considered to be abnormal.

In truth, however, it is very normal. As one Soul discovers either another Soul from Its Cluster, or encounters Souls from different Clusters who are in some way equal, but of either Higher or lower evolution, then the Soul on the trek must then decide which individual or group of like-minded Souls to align with. Many gifted people use their various forms of sentience to correctly gauge the amount of Light that another person emits. They see the various hues radiating around a person as either vast or minute energy streamers that accompany each person. *All of My Children* can perform this feat; it is just that so many of them have *"Temporary Spiritual amnesia."* From My vantage point, that is to say, My observation point and the point of perspective of all of *Divinity,* when this event of seeing beyond the density and constraints of Earth illusions occurs, the coloration that you each have, whether you are participating in the Act of using your sentience or not, initiates another "Feat of magnificence."

The activated energy streamers of rainbow prisms each contain a "Sound." Did you know that? I believe I have mentioned this before. Well, they do. The decibels of sound range from very low, almost muted, in fact, to very high. Each sound birthed by an individual is predicated upon the evolutionary status of each Soul ready, willing and able to transcend the mundane and release their individual notes **up the spiral staircase.** Each "Note" is part of a symphony. When a bevy of prisms carrying an **equal sound vibration** merge with one another then align with a set of prisms carried by 1 or more people, a crescendo begins and continues to expand. This equal sound vibration travels in forward momentum until it arrives in the *Matrix of Infinity.* It is music without end. As a refinement of each note occurs, it is then that the chords and the scales of the music begin to play **My Song.** They play **The Song of God.**

The refinement of the notes which I spoke of happens as individuals find deeper strength in their Spiritual beliefs. As the individual learns *"No fear,"* or finds more high levels of *Infinite Energy,* which succor the person by providing more and more Spiritual insight, then the "Personalized note," or in some cases "Notes," that the person carries become more and more pure and glisten accordingly. Those whose tones are muted carry a darkish looking coloration. This does not always denote a person who is "Bad." It can also mean that something or someone has a grasp on that person, which is suffocating the individual's Spiritual motivation. This, of course, is where *personal responsibility* must take place. It is incumbent upon each Soul to use all of Its Spiritual wits to break free of the fetters others try to impose upon them. Remember that, please.

In *"Time"* all of My Children shall be free of these monstrous holds. Because this movement to release all of My Earth Star Children has already begun, We shall see and hear many, many more musical notes cascading throughout My Universe. I hear the thoughts, dreams, visions and nightmares which each of you Children experience. I hear rhymes and reasons, quietude and logic. I hear the wondrous music and feel the quickening of your individual Soul Selves as you each ascend to your own *throne of power*. This is the power "To be all that you can be," simply **because you can**. To live a life of non-power is to not live a life. However, I must caution each of you: To attain your own power point is vital and not nearly as difficult as you may think, BUT to *maintain* your power requires faith in yourself, love of yourself and the ability to allow nothing and no-thing to come between you and Me.

Celest — God, I am only going to make a brief statement here so that David and Suzy can have their turns with this material. All right, I sometimes have wondered what if people could simply view their personal canvas, the canvas which contains both the microcosmic and the macrocosmic view which they each have. Would it make a difference in how they would continue living, or if it would be too much for them to bear? I teach people to acknowledge that evil still exists here, but I also teach them that each one of us can change the paint on the canvas any time we choose. On our own personal canvas that is.

God — Celest, I have heard your frustration and your dismay over the years as you have encountered people in all walks of life who have asked you for help, but the majority of them do not, and have not, acted on the help you have given them. I have never heard diffidence in your voice or in your thoughts. I have never known you to "give up" on anything, and remember, I have been with you *"For as long as you have been."* I understand what you mean when you refer to a person's life as *"A canvas."* I think that is a good analogy. Each person uses the paint, which is the coloration of their note, to literally paint their individual destinies and decide the size of their canvas. Some choose very large ones, filled with possibilities and probabilities which they may or may not fulfill in any one lifetime.

Others choose very tiny canvases because they are willing and able to be complacent and, heaven forbid, not allowing anyone to *"Rock their boats."* Yes, this second group is also a matter of individual free expression and, although quite limiting, you know that what they paint is from the microcosmic perspective. They have not allowed room for more than that simply because they do not want to. The others, however, *ahhhhhhhhhh,* they are a sight to behold. I hear the movements of their bodies and minds, their verbal and non-verbal expressions and the diverse ways so many of them show their appreciation of the true gifts which their mortality has to offer.

These are also the ones who do not become jaded as a result of their Earth Star walk experience. During their mortality when they see each person as a flower, I hear the buds slowly unfolding. Sometimes it requires centuries for the totality of the bloom to emerge, but emerge, it does. As they watch the stars and the moon and revel in the experience of being a part of the universe, I hear the great explosions of light permeate each of the Souls who are watching. When they see beauty in all things, yet are aware that some *superficial beauty* can hide something ugly, I hear the notes of discernment and **personal responsibility** playing a tune which beckons all others to *"Come and rejoice and be at ease with your God Self."* They do this because they know there is nothing to fear. As they accept the truth of this matter I hear bells pealing and angels singing because they are "Being in joy" for each Soul who is "In ascension." When Souls are "In ascension," they are transcending the moral turpitude that has long held sway over My Children.

When these industrious Souls relish life to such a degree that the very Light of all Lights sends speeding luminescence beams around the universe, touching each Soul who is receptive, then I hear the great majesty of the timbre of the note, *"God is Incarnate on the Earth Star Planet."* It is then that MY Canvas flourishes and expands, enhancing all other parts of My Universe. Celest, you well know that even you can only do so much. Long, long ago, I told you, *"You are a Light, translucent as a crystal with the Light of God shining through you."* As the days continue to pass, Celest, bringing shorter and shorter periods of "time" left for people to either change or leave this planet, remember My Words, *"In the end it will be fine."* Now, Child, take a break and go outside and absorb the rays of My Sun.

David — Tell us, God, how do these musical vibrations affect each of us and is there anything else connected to this personal experience beyond what most are consciously capable of realizing?

God — The tones define who you are and on what evolutionary level you are currently working on. David, your own musical chords are playing loudly and fluently across the limitless dimensions you call space. Each Soul emanates that which is their own song, their own chorus line of the **Song of God**, although many know it not. Some can feel and sense these notes while others simply acknowledge that they exist. Each Soul is right, for there is no wrong answer, only choice and situations that present themselves, you see? When all is said and done, each note which comprises the whole becomes more vibrant. Then the Angels do sing with happiness over all the new arrivals to the exalted state of the now newly *awakened ones.* Each awakened one, as their own choir refines their own personal note, joins into the ever expansive tapestry of life. This note then becomes a permanent part of them. Have you ever heard the term, "I heard your sword sing and even though I cannot see you, I know that it is you?" This is part of your personal "Trademark," and since you are your personal sword this all makes perfect sense. Each note also carries with it a certain fragrance that will alert you when another is near. Each note also denotes the specific colors that emanate from your auric fields as well.

Swords are wondrous tools, ones that all of you should become more in tune with. Each sword has a purpose and destiny in its own right. Each of you has more than one sword in your arsenal and each has a specific task which they were Created to perform. They are fundamental in cutting through obstacles that come in the Souls' individual pathways. Sometimes these obstacles can be dealt with. They can be scrutinized for their content and validity; another tactic may require going around the obstacle, or if the Soul is capable, going over the obstacle. Those who are proficient at Creating their own swords will use them for The/their *Greater Good*, challenging the intrusive forces and besting them at their own game. There are limitless possibilities when using the powers of Creation, and as such, each must use keen discernment when plying their trade. There are limitless possibilities awaiting each sojourn of destiny. I would like to encourage all of you to embrace not only the concept of what you truly are; I would like you to embrace the fact that nothing is impossible; your options truly are limitless. As you well know, what you think, you Create. I implore you to Create with the *Greater Good* closest to your heart at all times. When in this "Mind thought," you can do no wrong and you most certainly cannot Create any more karmic baggage which will later have to be dealt with in one form or another.

David — God, I would imagine that one of the questions in the readers' minds is going to be about their ability to hear clearly what Soul Voice, along with Yourself, and others of their extended families are trying to relay to them. Do you have any helpful hints to guide them along their chosen path in this endeavor?

God — David, I believe what you are referring to here is commonly known as having the **eyes to see and the ears to hear.** It has been noted in many of your religious texts that this is available only to the chosen few. I would like to correct this misconception once and for all. Each Soul, no matter if they are man or beast, plant or other supposedly lesser forms of life, have the ability to contact their Soul Voice and have It become an active, conscious, valued part in their lives. Each person who chooses this shall begin remembering information which they have *chosen* to forget. As this is a school house planet, this, too, is one of the lessons you need to re-familiarize yourselves with. As I stated above, each child born communicates telepathically with Me at all times. It is as natural as knowing how to nurse the young. Having *the eyes to see and the ears to hear* is just a thought away. First of all, this ability must be called to you by the process of exercising your own free expression choices. There are many people who choose not to exercise this option due to personal choices in their Soul contracts, for explicitly experiencing a lifetime without their natural abilities. They wish to see how it feels and how they would react differently if these abilities were not consciously intact.

At any time, *Soul Voice approval required,* you can unlock these gifts that you have denied yourself and start using them for your own good. Now I am not saying that this comes immediately, as you well know, David. You yourself learned to see clearly when the self-imposed blocks were removed by Us after your true desires had reached a specific timeline in your life. The hearing ability came later. Fortunately for you, you had a very motivated, talented and highly evolved teacher and mentor from whom to learn. You also took the time necessary to examine your life and start ridding yourself of all the unwanted, unneeded and most certainly, unnecessary, baggage that you had accumulated along the way. Your chosen experience in this lifetime was to live as most others did so that you could better draw from those experiences for the timelines that are presently at hand. What both you and Celest and so many others have taught people over the years is that *a lesson has to be experienced before it can be understood and shared with another.* That lesson is simple, as all of life's lessons are supposed to be. Simply stated, it means that no one can teach another well, if they have not experienced the same or similar type of event themselves. If they have not walked in those shoes, they have no business suggesting or telling another what is right or wrong, or the proper way for them to proceed from that point on. This, My dear ones, is a double-edged sword which does indeed cut both ways. Bear that in mind in the times ahead, or it can be your own undoing.

How many of you still have not severed the umbilical cords that you have either attached or let others attach to you? Do you not see that these *all too real* attachments are draining you, that you are feeding off others as well as they most certainly are nourishing themselves off of your energy fields? How many of you can honestly say that you can clear your mind of all useless chatter for a mere one minute? How much time do you devote each and every day to your own well being? How often do you clear your minds to see if there is anything else worth hearing coming in? How much time do you spend each day recharging your **Spiritual batteries**? Let's be realistic here, for I already know what your answers are. Do you really believe that a moment's prayer at the end of the day, asking for that which you would like in your life, is truly enough to bring it into manifestation? It is what I hear from so many of you that I personally find disturbing. Your self-serving interests must be expanded to encompass the whole of humanity to truly expand upon yourself. Have you taken the time to remove any residue of doubt and fear that you have accumulated along the way? Have you released all stress, tension, anxiety and frustrations to make way for other more notable, more beneficial feelings to encompass you? It would enable you to feel lighter and less bound to this physical existence. I hear groans and moans from many people about things that *I know they have the power to change.* I can tell by your thoughts that this is not the case for most of you; if you are willing to read My Words, then you can now see more clearly what I hear. However, those people that do spend precious moments on themselves, for themselves, are the ones who seem to be most at ease with all that their life entails.

David, I would like you to add after this paragraph the exercise that Celest put together for the purpose of aiding every-one's personal quest for finding and maintaining a *clear channel*. It enables them to be open to the Universal Mind and also assists in each Soul's quest to "Be more than you currently believe possible." Please insert that now.

"Bridging the Gap"

This technique merely requires concentration and focus; it functions as a wondrous way to alleviate and dissipate any and all interferences and interruptions in any "channeling" and interfacing with Higher Dimension entities and energy forms. It also means that those who are in contact with any of the Star Keeper Forces (known on Earth as extraterrestrials) can receive and transmit all pertinent information with great clarity and understanding. This eliminates a problem so many Souls are encountering, both here and in the Higher Dimensions, which is attempting to communicate through the density and the combustive energy of the third-dimension.

It also eliminates the problem of not hearing all the words that are being sent to you.

Simply take 3 small breaths and release them through your nose; close your eyes and be sure you are completely barefoot before you begin Creating this Bridge.

Using simple visualization, picture a pillar, one that is like the ancient Roman pillars, in this manner it is huge and round, not any other shape. The pillar is transparent; its size is at least twice the size that you are. Place yourself within the middle of the pillar and be sure that it extends down past your feet, into the Earth. The top should be many miles above your head, reaching into the "Heavens." When you can see and feel this, call a golden-white light into the pillar, remember as you do so, the light permeates you as well.

When the light is in place, call upon "The gold dust of God" to interact and intermingle with the light in the pillar. You will be able to see or sense the dust filtering up and down your chamber; now simply ask the pillar (chamber) to begin the spiral and circular dance of connection. You should be able to see and/or feel the topmost energy reaching and expanding upward and outward as it searches for the coordinates to establish the Golden Bridge. Now if you are already in contact with specific beings, simply call their names.

You will find that as you do so, they will immediately be able to communicate with you on a much deeper and easier to hear level.

If you are just beginning to connect with these beings, if this is still new to you, I encourage you, as well as those who have more experience, to always, ALWAYS check your sources. Be sure you really are connecting with who you think you are. When you have finished with the communication, simply state to yourself and those speaking with you, "I am signing off now." At that point the pillar will disappear until you require it again.

The more you use this method, the faster the pillar will integrate with you. For some people the total integration may take place after the first use. Those of you who are used to "hearing" the "INCOMING" clues can immediately put up the pillar. Do not forget, this is important for the beings attempting to reach you as well.

Salude Celest

God — Now, using this method, *along with* your other ways and methods of ensuring that **who** you are communicating with is **who** they say they are, will greatly improve your abilities to see and hear more clearly. Then, too, I shall not hear so many discordant notes in the Music of the Ethers.

There are those who enter into a lifetime who are the seers and the prophets, those whom you now term as psychics or remote viewers, who naturally see and hear clearly. Not all, mind you, of these particular ones are checking their sources. This has caused a good many of them to become part of the contagion which is now becoming known as the *return of the false prophets*. I shall not go into this matter more at this time; perhaps I shall in the next book. Suffice it to say that **discernment** must be exercised at all times in all the different arenas of life. I have said this before and I will continue to do so until all of My Children can hear Me.

Speaking verbally is a learned response, communicating through mind-thought is the universal language that all Souls are naturally born with.

David - So tell me, God, out of all the thoughts that are so predominant in the minds of Earth's current residents, which is the most prominent?

God — Peace.

David — Is that it?

God — What else would you like Me to say? Would you like Me to say that global peace is just around the bend? Would you like Me to say that it is something that will happen naturally with no

182

effort put forward on your parts? Many, many people incarnated on Earth now were **chosen** to be here for their abilities to rise up to any challenge. To quote My good friend Blue Star, *"There is no more time to be wasted on vacillators."* However, I do like your dear friend Thor's interpretation of what Blue Star said. He said and I quote, "Instead of vacillators, should it not be, *'There is no more time to waste on **vacationers?'"*** Give that some thought if you dare to look into the looking glass.

You all have missions to complete, some are personal and some have planetary connotations, in fact both are intertwined. Each mission is of equal importance to both your and Earth's elevation into the Higher Realms. Now I shall remind each of you that your ability to join Earth in Her new resting area is predicated upon each of you performing the work necessary to raise your own awareness. No one can do it for you, nor should anyone try. This is a personal mission that requires more effort by you than you have ever put forth before. I implore all of you to look at your life, look at the world, see what needs changing and do what you can, when you can, without interfering in another's free will choices. Make the difference by Be-ing the difference. Leave no stone unturned and please remember that *you do not have to do it all yourself.* There are no extra credit points for becoming **martyrs**. There may be a couple of demerits, though.

David, it is not My intent to embarrass you with My next comment, however, I do know that you do not become embarrassed anymore, for you have nothing to hide. David, do you remember that moment many years ago when you yourself were working so hard to clean up your past life and move forward? I am sure you also remember what I prompted Celest to pass on to you when you procrastinated on some issues. Those were the issues you thought you could secretly hold onto "For the time being." I believe My exact words to her were, "Tell David to *either get with the program or you, Celest, cut him loose."* You took that most seriously as well you should have.

David — I do remember that all too well and I did take it most seriously. This is one of the ideas that I try to impress upon people we first come in contact with. When Celest makes a seemingly *off-*

handed comment that generally goes past most people, they **really** should be paying attention. She always has a reason for her choice of words, as do You, and her timing is impeccable.

God — Now that is why you both make **great** teachers. David, unless there is anything else, I believe We should pass this chapter on to Miss Suzy for her questions and comments.

Suzy — Hi, God, I'm here. I have a question, but first I want to say that before I read what you told Celest, I never thought about each of us having our own musical tone and color despite what I've heard from some of my sources. Like what Matthew has said, that each soul has its unique frequency identification and the several things that auras tell about a person, also that in Nirvana the treatment to heal traumatized psyches is the customized mingling of musical tones, wafting pastel colors and aromas. Some of the representatives of highly evolved civilizations spoke about communicating in tones and colors and also that some "bodies" are primarily just those ingredients. Even though I've known about these things for years and attributed them to souls off-planet, I never pulled them all together and related them to us "Earthlings." I'm thinking that most likely I'm not the only one who doesn't always see that what applies to other souls may be applicable to us too. I don't mean always, of course, but I think this is another instance where relating "the universe" to ourselves makes life here and everywhere else more understandable.

OK, that's my comment, along with "Thank you" for expanding my knowledge — *conscious* knowledge, I should say! My question is about the "inner voices" that are such a natural part of children's consciousness early on. What goes wrong with the ones who become brutal and cruel, torturing and killing animals and even sometimes children, and the adults who kill and claim, *"The voices in my head told me to kill them because they're evil"* or *"because they're too pure to live in this world"*? Surely not all such cases can be attributed to these people being battered babies, or can they?

God — I knew I could depend on you to come up with this

question, my little Suzy, because it's been rummaging around in your/our mind for a long time, you just haven't thought to talk with me or Matthew about it. So, what is it that "goes wrong"? Well, maybe nothing. The term "bad seed" seems to have been coined for "demonic" behavior to satisfy the need to understand something that even mental health types can't account for because nothing in the child's earliest environment and influences would indicate that such deviance could ever emerge. OK, now you're wondering if "mind control" might be the answer, and with some older children and young adults, it is — I'll get back to that. But the answer to why some children develop cruel tendencies is that it's their pre-birth choice to experience the opposite of what was done to them in other lifetimes so they can achieve balance — by now, you know that this is the aim of not only every soul, but the entire universe, which is the composite of all the souls in it — and their behavior is natural, a part of that balancing act. Yes, the parents are in on this, whether it means they signed on to be gentle, guiding nurturers or baby-batterers. It couldn't be any other way, you know, because these agreements are designed by everyone involved for their own and the others' soul growth.

The answer is not so simple for adults who claim, and genuinely mean it, that they killed because "voices" told them to. This can be a matter of serious brain deterioration due to an advanced stage of mental or physical illness, the result of a terribly abusive childhood environment, a radically distorted perception of religious teachings, or any combination of those circumstances. The act of killing may or may not be a balancing provision of the soul contract and the same is so about the deranged mental functioning. And yes, it's also possible that the person acted under the influence of mind control.

Now let's talk about mind control as the means whereby individuals are virtually kidnapped, then involuntarily methodically brainwashed and specifically programmed by "handlers," and which, as Matthew also has told you, NEVER is a provision of any pre-birth agreement! So how then can "evil" become inculcated in an individual whose "inner voice" did retain the innocence, ancient wisdom and communication with soul self/my self even while publicly conforming to the superficial expectations of "society"? It goes back to the various compartments of the psyche that I spoke about in another chapter. Levels of both innate awareness/sensitivity and acquired knowledge/behavior can be separated, or blocked, from consciousness when intensive, prolonged brutally intrusive measures are applied over a long period, which they are by various methods to accomplish what the mind controllers need — a "clean slate" on which they can input specific stimuli that will dependably result in certain responses. "Mind" control actually is the altering of *brain* functioning — the brain is a computer and like any other computer, it requires data entry to respond as needed, and that is what the programmers do. So you can see that an individual under that kind of control *cannot* act according to conscience or any soul level choices, but rather only in the mechanical way that a robot is maneuvered by its designer's throttle. That *is* what happens — there's *nothing* natural about mind-controlled actions! With supportive trained helpers, some persons who are tremendously strong psychically eventually can be "de-programmed," but many kill themselves, just as they're programmed to do after completing their "missions," or they're otherwise "eliminated."

There are other types of mind control that also drown out the "inner voice," like much of what mainstream media offer as "entertainment." You could say that this is *covert* because it's not the blatantly cruel methods used to brainwash and program killers, or the rigorous training of military troops to kill a designated enemy or what's done to keep the sex slave and "illegal" drug industries going strong. But the results are somewhat similar because of the influences on weak, vulnerable minds to wreak the same kinds of havoc to selves and others that they've become inured to by the prevalence of violence on TV, in movie theaters and the popular computer "games." Or it's shallow "amusement" that dulls sensitivity and precludes thinking deeply.

Much of what is called "news" is intended to disinform, misinform and keep you uninformed about factual happenings when the reporting isn't focused on trivial events to divert your attention from what IS important. Further, the "news" not only tells you what to believe, it subtly or not so subtly ridicules or ignores independent reasoning that could lead ones to doubt official rhetoric and "expert opinion" or even actively oppose strong-arm policies and actions. Many millions are being force-fed what a mere handful of media owners — read that, "mind controllers" — want you to be preoccupied with, and this includes the chock 'a block menu of sports that arouse more emotional investment in them than in the sorry state of your world. Then there's the mesmerizing and persuasive advertising with its sexual overtones, "ask your doctor about this pill," and "buy, buy, buy." What kind of mentality and behavior do you think comes out of this sick conglomerate of *"don't listen to your inner voice"* producers?! It's Orwell's *1984* come to life in "real time."

Now then, from my point of view, religious indoctrination is pure and simple overt mind control — just think about your religious history that's bloodthirsty on a massive scale and the populace who weren't its targets cheered it on! While some religiously devout may derive comfort from their faith, mostly religions have kept the masses in bondage to the dark minds that devised those "rules," which don't include one iota of spirituality, or universal truths! Spirituality and universal truths are one and the same: The awareness, the KNOWING that each of you is a part of me — you're all god and goddess selves, inseparable from each other and all other life in our universe. For goodness sake — let me say it this way: For *God*-ness sake, which includes ALL of US — I've told you this over and over so you'll remember that you DO know it at soul level! Listen to your inner voice — that's your soul talking to your conscious self — and you'll start seeing what I hear.

Suzy, beloved child, thank you for your important question. All right, if this is such important material to cover, why didn't I just talk about it — what if you hadn't brought it up? Well, as I said, I knew you would, and I think it carries a lot more weight when "one of my parts" rings in on any subject. True, there's the advantage that I don't have to drone on and on and this book winds up an interminable monologue, but the much larger purpose served here is that your, Celest's and David's questions and comments are meaningful to others of my children who can relate to what you ask about and are dealing with "down there."

Suzy — OK, God, you're the boss!

God — No one is going to know unless I tell them that you're laughing, Suzy, and you didn't type what you were thinking: *"You da man, dude!"* It's moments like this when I WANT to admit how intensely I wish ALL my children could relate to me that familiarly, like the *family* we ARE! How magnificent life on Earth will be when you do — then you *will* "see what I hear."

Celest — I just wanted to mention something because of Suzy's question. As you know, God, I have been teaching people for many years that each Soul has an *individualized musical note* and an *indelible fingerprint* which is indigenous to the individual Soul. The fingerprints can guide them to and from places to move to, people to interact with, etc. Although they cannot be seen, they function as inner compasses and are imprinted in Soul Memory. People were not aware of this.

Each musical note manifests to a person at specific times in the individual's lifetime. The notes cannot be taught to anyone, each will discover their own notes sooner or later. For many people the notes can change from 1 note to many notes throughout an individual's mortality. Millions of people can share for instance, "C flat," but it is the individual's level of evolvement, missions to be accomplished, and ability to Create etc., which keeps each note from replicating. In this manner one note may be the same **but** is completely different to each individual who has the same note or notes. I have found that making people aware of this has caused their awareness to bring personal notes into manifestation more quickly. Then the person can consciously understand the musical chords much better. I consider this information of great benefit to receptive people.

God — Yes, you are correct, Celest. Thank you for adding the additional information for Me. I think this wraps up this chapter quite nicely.

Celest — I appreciate all your information about the entire matter and I thank you.

Chapter 11

2012

God (*received by Suzy*) — All right, let's talk about this topic that's looming larger as the days pass: What will happen when you cross off the last day of 2011 on your calendar and you pin up the one for 2012? The thoughts in many minds about that year range from the sublime to the ridiculous, and since the latter is so quickly addressed, that's where I'll begin.

No, your world is not going to end. Earth is an eternal soul inhabiting a planetary body, and now that it's back from the brink of destruction — thanks to the infusion of light from your "space" neighbors — and on the way back to its original vibrant health and beauty, she's going to keep it for a long time to come.

With "ridiculous" accounted for, what is the "sublime" that you can expect 2012 to bring? Like everything else that happens anywhere, the choice is up to individuals, the decisions each makes. What I can tell you with certainty is, you who make the trip with Earth into the higher planes will be living in the promised Golden Age. In numerous of his messages, my Matthew-Self has accurately described the changes and challenges during the transition between now and your world in 2012 with its astounding differences that you will welcome whole heartedly.

Suzy, I need your proficiency here, to find all the parts of his messages about this and organize and edit them so the information flows nicely and there's no superfluous or repetitious material. So, will you work with me on this?

Suzy — Well, of course, if that's what you want. But I'm curious — why you don't just talk about this yourself?

God — I know all about your curiosity, Suzy. My preference for Matthew's words goes back to this "umbrella God" of yours, the indivisible sum of every single soul in this universe, and to you, that collective multidimensional intelligence is inconceivable. It is to *everyone* there, and that's my point. I want the information to come from a highly evolved soul whose fairly recent life on Earth and love bonds with some souls living there is a *personal* perspective as well as an authentic account of Earth's journey into the Golden Age and what life there will be like. I can't think of a more appropriate soul than your dear son, can you?

Suzy — God, you know perfectly well you're playing up to my maternal genes, don't you!

God — And why not play my trump card here, "Mother"— I know how much work is involved in what I've asked you to do. After this "Essay on 2012" is in place, I may have a bit more to say besides "Thank you, my beloved child."

* * * * * * * * * * * * * * * *

Essay on 2012

by
Matthew

Those who have interpreted the year 2012 as the beginning of the end of darkness — never mind the total end of the world! — have misinterpreted its significance. Most simply stated, 2012 heralds Earth's entry into the Golden Age, and between now and then is a time of transition from life as you have known it into life totally in harmony with all of Nature.

Everything in the universe is energy vibrating at one frequency or another, and when Earth was in prime health, in times you know but don't remember, all of her life forms were vibrating harmoniously. When she was near death more than six decades back, there was no harmony whatsoever, no balance of Nature — there was hardly sufficient light to sustain any kind of life, including Earth's own. What is happening now, with the help of stabilizing forces, is the transformation of your world — Earth's rejuvenation and return to balance — reaching completion in 2012.

But that year no longer has the "time absoluteness" it once held in prophecies, and your calendar cannot accurately convey when the major transitional changes will be completed because linear time is disappearing. What you perceive as time passing faster and faster is the effect of the higher energy planes in which you are living now, where everything is accelerating as Earth makes her way into the continuum — or, more accurately, as your consciousness grasps the actuality of timelessness, the reality of eternity and infinity. The faster, or more intensely, the light infuses Earth, the more swiftly your "time" passes as she moves still higher into fourth density vibrations. So, just as in this moment your calendar week is passing in less than half the time of a calendar week a dozen or so years ago, 2012 will be coming increasingly more rapidly than your current calendar can indicate.

Now then, why does that year have historic significance universally? It involves celestial orbiting cycles and their influences on your planet as well as life designs made in total clarity by highly evolved beings who planned Higher Universal-MAN with attributes of spirituality and intelligence that far exceed that in today's Earth population. Opportunities to return to higher densities have been offered in prior cycles and missed, and this time when the energetic alignment is again optimal, advanced civilizations are assisting so Earth's desire to rise to her former vibratory level is assured. What happens on Earth affects the universe, so it is of utmost significance to those advanced civilizations that the dark ages on your home planet be reconciled within the light and you knowledgeably take your rightful place among your universal family.

Along the way there will be many profound changes, changes you can't even imagine, that will transform life as you have known it into life in total harmony with all of Nature worldwide and thusly flow out into the universe. Very little of the wondrous world on your horizon will be rooted in your systems to date — that is precisely WHY you are creating your new world! The goddess vibrations that already are showing effects will continue to bless you as individuals and as a civilization. The negativity that is the root of fear, greed, dishonor and violence will be gone in the Golden Age, and the vibrations of Earth's entirety will be LOVE. Love, which is the same energy as LIGHT but simply expressed differently, is the pure essence of Creator, the ultimate power in the cosmos. This energy is the composition of souls and the key to opening hearts and illumining minds, and it is flowing more abundantly on Earth than ever before. As the darkness continues to fade, love will replace conflict and tyranny with peace and cooperation; love will eliminate the superficial superiority of one group over another; love will enlighten those who regard others as possessions or dispensable and uplift those who have been subjected to living in those conditions. In short, LOVE is the power that is transforming your world.

Although no major strongholds of the darkness will cease abruptly, the transition will be like lightning in comparison to the long ages that violence, inequities, abuses and deceit prevailed. If you could see in parallel motion the pace of the past many centuries, when only intermittent flickers of light broke through the dominant darkness, and the pace of the past few decades of growing light intensity, you would marvel at the swiftness of the changes.

The progressive changes have required and will continue to require the help of extraterrestrials. Almost all of them are unknown to you except as we speak of them and in some cases, their own messages sent forth, yet some of the strongest, most experienced light warriors in this universe are right there among you, working behind the scenes to guide the essential changes so that as many as possible of Earth's residents will accompany her into the higher planes. This is how beloved and significant universally your planet is and how beloved and important YOU are! In keeping with universal law, it is your heartfelt desire for Earth's well being that is your invitation, your request to those civilizations for their help, but your bewilderment about how to heal the pervasive damage humankind has wrought also is part of their divine authorization to assist. You are in charge, however, because it is *your* homeland and you chose to be there specifically to participate in this process. That's why millions have been inspired to become actively involved or to monetarily support efforts to end violence and environmental destruction.

The first reforms are in governments. Many of the populace who are unaware of the ongoing transformation see governing policies leading to the brink of planetary disaster, and even among lightworkers there are concerns about what will happen in this critical world arena. Not only is it difficult for you to imagine systems dramatically different from what you are accustomed to, but in reforms of the magnitude required, it is realistic to anticipate confusion and foment. Please know that trustworthy souls with spiritual integrity and expertise in the various fields of governing are ready to take the helm and bring order as rapidly as possible as corrupt, tyrannical government leaders are unseated. A great deal of "shuffling" in the United States government will lead to ending its engagement in war and internal and international strife, and the unseating of other self-serving heads of state will end civil wars, genocide and longstanding conflict. Many wise and able leaders in previous Earth lifetimes chose to return to the planet to complete their groundwork for this unique time at hand, and others are members of your "space family" — many are your ancestors — who volunteered to assist during this transitional period. In no way are they there to "take over," but rather they came in response to your thoughts, feelings and actions for peace, fairness and stability in your world. The transformation at hand is your desire and soul level vision — if this were not so, it could not happen. Looking even farther ahead, during the past decade or two some souls have come in with the advanced spiritual clarity and ancient wisdom that will naturally put them in leadership roles.

Because money is the basis not only for commerce, but even more so, for concentrating power, the need for economic reforms worldwide is as crucial as changes in national leadership. The economy as reported is more myth than actuality. Only a comparative handful of people know how tenuous and corrupt the global economy is or that international trade and the stock markets are manipulated by the Illuminati, a group of darkly-inclined people who have passed their tight global reins from generation to generation. They have amassed vast fortunes through that control as well as by charging usurious bank loan rates and accruing mammoth amounts from their illegal drugs industry, and they use that money to buy governments; bankrupt countries and exploit their natural resources; keep billions of souls at barely subsistence level; and fund both sides in wars that they precipitate and perpetuate because from wars, they derive handsome profits. This cannot continue and it won't. The unconscionably inequitable allocation of money in your world will end. Although I cannot give you finite details of the changeover process, I can give you an overview and assure you that the honest, knowledgeable people who will manage the process will keep disruption at a minimum as they fairly distribute the world's wealth.

The Illuminati's illegally and immorally garnered fortunes will be put into circulation and their exploitation of natural resources worldwide will end. Since that power base is what enabled them to set government and banking policies and own multinational corporations, those corrupt controls also will end. The huge debts of the poorest nations were incurred by their state of desperation, often caused by Illuminati actions and influence; but the loans went to the despots ruling the countries and did not benefit the citizens, so those debts will be annulled and assistance given directly to the people. Many national borders have been set by the victors in war who wanted the natural resources, and that created "have-nots" who formerly were "haves." When the LOVE in souls ends all conflicts, borders no longer will be cause for dispute because all peoples will be "haves."

The coffers of the United States, which is erroneously considered the most fiscally sound nation in the world, have been empty for some time. The national debt, in large part due to the skullduggery of the Illuminati-owned Federal Reserve System and its IRS collection agency, will become manageable when that System is dissolved. The various currencies, especially dollars, have no foundation — daily transactions involving billions of dollars and other currencies are merely information passed from one computer to another and they far exceed the money to back them. The "new" foundation for currencies will be a return to an old one, where precious metals was a set standard for exchange, and "old fashioned" bartering once again will be an excellent way for nations and communities to conduct some business.

The basis for much of your current economy will change considerably and employment will change accordingly, but your greater spiritual clarity and usage of brain capacity in the higher frequencies will enable a joyful transition into fields that support cooperation among nations and harmony with Nature. The wanton destruction of your environment through oil and gas extraction, mining, logging and their resultant pollution will cease and all types of toxins in the atmosphere, soil and water will be eliminated. Forests will be restored to the levels required for the balance of Nature, and the need is great as well to preserve and expand habitats where animals have been reduced to countable numbers, just as the oceans must be returned to health so marine life can flourish instead of disappear. There are plans to achieve those goals as well as keep pristine land areas free of concrete incursions and implement alternative power sources. Technologies known but suppressed and the more advanced technologies that will be introduced by your universal brothers and sisters will clear the pollution and provide renewable energy, new modes of transportation, new types of building materials, and greatly enhanced food production methods. Your hearts will be gladdened at the amazing speed with which these changes will happen!

Natural building products that will come into wide usage along with plants that will be introduced include clay, strong reeds, straw, tropical canes and surface stones, and all will be used in conscious agreement with humankind. While there are countless levels between the lowest and the highest universal intelligence, which you may think of as omniscience, no thing is excluded from the mass consciousness. To be more personal — indeed, to be more *correct* — substitute "soul" for "thing" and you can see the inter-relationship of the totality of this universe. The higher the vibrations of any environment, the higher the levels of comprehension of all life within it, thus just as you are expanding in consciousness, so are all the elements of Nature in your world growing in their varying levels of awareness.

The fast-growing food crops, flowers, cotton and other fiber-producing plants, plants with medicinal aspects, canes and grasses, and all kinds of trees will agree to grow as long as needed to meet your requirements and then transmute their energy into your usage of them. Although much less lumber will be used than currently, the sacred relationship between trees and humankind includes their willingness to be used for decorative parts of building interiors and furniture in the short term, perhaps as long as the next half century. Acknowledgement of all these natural sources' importance and consciousness and gratitude for their willingness to give their lives for your use will become inherent in all peoples. Too, you will come to know and treasure the Devic kingdom that is so closely allied with the beauty and thriving of all that you consider Nature.

The allocation of food and other basic life essentials available in the richer countries will be shared on an equitable basis with the poorer countries until a global production order is achieved. Diets will change from meat and seafood to plants as people learn to respect and honor all animal life. The herds of food animals will decrease through the cessation of breeding and natural transition, and as plants become diet staples, any that were harmfully genetically engineered will shed those properties.

Animals in the wild will instinctively know not to overpopulate and those that are carnivorous will turn to the plant kingdom for sustenance. The albinos being born in several animal species have both spiritual and transitional significance. You associate white with peace, and these rarities that are appearing are symbolic of the coming changes in animal nature that will end the predator-prey food chain and restore the peaceable relationship that once existed among all species, including humankind. The instances of unlikely cross-species friendships and even nurturing of the young from one species by mothers of another are more indications of Earth's return to her original paradise self. Still, an extremely important factor in this is the inspiration in many souls to be advocates for the animal kingdom and alleviate their manmade plight.

The cetaceans' spiritual mission, to embody in huge bulk and inhabit your oceans where they absorb and anchor the light beamed to the planet from distant civilizations, soon will have been fulfilled. These whale and dolphin souls, which species-wide are the most highly evolved spiritually and intellectually on your planet, will soar to their original light stations when they leave physically, but they will continue to grace your planet with their love energy.

What are commonly known as "global warming" and "El Niño" are part of Earth's natural processes to return to her original moderate climate everywhere. While she is achieving this, glaciers will melt, the vast deserts will become arable, rain forests will flourish, and variations in temperatures will markedly decrease — ultimately, everyplace in your world will be comfortably habitable. Peoples now living in the coldest or the hottest climes will adapt, but it is unavoidable that the few animal species in the Polar Regions will disappear and some that live on the fringes will survive by migrating; the affected species instinctively will know not to reproduce or when to move.

Contrary to current count and certainly population projections, your numbers are decreasing and the birth rate will continue to drop but not precipitously. The balance of Nature no longer will require pestilence, so no disease-causing or transmitting factors will be present, and the common use of toxic chemicals and prescription drugs will cease. Medical treatments will drastically change until there no longer is any need for therapies because bodies, which will have a greatly longer lifetime, will become free of all forms of disease. New educational systems and resource materials will reflect factual universal and planetary history, and true spirituality will replace religions in accordance with the truths that will be revealed.

Those are some of the most significant changes under way and ahead, and all will have trickle-down effects that will permeate and uplift every facet of life on Earth. The Golden Age — the "second edition" of the Garden of Eden — will radiate the love, harmony, serenity and beauty of spirit that you, in your remembered awareness of being god and goddess selves, ARE.

Now I shall tell you some of the more "down-to-Earth" features that you can anticipate in that beauteous world. City life will be much more fulfilling for the spirit than it is today, due to the demolishing of substandard buildings and restoration of once fine buildings that fell into decay; the addition of many small parks and colorful playgrounds, vegetable and flower gardens, and neighborhood libraries, concerts, museums, and galleries with locally produced art forms; entertainment and recreational centers for all ages and interests; and animals, even those you now consider wild, roaming freely. Also, new transportation modes and a much fairer distribution of wealth will enable city dwellers to frequent the countryside, where a booming business will be "bed-and-breakfast" inns to accommodate the growing desire for those oases of respite from routine activity, and to travel to distant places as well. Still, millions now living in cities may prefer to move to the solitude and restorative energy of familiar rural, forested areas. And, like a new wave of pioneers, some of you will be motivated to relocate to currently uninhabitable places when those start flourishing and beckon the adventuresome, while other souls will choose to live in houseboats on the calm, restful seas.

Architecture will be limited only by imagination and choices, but no building will be ugly or inadequate for its purpose. Geodesic domes will be popular as will fanciful building designs that reflect the light-heartedness that so long has been denied the majority of Earth's peoples. Current and new technologies will produce construction materials similar in strength and appearance to today's concrete, steel, rigid and flexible plastics, and those along with natural products and quality simulations of fine woods will be widely used. So will glass, which will be altered from its present composition, because you will desire to live closer with Nature even when you are indoors.

By unified intent, no litter or eyesore of any kind will exist anywhere. Wherever you live or travel, you will not want the vista marred by the utility poles that now are necessary blights on land-scapes. The poles will be removed and where conduits are required, they will be underground; and other energy sources will be direct, without any need for connecting wires. Although telepathy will become a common form of communication, voice-to-voice communion across the miles will be as important as now, but the harmful aspects of the wireless methods you are using will be gone. Expanses of concrete gradually will be removed too, as new transportation modes will change the need for current fuels and highways.

All unjust laws and policies will be struck down and education worldwide will accurately reflect the universal truths. The writing, printing and distribution of textbooks will be done expeditiously in conjunction with computerized lessons, and the souls who are innately prepared to teach will step up to this mission they had chosen.

These and other marvelous lifestyle differences awaiting you are indeed gargantuan changes from life in this moment, yet the greatest transformation you will experience is in humankind, where love and higher consciousness are REcreating "miracles." Like souls on Earth and in Nirvana once again going back and forth between these physical and spirit worlds, travel that was common-place until third density limitations closed minds to this possibility. Like your transcendence from believing you are lone individuals to knowing your inseparability from all life in this universe, and embracing each other as well as members of extraterrestrial civilizations as the brothers and sisters you all are. Like life without anxiety or conflict as people of all countries and cultures are harmonious, cooperative, helpful, kind, high-spirited and delightfully good-natured.

Now I must tell you as well that the transition from this day to that world will continue to present challenges. To say otherwise would be neither truthful nor prudent as your expectations would not be met, and instead of successfully dealing with challenges — which you are well prepared to do with wisdom and strength of spirit and character or you wouldn't have chosen and been selected to participate! — you could become discouraged as Earth continues apace on her ascension journey.

Wars and other violence, injustices, deception and corruption will continue until that energy set in motion is played out. Although the dark forces, the vast force field of negative thought forms, has left this part of the galaxy, tentacles of that energetic influence remain and are making last ditch efforts to control the most vulnerable souls as well as attack those with the brightest light. Further, the higher frequencies now on the planet are magnifying all human characteristics, and those that are darkly inclined are showing that intensification through increasing hostility, greed, violence and apathy toward those who are suffering and in desperate need. So, while not all of the dark skirmishes are past, we urge you to be *encouraged* by each that arises — it means that the vanquishing of the darkness is that much nearer. Rejoice in knowing that its momentum is close to the point of exhaustion because all of you who are *living your light* are helping to speed it to conclusion.

Controlling the flow of money is the last mundane tool the dark ones have and they will keep it within their grasp as long as they can. The "rotten tap root," so to say, has been loosened and the tendrils are breaking, but until all have been eliminated, economic difficulties will affect many lives. Remember, you have the power to create your own abundance through the law of attraction, and sharing your resources is the best way to bring even more abundance into your life.

Prior to peace and harmony prevailing throughout Earth, many, many souls will leave due to the same causes as now — disease, starvation, injuries in wars and other types of violence, geophysical events — so the population will continue to decrease from those means. As sorrowful as these deaths may seem, the adversity that the souls experience beyond their pre-birth agreements gives them leaps forward in soul growth. They will greet their return to Nirvana knowing that if they choose another Earth lifetime, it will be in the splendor and glory of a revitalized world and the abiding love among its inhabitants.

Geophysical events will continue as Earth's natural and necessary cleansing process. The blatant disregard for human and animal life for millennia past — and still happening on a lamentable scale — caused a massive amount of negativity to accumulate. Although this has been greatly reduced via geophysical events, its remnants, plus what is being generated anew, must be released. It matters not whether this is by natural or manmade occurrences — the ridding of that negativity is what is important. The effects of these events, which will lessen in frequency and severity as Earth keeps ascending, are being diminished to the greatest extent possible by members of your universal family. Their technology cannot prevent all deaths and damage, but it is limiting the death toll and property destruction by leveling out over a wide area the energy releases via earthquakes and volcanic eruptions and is steering the strongest storms to less populated areas.

The record high and low temperatures, droughts and flooding

that are part of Earth's transition to her original moderate climate globally will present hardships for a while longer. Gradually some sea level coastlines will become submerged; this need not present anxiety as there will be protective and compensatory measures for any inhabitants of those areas. We are aware of the speculation that Atlantis and Lemuria may rise, but this will not happen. Those large land masses served their civilizations during that era on Earth, but their return is not needed; however, some souls living then have come back to assist in the ongoing consciousness-raising and spiritual renewal within today's populace.

That religions are teaching the "word of God" will be shown in the fullness of the deception that spawned that falsehood, and among the challenges you will encounter are the many individuals who will not believe the truths that will be revealed. Some will do battle, convinced that it is their divine right and duty to defeat the Anti-Christ or the infidels through bloodshed. You will witness the shock, confusion, anger, disillusionment, and yes, very likely fear — the deceivers who made a vengeful God have been masterful for eons — of people whose minds are not totally closed to the revelations. Provide a compassionate safe haven for their questioning and rely on your intuition for the best responses — they will be there when you need them. However, it is not your responsibility to convince them that the foundation of their beliefs — maybe even their very life purpose — is a lie. Rejoice, just as we shall, when your efforts succeed, but please do not feel despondent when they don't. The resistant souls, like all others in the universe, will continue their evolutionary pathways wherever their needs shall best be served, and the eternal and infinite love of Source will under-gird their way.

In summary we say to you, our beloved Earth family, know with your entire being that the world of love, peace and harmony you have been co-creating is close at hand. Remembering that you chose to be exactly where you are right now so you could participate in this unprecedented time in the universe will let your hearts be light-filled and your journey a triumphant adventure. Myriad light beings are with you every instant, enfolding you with the love and protection of the Christed light as you usher in Earth's long awaited "2012" Golden Age.

****

God — Suzy, thank you from my "umbrella selves," who can't think of a thing to add to Matthew's loving, enlightening words that you so efficiently organized.

Suzy — Well, he helped, you know. So then, God, I guess you and I are finished.

God — Yes, of course I know he helped, and my dear child, you and I are hardly finished, but I know you mean our work on this chapter, and to that I say *"Job well done!"*

David — In the upcoming future what do you see happening that will end the current cycles which will allow all the Earth changes to be complete by the dawning of 2012?

God — Well, here We are in the winter months of 2007. Much that needs to be done to complete this cycle in Earth's history is already under way. You see evidence of this with every stone that has already been overturned in the moments leading up to "now." In the days ahead you will find that the media can no longer control and filter what news is shared with the general populations of this world. The truth of what has been taking place and what is currently occurring will no longer be withheld from the masses. It is a wondrous time that presents itself, front and center, for all to receive and bring into their hearts as truth. It is a time of great upheaval, for the beliefs that so many of you have long treasured as truth will show the other side of the coin, the one you have long been denied. Their true colors will shine forth with all the brilliancy they possess. They (you) will also see that a great number of areas still need to have their energies transmuted and balanced.

I can only assure you that all the important illusions that have held you each captive on this planet will be revealed in the days ahead. There will be more civil unrest; there will be more earthquakes, perhaps some tidal waves and forest fires. This, My dear ones, is a natural cleansing process that your loving planet is performing to displace the remaining pockets of negativity that have held not only you, but Her, in bondage all these many years. I have told you all this before but perhaps it needs repeating. The release of these pockets of "displaced energies" is forcing those who are in opposition to the light to reveal themselves. It is also their wakeup call, the one that announces to them that their reign on this planet is long over and that it is time for them to relinquish their hold here, once and for all. My heart goes out to each of them, as should yours, for they are as much a part of you as they are of Me. As time passes there will be none left to interfere in the works that must be done in the days ahead. Yes, it is almost a time of celebration; it is also a time of great sadness which will be experienced by many. Those who will be leaving or "relocating" to another place will have much to deal with. You will also, for there is much that you will have to reconcile yourselves to. It is you who must clean up the aftermath of battles that should never have had to been fought. No, you are not going to carry guns and send them on their merry way. You will vanquish them with **Love** and revelations of truth.

Remember this well, many who will be leaving will be among your loved ones, your families, your friends. Would you not wish them all the best that their futures could hold for them? Will you not send them off with love in your hearts? Will you not release them from your emotional bonds and allow them the freedom to choose to move into *The Light* as you yourself have done? Miss them, but do not belittle them, for they too are your brothers and sisters and some chose to play the unpopular roles so that the greater good could be accomplished. Remember, I have told you that before. There is always balance to be had if you look deep within. With that having been said, I wish you all a safe journey, for the days ahead will hold many surprises for each of you and the time to celebrate will be many long hours away. You are entering the most difficult phase of your lifetime, live it well. Embrace it. Go in peace, live in peace and love with all your hearts. We await you.

David — Thank you, God, however you "forgot" to mention the completion of these changes by 2012.

God — David, I know what you are fishing for here and it is timely as well. Will everything return to their once pristine state? No, they won't. This too will take time. Will there be no more work to do? That, My dear ones, will never cease for you are evolving and evolvement requires change. I would like to add that you are all up for the challenges that lie ahead. Embrace them with passion and a zest for life and let us not forget to put a little *pizzazz* into it as well. This is a new phase in the tapestry of your lives that you are Creating here. Weave it with love and cherish each moment as if it were your first. **Be** the artists of Creation that you each are.

David — Thank you, I believe that covers it nicely.

Suzy — God, I'm back. I think that what you told David about the people "who will be leaving or 'relocating' to another place will have a lot to deal with" needs some clarification. Millions of souls will be leaving before 2012 for the same reasons they are now — disease, starvation, genocide and so forth — and for many, that's what's in their original or amended soul contracts regarding experience and physical longevity. That's a completely different reason for leaving than the souls who agreed to play the "heavies" so many, many others could wind up their third density karma and achieve balance; then those "heavies" were supposed to join the light forces, but they knowingly reneged on their contracts and continued creating widespread death and destruction. Because they have refused the light, which not only would bring spiritual awareness but also change their cellular structure into the crystalline form that would enable them to physically survive in the higher vibrations where Earth is heading, their bodies will die and by universal law, their souls automatically will go to a world where the energy is the same as the energy registered by their thoughts, deeds and intentions during this lifetime. Aren't they the only ones you meant who "will have a lot to deal with" in their new locations?

God — Yes, Suzy, they are, and I thank you for catching this. In my "relocating" statement, I wasn't including the souls who, in the pre-birth agreements that are designed to benefit all the ones who want to share the lifetime, play the "heavy" roles so others in the agreement can experience what they need for balance. Some of these folks will take leaps in soul growth because they've followed their contracts to the letter by listening to their inner guidance. Others won't because they didn't, but they'll be given another opportunity at that same level to experience what they signed up for this time but didn't manage to achieve. It is the ones, as you said, *knowingly* reneged on their agreements, who will indeed have a lot to deal with in their new locations. I'm asking you not to become obsessed with punishment for these souls while they're still among you — believe me, they won't escape the laws of the universe that will consign them to doing that to themselves by way of their "relocation" destinations. Instead, *focus on what you want for your world* — peace, harmony and cooperation among all humankind and with all of Nature. So, my little editor Suzy self, do you think that will suffice?

Suzy — Yes, I think so. God, this is an example of what I've done at times in helping to prepare this book. I forget to mention in my first go-round of questions or comments some aspects of a particular subject because I've received that information in messages to post on my site, and I mentally drop it into the gaps. Then when I read Celest's and David's questions and comments and your responses, that important information comes forth along with things that are new to me. Our four-way contributions are such a rewarding experience — it's a really "upbeat" feeling, getting both a refresher course *and* new information. Maybe it's somewhat like that for you and David and Celest. Well, I don't mean that your "umbrella God" self that is all of us here and every-where else has to remember or learn anything, but that we, your parts, are doing this. The important thing is, our combined efforts are giving readers what they need to comprehend the "big picture."

God — That is indeed our good intention, but I remind you, my beloved "part," that it was exactly your "umbrella God" that needed prompting to make that clarification. And I'm glad this happened! I hope it shows everyone that I am NOT religions'

Perfect Supreme Ruler. On the contrary, I'm much more personable, much more approachable, much more talkative, much more *human* than most people think I am. I am ALL of *YOU*, and an important purpose of this book is to show who I AM/WE ARE.

Celest — Blue Star has spoken about 2012 for many years now and his teachings coincide with the essay and Your statements, God. So between what I already know and everything in this chapter, I cannot think of any questions.

God — Good enough, Celest.

Chapter 12

Don't Shoot the Messengers

God (*received by Celest*) — All right now, I have deliberately chosen this chapter to be the final one in this book. I have spoken of many things to you and sought to bring to the forefront of your minds issues as well as answers to questions that I have heard *buzzing* around in the collective minds of the human race. When I first spoke to Celest and then to David and Suzy about what was to be included in My Book, I had already decided the topics I needed to address. My decision was predicated on the *amount of truth* you, the reader, could successfully assimilate and how you would each *react* to My "myth busting" information.

Of course My Desire was and is to give you the most important information to assist you in personal evolvement, and to communicate with you in such a manner that I could share *My Truth*. In this way I can show you the totality of the convergence of all Higher Realities. I can only do this with those who are receptive to **My Words**. If I could correctly define the term "Messenger" in a way that it would be easier, perhaps more palpable for your mental absorption of the understanding of the word, I think I would say something very simple. I would say, "A Messenger is an androgynous being, whether animal, vegetable or mineral, who walks among you delivering the truth and teaching non-radical techniques that would bring you a *better life*." They enable you to have the **opportunity** to live life in a better way. You could have the conscious understanding that without the complete comprehensive overview and the minute details relating to any of these selected subjects of Mine, then you would continue to be *"in the dark,"* so to speak.

If you notice, I prefaced that statement by saying, **"If I could."** Yes, Celest, I know you thought you did not hear Me correctly, but as I told you while you were writing the words, *"This is the way I want it to be written."* In the broadest sense of the word,

I used "if" so that I could show you the convoluted process that sometimes occurs when I am reaching out to you, when I am attempting to quell your senseless fears by sharing My Truth with each of you. Without the receptiveness of your mind and Spirit, I cannot be of any help to you. You see yourselves as humans with a *Soul*...somewhere. You do not see that you are *Soul walking in human form*. Although this is not true of All of My Children's perceptiveness, or lack of the correct perspective factor, there are still too many "in lack," from My assessment of the situation.

Ironically, people will listen to what other people have to say before they will listen to Me. Although in one sense I am sure it is a "behaviorism" that is more acceptable to the masses here, I often wonder how shocked everyone would be if they understood that many, many times when they are listening to others who also speak My Truth, they are actually listening to My Messengers. No, none of the Messengers say, *"Well, God is right here on my shoulder telling me what to say and ready to slap you across your head if you do not listen."* Nor do the messengers prance about like circus clowns seeking a soap box to stand upon and preach from. Each Messenger, regardless of his or her origins, is on a personal and planetary quest. On the personal level they are here to be the best they can be in order to help others of My Children. On a *planetary level* they are well aware that each success story they have, each person who listens to what is said without bias, without judgment, without attempting to interfere with the truths being told, helps to raise the vibrations of this planet.

Not all My Messengers are in human form. A flower will speak to you of such wonders it beholds as it gazes upon the beauty of this planet and upon your own inner beauty, *if you but listen*. An animal will speak to you of its desire to be of assistance to My Children On the Earth Star planet, *if you but listen*. The trees and all other life forms of My Creation speak to all of you in subtle and wondrous ways, *if you but listen*. As I see it, nobody takes the time to listen. They may "hear" but they do not "listen." My Messengers who are My human counterparts must be able to travel all roads, respect all life, and do what they can to assist in the convergence of the human race as *God I Am*. The Messengers in human form must cooperate with one another, they must adhere to all Universal Laws and promote **not themselves**, but promote the Words of God instead, My WORDS.

Yes, I have watched in sadness when one, sometimes many, of the human Messengers, are brutalized or murdered because of the truth they speak. You may consider these Messengers to be the world's greatest "whistle blowers." And you know how popular whistle blowers are on this planet! Therein lies the danger to them. Yet, conversely, people have been heard to say, "Please tell me the truth, but don't tell me anything bad." Brilliant phrase, isn't it! Then there is, *"Well I can handle the truth in small dosages, but don't tell me about realities that will rock my personal world."* Another good one! All right, we have Children who want truth but it is "Conditional truth." We have Children who want truth but only if it aligns with what is deemed "acceptable" to them. Then we have Children who want truth and will settle for no less than the absolute truth. My Messengers do not have an easy task; however, prior to their incarnation here, they accepted this responsibility. This is why I selected them above all others to share the Words of God. Nothing and *no-thing* shall deter them from their missions.

Think about the Messengers you yourself have encountered. Perhaps some were on a slightly lower level of evolution than you, while others were on a much higher level of evolution. But regardless of their evolutionary status, if you learned something from them that can help or is helping you in your own ascension, then they are doing what they should be doing, and just as importantly, so are you. Quite often as part of an individual's Soul Contract, a less evolved Messenger will receive assistance from a more evolved Messenger. If you continue to bear in mind that the Earth is a planet that still at times can cause you to feel as though you are walking in quicksand, then please give silent thanks for the fact that there are so many others of My Children willing and able to guide, protect, educate and teach, teach, teach by the examples they have set for themselves. *Teaching by example* is a time-honored tradition on most of My other planets.

It means that an individual is giving of themselves to others without any hidden agenda. They have no mission *"To be frantic about."* It is about living and being **Me** for all the world to see and then perhaps, just perhaps, *My Will shall be done.* I also ask each of you to remember that what the Messengers agreed to while "At home" is **in most cases,** masked from their remembrances while they are here on Earth. As Celest knows very well, more so than do most others who are *"Like her,"* is that the greatest gift the *Messengers can initiate with a person, is by allowing the person or persons to fall until they have had enough of the experience.* You see, it is only when circumstances, whether self-created, or engineered by unilluminated Children, cause an individual to experience personal dis-organized chaos in his or her life to such an extreme that they simply are <u>ready</u> and <u>willing</u> to accept change and assistance to change, can they honestly say "I am ready, help me please."

This is why I have cautioned all My Messengers to stand back, become "Passionately detached" and await the call for help. The mistake less evolved Messengers have made is to try to help others before the ones they seek to help are ready and receptive. No, I do not call it "Throwing pearls before swine," I call it "Casting God in front of non-believers." This accomplishes nothing good and increases the individual's reasons "not to believe." Celest, I am going to ask you a question now. I am going to turn the tables a bit. How many times in the years since you Star-Walked your way into the Earth dimension have you felt "alone, totally segregated from your 'Own kind,' " and helpless to assist the very Children you knew needed your help?

Celest — Well, God, I am glad I did not try to keep a record of all those times. It would have rapidly become a written text that wrapped around this planet *ad nauseam.* OK, God, I know what you are doing here; in this case I am going to head you off "at the pass." I already heard what you are getting ready to say. By the way, God, just so you know, sometimes you think very loudly!

I have had to learn to accept and live with the "aloneness feeling." Even though I am now married to David, he and I both still feel that "Loss of familial sensation." You know very well that we both understand why this happens, and yes, we have accepted it as part of our Star-Walk.

It is a common "anomaly" that affects all who are "like us." I will say that at times it can make life here more difficult but that is OK. In the Greater Sense, I feel that the more I can experience here by better understanding the mayhem and unhappiness which assails so many people, the better prepared I am to "balance the scales" by showing a greater quality of life that can be achieved by all people. You asked about "Helpless," I cannot say I can use that term when confronted by a person or persons whom I KNOW are in dire need of help, yet are not ready to hear what I can tell them. Sometimes I have to tell them "No," in order to tell them "Yes." I know you understand what I am saying. I think I would use the term "Acceptance" to best describe my feelings at those times. I cannot change what I cannot change. Nor should I. Until a person accepts personal responsibility for their actions or lack of actions, I can play no role in their life. Have I answered your questions thoroughly enough, God?

God — Yes, Celest, you have. I wanted My Children to hear your perspective, to hear all that you have just said, in order for them to exercise their free expression choices and perhaps be able to broaden their evaluations on life and particularly on themselves. I appreciate your candor and your willingness to **"Stand in truth."** I would have expected no less from you. By the way, *I will try to turn down My thinking cells,* just a tad.

I do caution all of My Children to practice great discernment when listening to others who SAY they speak for Me. If an individual, or a group of same-mind-thought people, converge upon any area and start to try to convince you that they are in "Communication with God," and that God has sent them to "Save you," then I suggest you turn around and run as far away from them as you can!

At one time this insidious practice was quite minimal here on Earth. However, in the present **"Now"** time of today, this devious behavior has taken on epidemic proportions, skillfully designed to feed your fears and pull you off the path of the Light of all Lights. Although all of Divinity was aware that this method of indoctrination would happen now, We must each do all We can, when We can, to lessen the impact of the lies and deceit. As We do this, more and more False Prophets shall be exposed, not only for "What" they are, but also "WHAT" they are listening to. If you remember that I do not Create, endorse, or enact "Hell and damnation" beliefs, then you should have no problem being able to tell "Left from RIGHT." Another thought for all of My Children to mull over is this: do you realize, any of you, that *I too am a Messenger?* I AM the Creator's Messenger. I AM the Divinity's Messenger. I have many roles to complete, but as Messenger of the Creation, I have an awesome responsibility to uphold. A full cycle of completion is also an aspect of My Own Divine Self that **must be fulfilled**.

So it is that as you each, Soul to Soul and heart to heart, accept My Divine Love and My Understanding without conditions imposed, you intertwine within The Divine Plan in a manner you have yet to consciously realize. You see, if you were all in conscious awareness of the totality of your part within The Divine Plan, there is no doubt many of you would try to change yourselves to fit your "Idea" of what your role should be. It is by living and being and doing all that you can without being in a full state of knowledge of your own individual outcomes that you shine the brightest. It is AFTER your period of incarnation is over, that you will find that you have also been *"Overcoming your former selves"* to the best or worst of your abilities. In the times to come, many of you may be selected to inhabit other planets as My Messengers. It is not "A crap shoot." It is YOU, as My "Shared Soul" in a sense, striving to find your place in the Omnipresent Universe.

I encourage you each to not waver in your beliefs, to not allow others to taint your mind, hearts or Spirits. I am ALWAYS available to speak with you, if you but LISTEN.

Celest — God, before I turn this chapter over to David and Suzy, I just want to thank You for asking me to participate in the writing of this book. I wish I could think of another word in the human language that would better describe my feelings about this. But languages on this planet are so limiting in expressing intangible qualities. Telepathically, I have told You, in my own way, how I feel and the "Why." So, that having been said, I will sign off for now.

God — Celest, you know perfectly well that it was not necessary to try to explain this to Me. I want you to remember what I am about to say, this means you and David both, My Child, it was decreed long, LONG ago, that you 2 would reunite in your great love for one another and work together to assist in the ushering in of "The Golden Now." You two are "A team, you are a match." As such the good works that you are both involved in, far beyond My Writings, are having great success in quelling the final vestiges of the unilluminated ones. Unfortunately, this has made you two rather huge targets for them as well. Celest, I know you remember what I had said to you long before your descent here. I see your memory cells flicking channels and imaging a certain part of My Conversation with you. I told you then, "As the days pass and you feel yourself being attacked for what you **know**, KNOW that I will be on your shoulder very much."

Even though I know that Blue Star is very much in evidence around you, protecting and encouraging you, even when you arrive at states of physical exhaustion, I simply felt the urge to remind you of what I said. Go now in peace as always, Celest.

David — "Bang, bang, shoot em up," comes to mind as I thought about the title of this chapter and where it may be leading. I sincerely hope we shall soon have all grown out of that particular stage of pubescence. Since I am well aware that our mission is not to stand on soapboxes and give people more information than they are ready to handle, I was wondering if you could clarify the statement that "Earth is a Schoolhouse Planet" for those who still do not understand this basic concept.

God — OK, let's try this one on, shall We. Every form of life on this planet is connected in the Greater Sense by their/its desire to be the best that they can be at any one given moment. Even if this is an unconscious desire, each life form is also aware that they are all connected in the Greatest Sense by and to the energy that Created them. Each has a role to play, some need to be the baddies and some get to be the good guys, as I have stated before. Although, remember, the roles are constantly changing as each individual life cycle ends and another one is birthed. If you believe, as I hope you do by now, that reincarnation is a reality and is another truth, then you will start to get a better understanding of why role reversal is so necessary in order to achieve balance and a more comprehensive complete grasp on the larger picture. As My messengers have told you many times over, you are here to do God's work, and part of that is to see through others' eyes. As such you are to expand upon yourselves by playing all the different roles that the societies of the different timelines have to offer, not all at once, mind you. However, "Be-ing the **all at once**" does come into play as the multitudes of people begin to realize that they are not just one astrological sign, they are not just one culture, one color or one sex. You each are a combination of all these diverse vibrations because you have each experienced what life has to offer in all varied roles you have played. Actors indeed, you each are. I wonder how many of you realize that your mother of today could have been your husband in another lifetime and so on. That should give you something to seriously think upon, and if so, perhaps, mayhaps, you will look differently upon those others who are currently in your present life.

I want to tell you that many of you take life too seriously. Have you forgotten that **"the art of work is to play?"** I watched your dismay when you have tried your hardest and still failed to succeed at the task before you. I have also watched and joined in with you as you laughed out loud at yourself for your mistakes and you each grew leaps and bounds **because** you had failed at something, but at least you tried and learned from the trying. I have sat in on your sessions with others of your Soul Clusters as you planned your next life experience. I silently chuckled to Myself as you reached for the brass ring, throwing a twist in here and there, to see if you could trip yourselves up. You are always challenging yourself to reach for the impossible, yet succeed you have, more often than not. Now might be a good time to tell you, *"No Mission is Mission Impossible."* Now I would like each of you to know that I do not interfere in what you choose to try, or choose not to try to accomplish. This is a Soul's choice, as well it should be. However far you may push yourselves, even pushing yourselves to the limit, you always succeed in one aspect. You either triumph or you fail. Bummer, eh... not really, each aspect of a challenge has its own learning curve to it.

A good warrior, no matter the level they are on, cannot be a "great warrior" until they have been defeated at least once in battle. To not know defeat leaves one vulnerable to thinking they are impervious to failure. Have you ever heard the term, "the bigger they are, the harder they fall?" In some aspects this is true, because your own worst critic is always yourself. **We (My** other Children and I) do not judge you for your choices, nor should you judge another because of theirs. A schoolhouse is a place to learn, to throw around ideas and discard those that do not ring true to you. A schoolhouse is a place where friends and soon-to-be friends congregate to play out their good fantasies, fuel their desires and ultimately become that which they were destined to be. Not all have chosen the road less traveled, however each will find their way home, **eventually** to reunite as one.

Celestial, in her infinite wisdom the other day, coined a phrase that all might well pay attention to, for "its information" has come full circle in this time long awaited. I quote her as saying, *"grade school is over, high school is over, this is life, so live it."* Most appropriately said, if I do say so Myself. Each of you has had many, many lifetimes to reach this point in your own personal evolution. What you do with that education is completely up to you. I am fully aware that not all of you will awaken in time to fulfill your Soul contracts and exercise the option in your contracts that enables you to complete the journey with My Beloved Earth, and that's all right. Each Soul will have ample opportunities to "get there from here"; it may just take a while longer than they planned. Having faith is believing in yourselves, knowing that you are doing the best that you can at every given moment, *to the best or worst of your abilities.* In school you always have required lesson plans to follow. You also have your extracurricular courses and the option to change, or enhance, your major course at any given time. You can then further your education in the direction that draws your fancy at any given time. Living life on Earth, or on any planet on any dimensional level, offers many of the same opportunities, just at varied levels.

Teachers are messengers, hopefully you would not shoot your Spiritual teacher just because you disagreed with what they were telling you... *would you?* If so, you most certainly still have a need for some remedial lesson plans. All of you have the right to agree to disagree. Ushering this world into the era of the Greater I Am and flourishing in The Golden Now is what you have all labored so long for all these many years. You should be proud of yourselves for making "the final cut," for not all who wished to be there now with you were chosen. With that I shall bid you, *God* day.

David — God, I would like to take this moment to thank you and all our "sponsors," as well as ourselves, for granting us the opportunity to receive a PhD in life.

God — David, you have all earned it, with high honors I might add. Thank you for all your efforts in getting **My** word out.

Suzy — Good morning, God. I LOVE it that you said flowers and animals are your messengers! I've long thought of them as Earth's gifts to people, and you know my very special bond with dogs, but I never thought of any of them as your messengers. Now I see that of course they are — they're your creations! When trees and flowers uplift our spirits and we admire their strong or fragile beauty, and when family animals share with us their loyal, devoted companionship and we're inspired to preserve the habitats of "wild" animals and plants — well, the deep emotions all of these lives evoke in us are their/your soul-level "messages" to us, aren't they?

God — Yes, little Suzy, that's how it is, and it's such a natural way for me to communicate with all of you, isn't it? Yet unless I spell it out, how will my children know that the souls of those kingdoms also are my messengers, especially since far too many of my humankind don't believe that I can speak verbally to their *own* selves? One purpose of this book we're collaborating on is to show that I not only can, I DO!

I know there's a matter you wish to discuss with me privately, Suzy, but I'm asking you to share this with readers. Please write what's in your mind.

Suzy — Well, God, I'm sure you have a good reason for this, so OK. This "time passing faster and faster" situation is really hard to adjust to, and the "timeless" continuum that we're heading into — which I do understand is what's causing this "time running out" sensation — is impossible for me to grasp. Since I've been receiving spiritual messages for almost 14 years, shouldn't I be dealing with this time thing better than I am?

God — Thank you, my Suzy soul. Now then, you *are* dealing well with "this time thing," you're just not giving yourself any credit for it. True, you're not achieving as much each day as you'd like to, but you've learned not to "buck the system" the way you used to, when you felt pressured to work until fatigue halted you. You stopped feeling that pressure, you prioritized your diverse responsibilities sensibly, you're getting as much sleep as your body tells you it needs, and your time with Bob and your "fur family" is more pleasurable because you're relaxed. That's not only dealing well with "time," it's a much more balanced life.

What is beyond your "grasp," as you say, is consciously remembering your experience in the continuum. When something works well for you in one situation, you apply it to another, don't you, and we both know that sometimes that works, sometimes it doesn't — *trying* is what *learning* is all about! I'm going to tell you what you haven't learned, not well enough, anyway, and that is that making comparisons works *very* well in one situation and *never* in others. Suzy, you need to stop comparing yourself with Celest and David. You need to accept that the Light *Warrior* aspect of their full mission requires their BEing in the continuum, their full awareness of the universe's inter-dimensional omnipresence. At soul level, you and all my other children have this awareness too, but at this point it's not necessary for you or most of my other messengers to connect with it *consciously* because it's not needed for your respective light services.

I'm going to mention your recent email exchange with Celest that started with your numerical typo. When she suggested that you really meant a specific larger number, you wrote back that you knew she would "use her crystal ball" and know what you meant.

To that she replied, "Suzy, I AM a crystal ball!" She is indeed, and that's a good example of an ability she needs to successfully fulfill *her* mission and you *don't* need for *yours*. Not right now, anyway.

I'm telling you this "publicly" because ALL my children need to know that comparison is good when it is measuring personal characteristics, talents and skills development, knowledge, goals, sensitivities, accomplishments, relationships, and so forth in this moment against the same a year ago, or ten years or twenty — this "yardstick" lets you know how far you've progressed, or not. But it's *never* good to compare your *perception* of self with your *perception* of anyone else! Now, it's fine to be inspired by others' achievements and emulate their qualities that you respect — that can help you aspire to and reach greater goals — but that's *not* the same as "using" those people as a comparative measurement of *yourself*. Of course this comparison business goes both ways, with ones feeling quite superior to others, and I don't have to tell anyone what thin ice you're on if you're doing *that!*

There's something else that has a place as ones progress on the lighted path — *humility* — and something that hasn't — *egotism*. Don't confuse humility with lack of self-worth or egotism with self-confidence — I don't think I have to explain how greatly those sets of characteristics differ!

Still on this comparison issue, I'm going to say again that ALL of you not only chose, but *were selected* to participate in Earth's ascension. Some of you were "born leaders," literally, but most of you have roles that by *your* comparison with those kinds of positions are minor, yet from my view — which surely you won't argue is higher than yours — *every one of you has equal importance in the collective purpose.* The street beggar is contributing just as is a person of renown for philanthropy, for instance. You may not see the connection, but both roles are essential for helping everyone achieve the balance that you as individuals require and, as Earth's population, she requires.

Well, my dear little Suzy, you didn't expect your question to get such a rouser reply, but you can see how it helped me make an important point or two.

Oh yes, one more thing, and this is for readers who may

wonder why I sometimes address Suzy as "little" — it is a term of endearment that gets a smile from this radiant goddess self each time I use it, like it is right now.

Suzy — It was sweet of you to mention that, God. And I want you to know that I will take your "comparison" advice to heart!

God — I'll help you, Suzy, just as I help and accompany all my other selves along their Earth lifetime journey. Regardless of the pathway each of you chooses, my love for you is infinite and eternal, and that, I believe, is the perfect thought to keep foremost in your minds and hold in your hearts as we come to the end of this book.

Celest — I am so thankful, so grateful for all the wondrous truths that have been discussed in this book. If each reader has either learned or relearned information that will be of aid to his or her life, then we have all done our jobs well.

We have now arrived at the conclusion of this book. It has been a great pleasure for me to work with God, David and Suzy in bringing information that God considers pertinent to all those who are receptive to His Truths. In a way, it has been strange to be speaking publicly about the Words of God. Until God decided He wanted this book to be written, my constant communications with Him have been personal and private with the notable exceptions of His dictating to David and I His "Letters from God." He and I have discussed everything under the sun, moon and stars and many, many times, matters well beyond this universe. So often we would join in laughter about many diverse issues, other times the matters were all extremely serious. I remember an incident when we were all just beginning this book and God was transmitting information to me so fast, I could hardly keep hitting the right keys on the keyboard.

I am used to my father doing that to me when he is having a "Pleiadian moment," but I did not expect God to have a "God moment." Silly me! I silently had the thought, "I wish God could type." Immediately, without breaking His stride in the least, God said, "I am typing." I was very surprised, but I said telepathically, "What!!" And then God said, "You're typing, aren't you?" If you are looking for a moral to that incident, it should not be hard to find.

I wish for each of you to have a better understanding of a universal truth. Although God is a Supreme Being, He is as close to you as you are to yourself. Have the confidence to speak with Him and have the discernment to listen to what He has to say. There is no mystery here, He will answer and if you are listening, you will hear Him. On a personal note to each of you and in response to the overwhelming email question of the ages, "How do I live life?" I ask you each to *"live life with passion."* Infuse everything you do and say with passion and a zest for life. Live life as though each day is your first day on Earth, and see life as the incredible gift it is. All that you have read in this book can be used as "life tools." Each tool is in itself a gift. If you have learned enough about what Soul Contracts are and are not, then stop thinking about what your own Contracts may, or may not be about and **live life in the NOW, with passion that will rival the stars by its own beauty.** In this manner you will be living an ordinary life, in a non-ordinary way. What else can you possibly ask for? If you are "being life" and "seeing life" in a clearer fashion, then "you can do no wrong."

Salude... Celestial Blue Star

****

Although we are at the conclusion of this book, I know that our work is far from over. In fact, in many ways it feels as if we have just begun. Each and every day Celest and I fill our days with laughter and love from the moment we awaken to the time we go to sleep. And then the fun begins all over again as we travel in our dream states to places most would not believe possible. I, for one, have always felt that life should be this way, where unconditional love was not only possible, that it was to be the driving force in our lives, whether we are in a relationship or out on our own. I cherish each moment and I never forget to acknowledge that it is indeed a great day to be alive. Celest, Suzy and I many times feel as if we are not doing as much as we should be or could be, and then God pops in and reminds us of all we have done up to now. He also reminds us that we do not have to do it all ourselves. His humor and patience is exceeded by none. He shares His wisdom and thoughts freely and openly, always allowing us the choice to proceed or take a different route. A greater example of good parenting could not be found throughout the cosmos. I laugh to myself when He and I have finished speaking at times and I have thanked Him for all that He had shared with me. He laughs back and causally states, *"I do have my moments."* Which is true, He also has all the precious moments of our lives which He experiences through us.

I remember a day long ago, when I was not hearing His voice in my head because I was too far into my intellect to hear Him, how lost I had felt. Fortunately for me, those days are long past. At one point early on in the book, when my mind was somewhere else and I kept interjecting my own thoughts, He stopped me and said, *"This is like the battle of the titans when your intellect gets involved."* Let this (my experience) be a key to your understanding that we should not cast our own shadow. This can easily happen if you are not aware of what is transpiring. My conversations with God range from the Spiritual to the esoteric, to the trivial and everything in between. Even our long talks about sex versus sensuality never flustered Him in the least. I refer to God as "He" for ease in speaking; however, I know that it is the Father/ Mother aspect *which* is God, that I am reaching. He is both masculine and feminine in His wisdom, for He draws from both equally and without bias, always looking at both sides of the picture. His love for me and His love for you is unconditional, He could not and would not pay favoritism to anyone, that is not His way. He has taught me so much; he has helped me remember so much of what I had forgotten that I can sympathize with all those who have not reached out and taken the time to re-unite with His presence. This is a small perspective of what awaits all of us in the days to come, and I look forward to the days ahead in a way that I have not looked towards anything else in my/this life experience.

I think I amuse God many times when we first start chatting and I *always* ask him for his "I.D." He patiently responds and then we casually resume. His presence is always unmistakable, as well it should be.

I hope you all receive from this book what He intended for you to understand. The more times you read it, the more you will receive from it. Many phrases are repeated, I always take that as a sign that the point He is making is important. When we are finished each day and I think about what information was shared that day, it always amazes me how simply and fluently He expresses Himself. I encourage all of you to open your hearts and minds to the real God, not the one that has been depicted in your holy texts or spoken of by your neighbor or friend. There is far more to Him than what you have conceived of before. Look at yourselves, or a child, a bird, a flower or a person walking by, He is each of them and each is unique, as well they should be. Now picture in your mind's eye a person, a Be-ing, that has all those qualities all rolled up into one. Now you have the picture. Speak to Him, He awaits your call. He always answers. Ahh, if we would all take the time to listen.

Thank you for sharing this time with us; it has been a unique experience for me and an honor to take part in *His Book* with Suzy and Celest. Ten years ago, five years ago, I would never have thought that I would be here now, taking part in this venture. None of us really knows in entirety what our Soul Contracts say or what our chosen missions are, until they present themselves to us. I, for one, would not want to know everything ahead of time, that would ruin the *"SURPRISE"* element.

I have learned not to push myself, some things take longer to assimilate and understand than others. I have found that if I am not grasping a concept right away, then perhaps I am not ready for that level of truth. This was just a thought of mine for you to ponder upon. Everyone moves at different paces. The more we open our hearts and minds to the truth and change our beliefs accordingly, the more truth is revealed to us. God is as much a part of my everyday life as I am myself, there is no separation. I can find Him anywhere, everywhere, anytime; all I have to do is slow down and look.

David of Arcturus

****

The influence of 35 years of faithful attendance at Christian churches from Sunday School onward, even choosing to go to a church college, was the solid foundation of my life. Even after our family situation disrupted my regular attendance and active participation in all aspects of church life, those years of indoctrination still had a firm grasp on my beliefs, with one exception: I no longer believed that telepathic communication was impossible (that is, unless one was hearing from Satan).

Many years later, when I was receiving messages for the Matthew Books, it was with continuous amazement — what my many sources told me was light years beyond anything I had ever heard before. Equally surprising was the closeness I felt with all of them and not only with Matthew, my son who was fatally injured in a wreck when he was 17, with whom the love flowed perfectly naturally.

In the beginning, I questioned some of the information from those highly spiritually evolved beings because it was totally foreign to what I knew, and I questioned almost everything that

God said because it was so different from what I had been taught about him. As our conversations went on, I started to realize that the God of my church years was always in my head and never touched my heart. It took me quite a while to shed all the dogma and accept the truth that each of us is a god/goddess soul, an integral part of God and inseparable from every other soul throughout this universe. But once I did that, my heart opened to the personal relationship with him that I have now, the ultimate bonding with a loving friend and constant companion.

Just as Matthew and I chat daily about myriad subjects, so do God and I. Some things are significant, really insightful, and others are trivial and we laugh about them. Sometimes he compliments a specific accomplishment or gives helpful suggestions; other times he chides me for letting my self-confidence ebb, and when I waver in trusting my intuition, he gets me back on track. Whatever we discuss, it's filled with his encouragement, guidance and unconditional love. Occasionally he says he wants me to record what he's going to tell me, so I'll have it for reference — of course, he knows how my memory works!

As David said, God isn't "him" or "her." He/Him is religion's emphasis on male as the authority figure and, as intended, that dominant masculine concept permeates all avenues of life, and I use it just as David did, for "ease of speaking." After all, we refer to an animal or a plant or a rock as "it," and they're all parts of God too — no wonder so many of us have special feelings for them! Since I don't capitalize "he" or "him," you may wonder if my completely comfortable relationship with God has led to a familiarity that has a touch of disrespect. NEVER! It's an issue that came up when I was recording our early talks ten years ago and was capitalizing "You" in my questions and comments. He told me to stop doing that, to not capitalize any word that referred to him because it was reinforcing my feelings about the vast distance that I had allowed my religion to put between God and myself.

Everyone can feel the same kind of closeness with God that Celest and David and I do. You know from what God has said in this book that you are as much a part of him as we are, you are unconditionally loved just as we are, and he doesn't judge your choices any more than he judges ours. The "peace that passeth all understanding" comes when we receive the love that God feels for each and every one of his creations and we let the power of that love flow through us and out into our world.

Suzanne (Suzy) Ward

****

This is the first of a series of letters that God asked David and I to write down and place on the www.godumentary.com Web site. We have only had time to place the first three letters on the site, however we plan to post some of the others "in due time."

"A Letter from God #1"
Received May 23rd, 2005
"A Dark Night's Journey Into the Sun"

God (*received by Celest and David*) — So it is that I have returned to speak with all those of you willing to listen to My words. I AM <u>The Word and The Word is My Law</u>. I have chosen to address you, Children, of My loins, Children of My Son, Children of My Sun, on this auspicious occasion. Today is the first day of the beginning of your rebirth of who you are. I informed Celestial that she and David were to each act as My chosen scribes for this narrative. My Celestial daughter inquired as to what language format I would deign to use. She was a bit perturbed, wondering if this Godumentary would mean a barrage of "thee," thou," and "thine." I was amused as she struggled to remember the olden days when we walked this earth together and used that vernacular simply because it was the language format of the times.

Since civilized mankind has bethought themselves to be a now "progressive civilization," I will of course "speak" on the same level as do you. I have arrived at this time bearing acknowledgements of the fruits of your labors. I am always aware of the turbulence that besets you, I am always aware of the intense struggles that are within so many of you as "right" fights against "might." I see the pain and distress that so many of you undergo in your determination to be all that you think you can be; I see the non-understanding in your hearts and minds as you fail to realize that there is no need to "think" of what you could be, rather there is a <u>need</u> for you Children to better comprehend that *you are already there.*

I see disbelief in your eyes and inner minds as cultures, races and religions argue as to who the "chosen ones" are. I see the desperation in your thoughts at the non-dispensation of justice in this world; of the vain and the mighty who have fallen so low that they are now the lowliest beings on My planet. I see glimmers of hope in your wondrous and beatific personal magnetic fields as small revelations are transmitted to you just when you need them the most. I encourage My angels and My Star Keeper Children to assist you all in all ways and all-ways. I watch as tears cascade down the faces of My innocent ones, My kind-hearted and brave soldiers, teachers, healers and those who have walked-into human form. The form that is "I AM."

I hear so many of you wonder and wander in your thoughts about the preposterous situations that you confront each day; there is so much reluctance to accept a reality that is not found in your abrasive school books. One that is <u>The Greater Truth</u>. You question "the why." "Why am I here?" I do not remember ever agreeing to undergo these torments, putting up with these restless, invasive things that go bump in the night and daytime as well. The truth is self-evident here. You see it is not in truth a question of your faith in My Greater Force of Creativity, it is not a question of you not having enough or not being good enough for others. I intentionally and with My Divine Foresight implanted the veils of illusion over each of your minds but NOT your hearts nor your Souls. You each thoroughly understood this prior to your descent into gross matter. You each happily capitulated with the understanding of the total acquisition of the great benefits you would reap as you sowed new seeds in the newer fertility of the human race as a whole.

When I gathered you each to My bosom so many, many, light years ago, I encouraged you to remember only that which would benefit you as a human form of My Expression. I shared with you My endless compassion and endless love for your strength and willingness to enter into the dimension of madness, of disorganized chaos, of violence and non-love for others. I did indeed remind you each, over and over again, that the non-remembrance of so much of your Sacred Covenant would become troublesome to you as you journeyed forward as a human being... yet again. It did not make sense to you at the time; perhaps it did not mean much to you then. You were each emphatic in your determination to succeed and of your understanding of your individual missions and your Soul Cluster connections. None said to Me *"hell no, I won't go."* Sometimes you wonder about that wisdom now. Remember, as Celestial has recently stated, **"wisdom is knowledge in a training bra."**

In those times that were the gathering of the bravest, most industrious of Souls, who committed themselves to My request for assistance to form a better world here, I gave to you each a promise. I said, "A life well-lived is its own reward, as you each traverse the density of the grossest of earth times, you will find a pot of gold at the end of your rainbow. It will be all that you have ever been, all that you will ever be. It is God-in-motion." I gave you forewarning that you would not be accepted for who you are, rather that the multitudes would attempt to convince you that at best you are My Emissaries. At worst the devil incarnate. NO, YOU ARE NOT MY EMISSARIES in this sense! NOR DO YOU BEAR THE MARK OF THE BEAST! You are Me in physicality. I express Myself through you. I experience life in human form through you. So a cycle of a life experience centering on the illusions of "forgetting" is now being lifted as I promised you I would. Promises made and promises kept.

I had patiently and explicitly explained to you each how easy it would have been for you to deter from your chosen paths. If you had been able to use all the activated memories, if I had permitted this, and allowed you to attempt to save people from their own dramas, you would also have altered your own personal paths of destiny. I could not allow this to occur. Nor indeed could I permit you to interfere in others' fates; others' choices and non-choices of a life not well-lived. It is not your responsibility, it is not your business. The planet's history books speak of ancient times they called **"the dark ages."** Ironically and sadly, I must dispute this fiction. You have been living in the dark ages since the inception of this planet.

If only these "learned" peoples on this planet could but see what I hear. Your goodness, your earnestness to help others here, that do not always deserve your help, has not gone unnoticed. Nothing that you do ever does. I permit you "free expression," that which many call "free will," in order that not only you can Create wonders galore but that I, too, may experience them through you.

I am not a static energy, therefore neither are you. I arranged, with the aid of my Star Keeper Children, that as you each progressed into a greater maturity, specific strands of your DNA would alter. As this grand event would take place your cellular memories would be gently reawakened one by one, so as not to overload your human minds. This is a "positive-positive" sequential progression that all of you must honor. I hear your prayers and your pleas for enlightenment, yet wonder why do you ask for what you already have. Praying is but asking. I already know what it is that you want, need and deserve to have, for I AM you and you are Me. As each step of your journey coalesces into matters of either a negative or disquieting experience, those issues then function as predestined and necessary catalysts. It is then, during these well timed episodes, that you MUST undergo *transitional times.*

The "transitionary" process was programmed into each Soul who has accepted the challenge of walking in a third-dimensional world. The cause and effect of moving through different stages, different periods of development and growth, are to say the least an endurance task, a completion of a cycle. Everything must come full circle for the beginning to meet the end.

A transition is basically and fundamentally a change in matter of one perspective to another. Each phase is an accomplishment; it is a realization of the truths that have been purposely hidden in plain view in order to allow each individual Soul to evolve at his or her own pace. For in truth we are all the same, yet different, each Soul is unique. The distinguishing factor is the life experiences and lessons that each have chosen along the way. All knowledge is to be accrued; each must experience in totality the lesson at hand. It is the realization that one has had enough of any one experience that allows them to move forward. Throughout each transitional phase is a learning curve, one that sets each individual apart from others of their Soul clusters. It is the combining of the accrued knowledge, unconsciously, that raises the entire cluster up yet another level, until such time as all the experiences desired, or manifested along the way, have been fulfilled. It is at this point where the re-joining with Source returns to full circle. When you begin a cycle, you must complete that cycle, and then you will begin a new one again. Life is about change.

Transitions can be seen as a momentous occasion, a realization, an affirmative action. It is during these periods when the mind (the intellect) comes into a greater understanding of all which the Soul and the Heart already know. There was a time when the intellect was a receiver of information, a vessel to be programmed as a safety measure to co-join, to meld in complete harmony with the Soul. Unfortunately over the years it has taken control of most human realities. It is time to restore the harmony, peace and balance that once was. When an individual is undergoing a transition it will be easier to transit if each one remembers to allow the process to flow and thus pass as quickly as possible. Over-dramatizing the event only distorts the beauty and magnificence of the growing and expanding experience. I am not insinuating that it will always be an easy feat. At times it can be quite painful, your head may feel as if it is about to explode. A migraine can pale in comparison. Fear not, this is simply a buildup of energy, an expansion of the chakras and it is a natural occurrence. To hasten through a transition, all one needs do is to simply acknowledge its presence, sincerely thank it for the experience, then release it. There is no need to continue recreating an experience that has arrived at its climactic conclusion. It is essential, My Children, that you understand the enormity of the transitional process, the depth and breadth of the experience. To KNOW when to accept something is of equal importance as to KNOW when to release.

There will always be a plentitude of transitional times along the way; it is part of walking as a true human being. These are meant to be "Spiritual guide lines" to challenge and test your mettle, your desires and your determination to experience all that life has to offer. My Children, without these phases of life, you could not live well, you could not evolve, you would cease to be.

Mayhap if I give to you pertinent information that is all encompassing in regard to those times of turbulence, it will reassure you that the "changing of the guard is but a part of your covenant." Without these alterations, dear hearts, what will you have learned?

1 — This state of mind, the fluctuations of emotions, is not permanent. You will pass through this as quickly as a blink in My Eye.

2 — Your Acknowledgement that these occurrences are gifts and the understanding of the uniqueness of this present allows it to pass.

3 — Releasing this "phase of traveling" does indeed Create more space for the birth of new transitions.

4 — Here are but a few exercises that I strongly encourage all of My children to learn. You see, I do indeed have a great sense of humor, contrary to what the religions of the day state. First, I speak to you each of the discomfort and melancholy that at times accompanies the transitional process, then I offer to you the antidote.

5 — Hold on to a wall within your home to release excess energy from the physical body. The body knows well it is undergoing a change, so allow it space to expel the over-abundance of energy. What is meant by "holding a wall?" Simply that I encourage you to place both hands on a door frame or a wall, then spread both feet apart and tell yourself, *"I release all excess energy from my mind, body and Spirit."* As you go through the changes and the refinements into your new light body, there will be many instances when you will endure an excessive internal buildup of energies. This technique will help alleviate all of them. I do not give you difficult tasks to perform.

6 — The use of "Sea Salt" has great importance. Sea salt is natural and has what your body is craving. A pinch under your tongue will help to balance your system. Salt is as natural and essential to the body as are air and water. A pinch of sea salt under

the tongue at least once or twice a day aligns the chemical structures housed within the brain. When you are in the throes of a transition, the electrical impulses within the human body have great need to be accelerated in order that luminescence can enter the cellular structure of the body.

7 — Drink a great deal of water. Water is the catalyst that keeps the energies in the human body in motion. Water is a conduit for the electrical impulses as well.

8 — All excessive energy, whatever its place of origin, requires an opening, a destination. It matters not if the energy is expansive or if it is an energy that requires grounding. If it would be more convenient to release excessive energy while outdoors, then please, by all means, release that matter into the ground. Place your hands or feet into the soil and state your intent to **release**.

All of these measures are predicated upon the personal enlightenment that you desire. As you transform in a personal manner it impacts on My planet and thus planetary changes occur. Enlightenment is achieved through understanding, through acknowledgement and allowing yourselves to remember that you are each God. I belong to no one, yet I belong to all. You are enslaved to no one.

I am declaring a moratorium on all ego-based issues. Those already in motion must run their course; however, those who indulge in this hellacious practice shall not be rewarded with transitional times. This year of 2005 is the beginning of the year(s) of great changes. These years will be heralding the fall of institutions of great learning. Many of those who perceive themselves as the upper echelon of the human race will be called upon, especially this year, to face their greatest fears......... Disgrace and revelation. Many prophecies have been issued in My Name, this does not make them true, this does not mean that they are in fact My words. I am here now to issue certain revelations, to correct procedural policies that in truth are not Mine, but belong to those who seek the down-fall of the human race. The human brain has been overloaded and undermined with falsehoods and untruths.

I am issuing certain challenges at this time. The Kingdom of God is for those who obey and honor My Laws, not the laws of man written by man. Who among My Children remembers the definitive battles between the Serpent and the Viper? Who among My Children dares to take the initiative and cut off the heads of the Vipers that plague My planet, My people? Who among you Children of My Light remember MY SUN? Who among you Children remembers well ONE of my Sons, the man called Jesus? I ask you, My beloved ones, <u>are you willing to live for your beliefs?</u> <u>Are you willing to LIVE your beliefs</u>? There shall not ever be a smoting of humans by MySelf or any of those who so well guard Nirvana! You are MY CHILDREN, I bring you life everlasting, and yet so many choose to question not ONLY MY WISDOM, but also doubt My Words.

I shall not destroy "the ungodly," they are destroying themselves. I do not pass judgment upon those who seek to debase Me. I offer them compassion for their grievous lack of judgment, I offer to them My undying Love. No one has the right to sit in judgment on another. Each individual Soul must either honor itself and in so doing honor Me, or disgrace itself, thereby relinquishing all rights to ascend with Me until those Souls have rejoined the Serpent Clan by their own "free expression." Each Soul must pass through the portals of the dark journey until the Soul's <u>self-appointed</u> timeline has emerged into My Light without regret, without remorse, without coercion. There will always be room in The Kingdom of Heaven, My Mansions in the sky, for all who honor their truths. *"Thy Will be done"* is an expression that is least understood, it did not originate from Me, but from early man. It is not MY Will that shall be done, it is your own. I said, *"you shall reap what you shall Sow."* From this moment on, let no man stand in judgment upon another, lest the judgment mirror back upon the man.

As the changing times reflect the crimson tide that is upon My planet, I ask of you to remain firm in your beliefs, to clearly ascertain the relevance and truthfulness, the ORIGIN of those alleged truths, that another tells you. To remain apart from the mayhem ongoing on My planet, you must first practice compassion and discernment. I leave with you now a special gift, it is to further your determination not to be swayed into the realm of False Prophets; in the soon-to-be difficult times, as you observe others gnashing their teeth and seeking REDEMPTION from an illusionary projection that proclaims ITSELF to be Me, remember your truths, your unconditional love, your abilities to stand erect and how to say "NO." Above all, remember *"MY SONG."*

"My Song is My Wind, My Song is My Tree, My Song is My Truth,
My Song is My Sun, My Song is the everlasting Love of God."
Write the life that is your own,
let no man come between you and yourself!
Children, BELIEVE in yourselves, BELIEVE in your special-ness,
BELIEVE in your unlimited abilities to <u>co-create</u> with Me.
All you need do is
remember ... remember ... remember ...
that you are not alone,
You never have been.

Celest and David — Until next time, we leave you with a thought of our own:

<u>"The destination is well worth the journey"</u>

Celest — God thought it would be a good idea to include this writing at the end of His book. Although I wrote this years ago, I am very happy that it has helped many people. Perhaps you can benefit from it, or you may know someone else who can.

"Spirituality 101"
"A Guide for Those who have "Forgotten"

"Forgotten" defined as... misplaced, temporary amnesia,
left-brain vulnerability, Spiritually deprived.

Throughout the Earth's history, individuals have discovered that he or she knows very little about the true "Spiritual path." It is a very human trait and happens quite often that people confuse the Spirit with the religious dogmas which are so prevalent on this planet. It is NOT that religion itself is "bad," rather it is the method of indoctrination and, in many cases, the manipulation of those who are Spiritually feeble, which is the causation of much pain and mis-information. For many people it is necessary to have an icon, be it a statue or a stone, or bible, in order to feel the existence of The Godhead. This is also where they affix blame for their personal and professional failures. It is also these very same people who willingly believe that another mortal has the right to expunge other people's perceived "sins." How can this be possible? How can any one person possess the empathy necessary to eradicate matter from a Soul? NO MORTAL has this capability; only the individual Soul and The Creator may do this. Yet humans continue to flock to churches, temples, and synagogues with the explicit intention of "finding God," of finding Soul redemption. One cannot "find" that which is not lost; you may lose yourself, but God is always present. Each Soul possesses the ability to erase from their SOULSELF, any and all perceived transgressions and then to forgive themselves.

However, please bear in mind that it is a violation of God Law, of the Universal Laws, to presume to release another from their understanding of their own wrongdoing. Each person evolves or does not evolve at any given time at his or her own speed; with his or own <u>intent</u> to do so. DESIRE is the key. Even then, so many that have the desire do not perform the necessary work, so it is that they shall remain in that "condition" for many, many lifetimes. Does this behavior make that individual or individuals wrong? NO, it does not! Nor does it mean that the individual in question loves the Supreme Being less than do you. Each Soul is permitted and yes, encouraged, to learn the path of Spirit by first determining what true Spirit IS NOT. Once that particular Soul has arrived at a crossroads in their Spiritual life, one that causes the manmade ideas of God to no longer ring true to that person, then and ONLY THEN, shall all truths be made manifest. This is when all that was formerly thought of as "impossible" is understood as "possible; "this is when the reality hits hard," that "impossible" was but a "crutch," now the crutch is a non-feasible idea. The new thought-forms send people messages of the innate and dormant understanding that God lives within each person, each life form. The "dormant" then becomes the kinetic energy needed to continuously move forward. They see that each leaf on a tree is an aspect of the totality of the tree, that each person is an aspect of the totality of the Creator and the Creation. This is how that person then gifts them-self with the Greater Truths... They realize that God arrives wearing many races.

As a child you KNEW many things, as a child you SAW many things. As a child you HEARD many things; as a child your INNER-KNOWING was faultless. You were sin-less, for indeed on a deep inner level of KNOWING, you KNEW that sin does not exist. This state of grace continues with all children until they reach the ages of 6 or 8. Then well meaning adults radically alter the child's perceptions of reality, to such a high degree, that the once pure-visioned chela then becomes but a carbon copy of the jaded adult. So commences "the loss of innocence."

All cultures have borne witness to their societies' children "speaking" to unseen entities. Yet the children have been empathetically instructed to not indulge in speaking to "imaginary playmates." They have been warned that it will make the children "crazy." The truth is that these children have been seeing beyond the physical, they have been viewing life through the eyes of God. As a child, the Soul is aware that all that is natural and simple, all that is beheld as normal, is in fact the natural state of grace, the living, not merely the existing, as a perfect being. A perfect being is a fine piece of life eternal within the greater universes, within the Soul's Higher Consciousness, within All That Is.

The once simple truths that the child has known now becomes a complex maze of small bits of truths, heavily coated with dangerous lies; also with limited straitlaced perceptions of God; with the wrath of God overshadowing human life and the pitfalls of the "devil" waiting on the left and the flaming sword of God on the right, prepared to smote the hapless child who ventures either too close, or commits errors of judgment. The loss of innocence! In this still continuing scenario, if the one doesn't get you, the other one will. It is little wonder that this planet is so constrained, so un-God-like, for how can you emulate that which you no longer understand?

All those who are now "adult children" had, at one time or another, experienced this mishmash of non-reality; of "things that go bump in the night;" of the ever present, but sometimes silent, presence of your true guides and teachers. These wondrous entities who had patiently and lovingly allowed you the gift of re-learning, of re-evaluating all which you have been told, then weighing it against what you "<u>KNEW</u>." So it is that I, who am living the experience of my Soul Cluster reunion, am writing this truth predicated not only upon my own experiences, but writing also of what I KNOW, of what I have SEEN, FELT, HEARD, with my non-third-dimensional eyes. As for myself, life will never be the same again... nor would I want it to be. You see, my greatest challenges here on this planet have been to understand that, unlike my home planet, I cannot simply trust all those I encounter. I have long ago forsaken my wish to wave my magic wand and "fix it" for everyone. I live "passionate detachment" in all that I do here. I have come to terms with the anomaly existing here... that the cliques, which I do deplore, are the status symbols, the "yardstick," by how my brethren and I are perceived. In other words, I accept most heartily the fact that "it is OK not to be human."

Salude, till we meet again... Celestial

Our Biographies

Celestial Blue Star — "Celest" is a Pleiadian walk-in and her father is Blue Star. She entered the Earth's dimension on July 26, 1989. She has been teaching and working with all races of people on the planet ever since then. She is here to also teach the teachers to be all that they can be, in order to best serve the God of this Universe as well as the people being taught. Celest has traveled extensively conducting workshops and lectures across the country, speaking on many diverse issues. She has taught of the Pleiadian ways and truths, the Universal Laws and disclosing the truth about the Illuminati. Celest has taught people how they can protect themselves from invasive forces. She works with all races of people, those who are walk-ins and those who are not.

Over the years she has written hundreds of lengthy articles pertaining to personal and planetary evolvement. She began the Blue Star Spiritual Counseling Agency and was kept very busy by the people who called her for help. Celest closed the agency down after 7 years because her schedule was so limited in what else she could accomplish in her spare time. She did continue to provide private counseling sessions, however, until 2005. Celest began "The Awakened Hearts Conferences" and held 3 a year until she became too busy to continue hosting the programs in different states. Among many other things Celest is involved in, she is writing book two of "The Blue Star Trilogy" and co-authoring several other books as well. Celest began the "Blue Star transmissions" on the Internet on December 12, 1997, at the behest of her father, Blue Star the Pleiadian. Celest, David and Suzy co-hosted their monthly teleconferences until they no longer had the time to do so.

At the time of the publication of this book she had already endured 13 near-death experiences and many, many attacks by dark energies. Celest is a warrior and a warrior-teacher as well. She and her husband David have co-joined their Spiritual energies and work together to do what they can while there is still enough time remaining for the Children of Earth to begin living a better life in a better way. Celest and her husband's Web sites are listed below.

David of Arcturus — David is a walk-in. He arrived on the Earth Star planet this time around approximately 43 years ago. It was long ago decreed that he, along with his wife Celest, would once again reunite to work together to help usher in the Golden Age of God. David and his wife have in previous earth incarnations been married a total of eight times, they have a total of 13 children from these previous unions as well. Due to the severity of the times that are currently upon us, they chose not to bring children into their lives during this present incarnation. Although David's origins stem from Arcturus, he has lived life on many other worlds. His approximate age of 157,000 Earth years may seem extraordinary to some; however, in universal terms that is considered comparatively young. He is an explorer, a teacher, a student of life, a healer and a Spiritual warrior. He is here at the bequest of the God of this universe, to make a difference by be-ing the difference. He teaches by example and he practices what he teaches. He has lived an ordinary life in order to better understand the injustices that have transpired against the human race so that he could draw from these experiences to better teach others. His communiqués with the heavenly hosts are accomplished at Soul level. His wife and he currently have three Web sites on the Internet which were built and are maintained by them. These sites are consistently viewed and have been translated all over the world. The Web sites are:

"Blue Star the Pleiadian — Blue Star Speaks"
www.bluestarspeaks.com

"Awakened Hearts"
www.awakenedhearts.com

"Godumentary"
www.godumentary.com.

David of Arcturus has battled against the injustices of the Illuminati and tried to bring awareness to people all over the world who would listen. His wife and he are currently working on a number of controversial books. They have co-hosted the "We the People — Speak Out, One World, One People" teleconferences until the summer of 2007.

A number of years ago David took a much needed respite from everyday life. He stopped and took a hard look at all the madness that was ongoing on the Earth. He began to realize not only his life's true goals; he also started to remember that there is so much more to life than what he had previously conceived. David found that life had far more meaning than he had supposed, it had a purpose, and he had a purpose, far above and beyond what he previously knew. Since then, he has reunited with his Higher Self and he has reestablished his connection with All That Is. David is now experiencing life as it was always intended to be. He no longer casts his own shadow and is fulfilling his destiny by be-ing his destiny.

Suzanne (Suzy) Ward — Unlike Celest and David, who know "who they are," Suzy has no conscious awareness of anything she experienced before this lifetime. The dramatic turning point in her ordinary existence came in 1980, when her 17-year-old son Matthew died in a vehicle wreck in Panama. She tried to cope with her grief by contacting mediums for news of her son, and all of them told her that when the time was right, she would communicate with him directly. Due partly to 35 years of immersion in Christian dogma and partly to her belief that telepathy is a rare gift and she didn't feel worthy of it, it was hard for her to believe that she and her son would ever talk again, but she never stopped hoping that they would.

Early in 1994, almost 14 years after Matthew died, Suzy heard him speaking to her as clearly as if they were sitting side by side. During the first weeks of recording their long conversations at the computer and receiving the images he sent of himself and his surroundings, she felt both joy and doubt: *Was all of this her imagination?* When Matthew's messages turned from life in his world to energy, universal laws, mass consciousness, the spiritual hierarchy, the cumulative soul and other topics beyond her comprehension, and he introduced souls from highly advanced civilizations who gave her equally astounding information, she knew this communication wasn't originating in her mind, it was flowing into it.

Matthew told his mother that her profession as journalist was not by chance; it was the experience she needed to organize for publication the hundreds of messages she was receiving from him and the other extraterrestrial souls. Matthew said that in their family's pre-birth agreement, her primary mission was to make this spiritual enlightenment, guidance and encouragement available to all receptive people during this era of unprecedented changes on Earth and in individuals. Thus the four Matthew Books were born — *Matthew, Tell Me about Heaven, Revelations for a New Era, Illuminations for a New Era* and *Voices of the Universe.* English language editions have sold in 26 countries and have been translated into nine foreign languages. After publication of the fourth book, Matthew's messages continued and are posted on:
www.matthewbooks.com

In further sharing of this vital information, Suzy speaks at conferences and to smaller groups, was a panelist on "We the People" teleconferences, is guest on teleconferences and radio programs, and hosts the monthly "Matthew and Friends" show on BBS Internet Radio.

With their family of adopted dogs, Suzy and her husband Bob live in a rural area of SW Washington and will be relocating in accordance with her guidance. Matthew's sister and two brothers and their families live in Latin America.

****

God — I AM

Celest and David's Upcoming Books

Like Life,
Are a Work in Progress

"Letters From God"
A compilation of letters transmitted by God to Celest and David

"The Book of Universal Laws — AKA — The House of Flounders"

"Quantum Thoughts and Inspirations of Blue Star the Pleiadian"
Past and present "Transmissions" with updated information

"And Then God Said... Then *I* Said... Then He Said..."
Volume #2 of a two book set

"Effervescent Effects — A Bountiful Harvest"
The Terra Chronicles

Send an email to
creation@godumentary.com
If you wish to be put on our Book Notification list.
Please put Book Notification in the subject line.

Made in the USA
San Bernardino, CA
04 November 2012